Baptists and Worship

Monographs in Baptist History

VOLUME 14

Ours is a day in which not only the gaze of western culture but also increasingly that of Evangelicals is riveted to the present. The past seems to be nowhere in view and hence it is disparagingly dismissed as being of little value for our rapidly changing world. Such historical amnesia is fatal for any culture, but particularly so for Christian communities whose identity is profoundly bound up with their history. The goal of this new series of monographs, Studies in Baptist History, seeks to provide one of these Christian communities, that of evangelical Baptists, with reasons and resources for remembering the past. The editors are deeply convinced that Baptist history contains rich resources of theological reflection, praxis and spirituality that can help Baptists, as well as other Christians, live more Christianly in the present. The monographs in this series will therefore aim at illuminating various aspects of the Baptist tradition and in the process provide Baptists with a usable past.

Baptists and Worship

Sitting Beneath the Gospel's Joyful Sound

R. Scott Connell

Foreword by
Michael A. G. Haykin

☙PICKWICK *Publications* · Eugene, Oregon

BAPTISTS AND WORSHIP
Sitting Beneath the Gospel's Joyful Sound

Monographs in Baptist History 14

Pickwick Publications
An Imprint of Wipf and Stock Publishers
199 W. 8th Ave., Suite 3
Eugene, OR 97401

www.wipfandstock.com

PAPERBACK ISBN: 978-1-7252-7157-9
HARDCOVER ISBN: 978-1-7252-7158-6
EBOOK ISBN: 978-1-7252-7159-3

Cataloging-in-Publication data:

Names: Connell, R. Scott, author. | Haykin, Michael A. G., foreword.

Title: Baptists and worship : sitting beneath the gospel's joyful sound / by R. Scott Connell; foreword by Michael A. G. Haykin.

Description: Eugene, OR : Pickwick Publications, 2020 | Series: Monographs in Baptist History 14 | Includes bibliographical references.

Identifiers: ISBN 978-1-7252-7157-9 (paperback) | ISBN 978-1-7252-7158-6 (hardcover) | ISBN 978-1-7252-7159-3 (ebook)

Subjects: LCSH: Public worship—Baptists—History. | Worship—History. | Baptists—North America—History.

Classification: LCC BX6235 C66 2020 (print) | LCC BX6235 (ebook)

Manufactured in the U.S.A.   NOVEMBER 20, 2020

To my beautiful wife, Mary,
whose two-time battle with cancer coincided
with the writing of this book
and who insisted through treatment that I must continue
to study and write.

This is a trophy of your perseverance.

You make everything in my life better, including this book.

You are my Favorite.

Contents

Figures

Foreword

THE SO-CALLED WORSHIP WARS within late twentieth-century Evangelicalism made sure that the subject of worship was front and center not only in the life of local churches, but also in terms of various academic studies. Yet, in all that has been written about worship in the past forty or so years, there has been really very little done by way of examination of what worship actually looked like in specific congregations of the past. And of all Christian people, Baptists, who prize congregational autonomy, should have been eager to have done such examination. But in truth Baptist scholarship along with that of other Christian traditions has been woefully lacking here. Hence, the importance of this study by Scott Connell, which carefully examines the shape of Baptist worship in specific North American congregations from the colonial era to the modern day (the inclusion of Jarvis Street Baptist Church in Toronto is both heartwarming and encouraging to this dyed-in-the-wool Canadian).

Unlike other Christian traditions, which have an order of worship that is more or less followed—for example, the Anglicans with their Book of Common Prayer—Baptist worship has theoretically been committed to the "freedom of the Spirit." Yet, broad patterns of order are discernible, as Connell ably shows, and knowledge of these is indispensable in our day when the foundations of so much in Baptist life is up for question. All who love the Baptist tradition are deeply in the debt of Dr. Connell for this fine work.

Michael A. G. Haykin, FRHistS
Dundas, Ontario
December 1, 2019

Preface

IT HAS BEEN ALMOST thirty years since I first sat under the teaching of Bruce Leafblad, a former church music and worship professor at Southwestern Baptist Theological Seminary. Having moved to Fort Worth, Texas, in 1992 to respond to the call upon my life to lead worship in the local church, I thought I was going to learn about church music. What I learned most during those years was that which about I knew the least. Until that time I thought that worship was what one attended on a Sunday morning that involved singing, praying, preaching, and an altar call. From the perspective of my twenty-something-year-old self, worship was primarily an event that helped people get saved. Though I had only just begun to become aware of some problems with this model (this was during the height of influence of the Seeker Service movement), I knew there had to be more to worship. Until then, I felt as if I were more of a spectator in worship rather than an active participant. I thought my role was to try to help God affect unsaved people in a way that would persuade them to become Christians by the end of the service. I had no real understanding that worship was really *God's people* in dialogue (i.e., "communion") with him. Furthermore, I had no idea that it was relevant to all of life because of its connection to the power and work of Christ through his gospel.

Many of us who were in Dr. Leafblad's worship class can still recall his prescribed definition of worship: "Worship is communion with God in which believers, by grace, center their mind's attention and their heart's affection on the Lord, humbly glorifying God in response to His greatness and His word." I had before never considered worship as being anything like this. What was more compelling was Dr. Leafblad's ability to take us to the biblical text to show us that this and this alone was true worship. Passages of Scripture that I had previously glossed over, if I had read them at all, became alive and inspiring as the true nature of worship leapt off the page before my eyes. Scriptures like Exodus 3, Exodus 24, Isaiah 6, John 4, Revelation 3, Revelation 4–5, and so many others now stood as mooring points for a true and better understanding of the reality of worship. Worship had new meaning in the context of a dynamic relationship with God through Christ and in the power of his Spirit. I now understood that worship was only for believers because only converted people could truly *commune* with God.

The most compelling thing to me during those days was watching Dr. Leafblad worship. It became clear to me that while he and I knew the same God, Dr. Leafblad knew him in a far more profound and intimate way than I did. Each class period began with prayer. To this day I can close my eyes and remember what it was like to sit in his classroom as he prayed. It seemed as if heaven itself had descended upon us when he spoke to God on our behalf. On many occasions I had to peek to see if what I was beginning to see through eyes of faith could be seen with my natural eyes. I would not have been surprised at all if I had opened my eyes to witness something like what Isaiah saw in the temple or John depicted in heaven's throne room. Jesus had become very real to me and worship had become very engaging and powerful. Through worship, the Spirit was transforming me and empowering the way I lived my life. I now understand that he was doing this by showing me the glory of God in the face of Christ. This is what the gospel does—it reveals Christ and in doing so transforms the worshiper.

I served as a minister of music in one of the mid-cities between Dallas and Fort Worth during my seminary days. It was thrilling to have a place to return to each Sunday to apply some of these things that I was learning in seminary. The people I served were kind and patient, and they tolerated more than I will ever know from a young and overzealous music minister. What I longed to do most was to show them how to worship God in the manner in which I was learning from Dr. Leafblad. I wanted to teach them to worship, but I had only barely begun to understand it myself. I decided I would approach my inspirational professor with the most *Baptist* question I have ever asked: "Is there a curriculum I could buy that would help me teach my people how to worship?" I have carried his gracious yet profound answer around with me for the rest of my life: "Scott, you cannot teach people to worship from a curriculum. You need to get before him and worship God yourself. Love him with your whole heart, soul, mind, and strength. Experience him firsthand and then return to take your people where you have been." I am still stunned by that answer (and my absurd question).

I have spent almost thirty years pursuing what he helped me understand during those days at seminary. In many ways, what follows is a reflection on that journey.

At the end of my program of study in 1995, I wrote a master's thesis with Dr. Leafblad as my supervisor. I had been meeting regularly with him for several years about worship and wanted to write a substantive research paper on the history of worship in the Baptist Church. I wanted to find out how worship had become what it had among Baptists. What I produced (through no fault of his) was poorly researched, shoddily written, and overly judgmental. I still have that paper and shudder at the thought that anyone would read it today. I have returned to that topic in this work, but in a much different manner and with different motives. My attempt in 1995 was to condemn the state of worship as I felt I saw it at that time—under the influence of the Seeker Sensitive movement. To quote my original paper: "The tree of Baptist worship was vast but hollow." There is much more to the story and it is a much more *redemptive* story than I would have acknowledged then. I have learned much in the years between then and now. Baptists have a rich history of true worship that needs to be told. I still have much to learn, but this work is the product of almost three decades of trying to do exactly what my professor instructed me to do: "Experience God firsthand and take people where I have been." This is the story of other Baptists who sought to do the same.

There are some Baptists whose story will not be told here. My parents, Moody and Pat Connell, were married at that great old Baptist lady in Marion, Alabama—Siloam Baptist Church (one of the churches featured in this book). They stood on the platform where James Devotie's voice previously had thundered the gospel story over a century before. My mother was raised in that church and it was only fitting that when it was time to be married, she should return to the church that had seen her come to faith, grow in that faith, and participate in ministry as a child of Baptist parents. She also was a student at the historic Judson College, which was just down Early Street from Siloam. Devotie was long gone by the time she was born, but I am a personal benefactor of the gospel legacy he left at this bastion for the kingdom of God in the black belt of Alabama. The family that was formed in his church over a century after he left the Siloam pastorate became a means of grace to me.

Finally, there is one person who has read this manuscript almost as much as I have and contributed positively to it more than any other. She did so while undergoing numerous surgeries, chemotherapy, radiation, and recovery during not one, but two bouts with breast cancer. When she was diagnosed the first time in 2010, she made me promise two things: (1) not to miss a day of work, and (2) not to stop the work on this manuscript. She is uncommon in so many wonderful ways. By God's grace she continues to inspire me with her passion and perseverance today. She not only was spared cancer's worst outcome, but she loves Jesus and his gospel more than ever because of her journey through it. There is no greater love in my life and together we have the privilege of raising seven children to rejoice "beneath the gospel's joyful sound" in worship! This book is dedicated to her as she is the most authentic worshiper I have every known.

Scott Connell
Jacksonville, Florida
September 2020

1

The Role of the Gospel
in Baptist Worship

Introduction

WORSHIP IS DIALOGUE. IT is more than that, but it is not less than that. Worship is a conversation between God's people and him. As a result, a worship event conveys something about those people and their understanding of who God is. It also communicates insights about the people's perception of the nature of their relationship and how it came to be. A worship encounter cannot take place in isolation from what brought them to the place of worship, nor can it deny their understanding of its present purposes or future hope. In short, a worship service is a snapshot within the context of an ongoing relationship between worshipers and their object of worship. Every act of worship is informed by some combination of priorities, convictions, and beliefs. These values serve as internal constraints that shape the worship; and as a result, the worshiper. All that occurs in a worship service is a part of a greater narrative that forms the worshipers' metanarrative. The Christians' metanarrative is called the "gospel," which is the good news that God has redeemed people who were estranged from him, but now through the death of Christ have been reconciled to him. It is because of the gospel and by the gospel that they first came to know God and now worship him. All of this takes place through the person and work of Christ, who is the central figure in Christian worship.

How then should the gospel inform worship? How should it affect the worship conversation? If it is by the gospel that Christians have been turned to God, does not the gospel have a continuing role in the deepening of this relationship through the dialogical nature of worship? Should not the gospel's ongoing work be evident in the way the church worships? In a liturgical tradition, this role might be ensured through the liturgy; how might the gospel be evidenced among the tradition of a people where formal liturgy is not just absent from practice, but vehemently rejected? Does historic Baptist worship reflect the gospel? If so, how can one "see" the gospel in a Baptist tradition?

Christopher Ellis in *Gathering: A Theology and Spirituality of Worship in Free Church Tradition* explains the nature of what can be derived from examining worship:

> Worship is a communal event. It is something which Christians do together. In fact, it is the central activity of the Christian Church. There are, of course, other things which the Church is called to do, such as share the good news of Jesus Christ in word and action—which is usually called "mission." But worship is the *central* activity of the Church because it is here that what it believes is most clearly expressed and it is here that it regularly encounters God and is confronted with what God has done in the past and what God has promised for the future.[1]

In his book, Ellis attempts to derive the theology and spirituality of English Baptists from their examples of worship from the earliest days of the seventeenth century until today. His work is an example of liturgical theology by which the beliefs of a particular Christian community are studied via its worship practices. Ellis explains, "In liturgical theology we observe the worship practices of a community and then draw from them what we perceive to be their theological meaning."[2]

Due to the nature of Baptist worship, this process cannot be simply accomplished by examining prayer books or historic liturgy. Neither exists in the Baptist tradition and the history of Baptist origins reveals their deeply held conviction to be free from such prescribed ritual. However, information exists in other sources that reveals the form and shape of worship in Baptist congregations, as well as the content. As Ellis has demonstrated with English Baptists, even so there is enough data available to undertake a similar study of Baptist worship in North America. While this effort for Ellis was challenging due to the scarcity of records concerning the nature of Baptist worship, he was able to derive conclusions concerning Baptist worship in England as well as the spirituality of those Baptists. He was able to do so

---

1. Ellis, *Gathering*, 4.
2. Ellis, *Gathering*, 14.

"fountainhead of the Christian good news."[13] Looking back at the definition from 1 Corinthians 15 above, Gilbert's "God-man-Christ-response" structure is evident. While Gilbert warns this should not become some "slavish formula" and that the gospel may be presented in a "variety of ways," these four words represent the "critical truths" of the gospel.[14] Therefore, the working definition of the gospel for this work is *the historic narrative of the life, death, burial and resurrection of Jesus Christ that secured the promises of God for his people,* and will be represented by Gilbert's shorthand phrase: "God-man-Christ-response."[15]

Many attempts have been made to define worship. As with the gospel, two aspects of worship[16] require biblical description: (1) the "all of life" aspect of "present[ing] your bodies as a living sacrifice, holy and acceptable to God, which is your spiritual worship" (Rom 12:1–2);[17] and (2) the individual and corporate "acts" of worship that characterize what we know as a "worship service"—"when you come together" (1 Cor 14:26).[18] While the "all of life" worship described in Romans 12:1–2 is the stream from which individual and corporate worship events converge and return to, corporate worship is specifically in view in this work. The definition will be crafted with that focus in mind.

Some specific characteristics of this dimension of worship must be considered before a definition may be offered.[19] Life (and our struggle with

13. Gilbert, *What Is the Gospel?*, 32. Gilbert explains that these four major points are also evident in Paul's description in 1 Cor 15:1–5; Peter's sermons in Acts 2:38, Acts 3:18–10, Acts 10:39–43, and Paul's sermon in Acts 13:38–39.

14. Gilbert, *What Is the Gospel?*, 35–36.

15. The "promises" of God should be seen as a play on words to include the third Person of the Trinity as the "Promise of the Father," in addition to what he works in the believer through the myriad of gospel promises such as conversion, redemption, justification, adoption, sanctification, glorification, etc.

16. Christopher Ellis refers to this as a "double meaning" of the word "worship." His reference to Rom 12:1 is that of an "attitude of the heart and mind which is the only appropriate attitude of creature towards creator. In this sense 'worship' implies wonder and humility, attention and obedience, confession and self-offering. Such worship is not contained within the walls of a church building and is not restricted to what happens within a worship 'service.' Indeed this root meaning of 'worship' is an attitude of life and a way of being Christian" (Ellis, *Gathering*, 3).

17. Rom 12:1. Harold Best writes about this aspect of worship in *Unceasing Worship* (2003), which is one of the few texts devoted to this dimension exclusively, though it is intended as a tome specifically regarding the practice of the arts in "unceasing worship."

18. 1 Cor 14:2. See also Acts 2:42, "And they devoted themselves to the apostles' teaching and the fellowship, to the breaking of bread and the prayers."

19. This discussion and worship definition are built upon the same effort by Christopher Ellis in *Gathering*. Since his approach to "liturgical theology" and the study of

sin) has a way of throwing us off course with our "way things ought to be" lifestyle worship (Rom 12:1–2). We need to gather with other believers who are journeying along the same narrow path in life. This gathering has the horizontal benefits of fellowship and encouragement, but the primary benefit results from the vertical encounter with God as a gathered body.[20] We have not ceased to be the church while scattered in our various avenues of life, but something profound occurs when we come together for worship. The first characteristic is rather logistical in that it requires an agreed time and an agreed place for a particular event. This is so the church can experience what Ellis describes as "an occasion when what should be true *all* the time becomes true for a short time."[21] A second characteristic of corporate worship is that while many of the elements can be practiced in private (e.g., Scripture reading, prayer, singing, etc.), this is specifically a communal event with other believers identified in a local expression of the church.[22] The horizontal aspect of worship is highlighted in this quality. The third characteristic of worship is demonstrative of its quintessential and vertical reality. While God's people set the time and place, they have gathered because they are the *ekklesia* ("called out") of God. Worship is a response to God who called them out. Ellis explains: "Worship is the place where the Church is gathered by God . . . the place where God's Word is encountered communally and where the Church is confronted by its divine vocation."[23] God's people are the "called out" ones in other aspects than this, but their gathering in worship is a heightened expression of this identity. When gathering for worship they are reminded of their alien nature in a dark world, and the calling of God to live their lives affected by the gospel.

Ellis has provided an extremely helpful framework and model for this work in his study of English Baptist worship. A similar model can be used

---

English Baptists serves as the impetus for this study of North American Baptists, his approach to and definition of worship is utilized as well.

20. Ellis calls this a "journey into God" (Ellis, *Gathering*, vii).

21. Ellis, *Gathering*, 3; emphasis Ellis'.

22. Only the gathering of a local church body may practice the ordinances of baptism and communion. These are elements of worship given to the church by Jesus to be practiced under the authority of local church leadership and in the presence of the gathered church (see Acts 2:42). These should not be practiced in private devotion.

23. Ellis, *Gathering*, 5. Ellis believes that the church only becomes the *ekklesia* when gathered, thus the need for a place to gather. While the corporate gathering is significant, and it is the primary subject of this study, insisting upon a place as part of the description for worship seems to skirt the teaching of Jesus in John 4:21 in which he disregards the need for a particular place for worship that is "in spirit and truth." Ellis' point is likely that any place will do, rather than a specific place being required, as the woman at the well was intimating in her question.

with North American Baptist worship. It is only fitting that Ellis' approach to a worship definition be considered for this study as well. Ellis suggests the following definition: Worship is "an encounter in which God and humanity are active participants and in which 'something' happens."[24] Three critical adjustments are made to Ellis' definition for the purposes of this study. First, though implied in Ellis' definition, the adjective "dialogical" is added to the noun "encounter" to emphasize the concept of a worship conversation. Second, the necessity of the gospel in worship is emphasized by adding the prepositional phrase "through Christ" after the word "participants" to demonstrate the requirement of Christo-centrism in worship—Christ must be central in Christian worship. Finally, more specificity[25] is required regarding the "something" of Ellis' definition by inserting worship's fruit of "transformation" from Romans 12:1–2 and specifically 2 Corinthians 3:18.[26] Therefore, the following definition will be utilized for the purposes of this study: *Worship is a dialogical encounter in which God and humanity are active participants through Christ and in which transformation occurs.* The nature of this transformation is specifically Christlikeness—becoming like the one who is held in view in worship.

A third aspect of this thesis requires the merging of the first two facets of gospel and worship. Can the gospel have a shape? If it does, how can it be recognized in corporate worship?[27] Here I want to return to Greg Gilbert's

24. Ellis, *Gathering*, 6–7.

25. Apparently Ellis intends to keep some mystery about what takes place in worship. While there are some things about worship that are not quantifiable in this life, it is helpful for the purposes of this study to focus on the transformation that should occur as a result of worship. I will leave the rest of the mystery of worship to other studies and ultimately to the clarity of the day of glorification.

26. Rom 12:1–2: "I appeal to you therefore, brothers, by the mercies of God, to present your bodies as a living sacrifice, holy and acceptable to God, which is your spiritual worship. Do not be conformed to this world, but be *transformed* by the renewal of your mind, that by testing you may discern what is the will of God, what is good and acceptable and perfect"; 2 Cor 3:18: "And we all, with unveiled face, beholding the glory of the Lord, are being *transformed* into same image form one degree of glory to another. For this comes from the Lord who is the Spirit." This transformation is the "un-conforming of the life to the world" through the process of "renewing of the mind" that results in conforming the worshiper to the image of Christ having "beheld the glory of the Lord" in worship. To borrow the antithesis of the concept regarding idolatry from Beale, "We Become What We Worship," in his *We Become What We Worship*.

27. This part of this study has two goals. The identification of gospel content is one goal and slightly more important to my study than the second. However, the presence of gospel shape in worship is a more fascinating discovery. It would be impossible to have gospel shape without gospel content. But it would be possible to have gospel content without gospel shape. Gospel shape is preferred, but accurate gospel content is fundamentally important.

four-word shorthand structure of the gospel: "God-man-Christ-response."
A shape emerges from this that can become very useful for analyzing and
evaluating corporate worship of North American Baptists for gospel form.
A few points of explanation will help clarify. First, God is the initiator in
the gospel, and he is therefore the initiator in worship. Second, man is the
responder to God in the gospel and subsequently the responder to God in
worship. Third, the nature of God's initiation and man's response is characterized by the revelation of God's holy perfection and realization of man's
sinful need, which brings the necessity of the central figure of Christ into
view through the gospel. Significant implications exist for worship regarding the representation of God's holiness and man's sin, and the recognition
of the centrality of Christ and his work on the cross.

Additionally, there is a response to the gospel that is also inherent to worship.[28] Ellis refers to this as the church being "confronted by its
vocation."[29] Because formal worship services are intended to transform the
worshiper for living out that worship in all of life, greater Christ-likeness
should be the result of encountering Christ in worship. Man's response to
the worship service event should be a life lived as worship and there should
be elements of the worship event that point to both this implication and
command. How does that which occurs on Sunday, prepare the worshiper
to continue that system of priority, values, and convictions (e.g., Godward
orientation through Christ) to be evidenced Monday through Saturday?

Brian Chapell has identified in his study seven elements that he
considered "consistent elements" in gospel-centered historic liturgies: (1)
adoration, (2) confession, (3) assurance, (4) thanksgiving, (5) petition and
intercession, (6) instruction from God's Word, and (7) charge and benediction.[30] As Gilbert asserts regarding the variety of ways the gospel is presented in Scripture while still being represented by his four-word structure,[31]

---

28. This fourfold model also demonstrates the "back-and-forth" dialogue that is inherent in worship. God speaks, man speaks, God acts, man acts, etc., is demonstrative
of the exchanges that take place in worship as well.

29. Ellis, *Gathering*, 5.

30. Chapell, *Christ-Centered Worship*, 100. These elements by Chapell are representative of conversational markers in the dialogue of worship. Each is reflective of one of
the two parties speaking in worship (God and his people) and the summation of the
talking points demonstrates the shape and contour of the worship dialogue. While each
element is represented by dialogue, in actuality, there is much more than the exchange
of words taking place in worship. As in a conversation between two lovers in a deeply
meaningful relationship, the words are attempts to express the deeper reality of affection, commitment, and devotion. We use the words in worship to express and denote
what is taking place at the much more serious and lasting level.

31. See Gilbert, *What Is the Gospel?*, 31–36.

Chapell's model for gospel-shaped worship can be applied similarly. While a variety of components may be used to show gospel contour, a consistent shape emerges. Additionally, Gilbert's fourfold structure of the gospel correlates with Chapell's seven elements of gospel-shaped worship, demonstrating the commonalities of the two and the effect of the gospel.[32] The dynamic exchanges found in the gospel—and therefore of gospel-shaped worship—will be sought for identification in historic Baptist worship in North America (e.g., God's initiation, man's response, the interposition of Christ and his work, and the commission to live a transformed life). Finally, the historic information gathered will be evaluated for accurate gospel content (e.g., both the historic narrative of the gospel as well as the effects of the gospel in the believer's life). Accurate gospel content is essential for gospel-shaped worship. In summary, historic Baptist worship will be evaluated for three components that will serve to denote the presence of gospel form in addition to gospel content: (1) Is Christ central to worship? (2) Is the gospel content present in terms of historic narrative and effects in the believer's life? (3) Is the gospel faithfully "re-presented" according to the proposed "shape?"[33]

One significant caveat to this part of the study must be raised. Just as Gilbert cautioned against the concept that any structure of the gospel might be seen as "slavish," no model for gospel-centered worship should be used this way in the Baptist tradition either. A formal liturgical model will repeat the same movements in worship each week as Chapell demonstrates in *Christ-Centered Worship*. Changes in these historic liturgies are rare once

32. Other models will be considered in this work such as one in Leafblad, "Evangelical Worship," and one in Hotz and Mathews, *Shaping the Christian Life*. Leafblad's model begins with "revelation," which demonstrates the initiative of God in worship. Chapell's model assumes this and begins with "adoration" as a response to God's revealing of Himself. In either case, Gilbert's declaration of God's initiative in the gospel correlates with both of these models. "Man" follows this in Gilbert's model that correlates with Chapell's "confession" and "Christ" correlates with "assurance." This back-and-forth dialogue continues in Chapell's model with "thanksgiving," "petition and intercession," "instruction from God's Word," and finally the "charge and benediction" to send the worshipers out to live a transformed life. All of this shows the dialogical nature of both models and that man ultimately is the responder to God in each of them. This is the implication of Gilbert's "response" at the end of his fourfold structure of the gospel.

33. This question is evaluated in a less stringent manner than Chapell did with formal liturgy. In a Baptist model, the representation of seven or eight conversational elements is unlikely to be identifiable in any consistent manner. However, the presence of elements that characterize God's initiative and man's response are much more likely. Also, the presence of elements that represent the central work of the cross and the sending of the church in its vocation as a result of worship are also likely to be present. This shape is represented by a simplified threefold model for evaluation: revelation and response; mediation and response; and exhortation and response.

established, and liturgical churches are faithful to enact the same liturgy each week. However, the Baptist tradition is not so predictable. This will not only pose a challenge initially to identify these elements, but also a delight ultimately to explore the myriad of approaches utilized in Baptist worship that emphasize and celebrate the gospel.

Fourth, there must be some delineation regarding which churches will be considered in a study as potentially vast as this one. Thousands of churches are representative of Baptist history in North America. The goal of this study is to trace a portion of the Baptist story of worship as it has been shaped by some of the most prominent influences through its history. Where there are branches in the Baptist worship "tree," the path that leads to the development of Southern Baptist worship today will be followed.

Finally, there are potential benefits for worship planning in today's Baptist churches that may be gained from this study. Inherent in the traditions of the past are lessons for the future. The principles gathered from this study should demonstrate principles for a potential methodology that could inform current and future worship planners. Baptists (and others in free church worship traditions) will want to keep the gospel form and content clear in worship while avoiding the slavish ritual that Baptists have historically rejected. Worship should be informed by Scripture and at the same time emphasize pneumatological freedom. This has been a hallmark of Baptist worship historically and its worship today should reflect the same. Gospel-centered worship is a reflection of the myriad of facets of the word of God and the gospel. There are common principles, but potential for flexible applications is vast.

The purpose of such intentionality in worship design is both corrective and instructive. The corrective aspect is intended toward those worship services where little or no thought has been given to the principles discussed in this study. In these cases, the elements of worship are often thoughtlessly thrown together. Worse, the template from last week's worship service is often simply filled in with different content, thus defaulting to a rigid liturgy that defies a main principle of Baptist worship.[34] This lazy practice is a poor use of the opportunity that worship liturgy affords. Churches should utilize worship as a means of retaining the gospel weekly and ultimately, generationally. As Chapell warns, "Where the gospel is lost, worship becomes

34. "Filling in the blanks" is the more common problem in Baptist worship design, especially with electronic and web-based worship planning resources. As creatures of ritual, we tend toward patterns and rigidity (e.g., the proverbial rut). Some pattern of repetition is healthy and instructive. We need some predictability in life and worship. However, there is room within the structure of healthy predictability to creatively *surprise* the worshipers with new aspects of familiar gospel themes.

reflective of a dead tradition or an evolving heresy." In contrast, "Where the church remains true to the gospel, her worship reflects the truths she holds most dear."[35] I submit that where the gospel is maintained faithfully in worship, the church remains true to the gospel.

Gospel-Shaped Worship

The gospel is how man relates to God. It is how he came to relationship with God through Christ and it his how he accesses God's presence in worship through the mediator, Jesus Christ. Bryan Chapell writes,

> Because it was the eternal intention of God to use Jesus to deliver his people (Eph. 1:4,5; Rev. 13:8), Christ cannot be rightly considered apart from his redemptive purpose. And since he is the most complete revelation of the glory of God, we learn that God's glory—while including power, holiness, wisdom—also necessarily includes the qualities of redemption: mercy, grace, love.[36]

God not only intends to shine his glory through Jesus via the gospel work (e.g., see him), but by the same manner he intends to share it with believers (e.g., become like him). Peter writes, "His divine power has granted to us all things that pertain to life and godliness, through the knowledge of him who called us to his own glory and excellence, by which he has granted to us his precious and very great promises, so that through them you may become partakers of the divine nature" (2 Pet 1:3–4). Paul writes to the Thessalonians that it is by the gospel that believers "obtain the glory of our Lord Jesus Christ" (1 Thess 2:14). Chapell later concludes, "Since the glory of God is inextricable from his work of redemption, the message of the preacher necessarily includes a redemptive focus."[37] This is not just true of the preacher's sermon, but it must be true also of the entire liturgy of worship. In other words, in order to see the glory of God in Christ and be transformed by it, one must look no farther, and nowhere else, than through the lens of the gospel.

Many hear the gospel preceding their conversion and then believe they are to move on to other things now that they have been saved. The gospel is not just evangelistic methodology; it is relational methodology between God and man. In other words, it is not just the front door to the Christian

---

35. Chapell, *Christ-Centered Worship*, 101.

36. Chapell, "Pastoral Theology," 192.

37. Chapell, "Pastoral Theology," 197.

life; it is the entire house within which we dwell with the Lord![38] As Paul
writes above, the believer receives the gospel at salvation, stands upon the
gospel in life, and is being saved (σῴζεσθε; present passive indicative in the
Greek) by the gospel throughout the work of sanctification until the day of
glorification when salvation has completed its work and the full weight of
his glory is revealed.

Jared Wilson seeks to awaken a better understanding of the gospel
among God's people by capturing the gospel's many facets in the phrase
"gospel wakefulness," which he describes as "treasuring Christ more greatly
and savoring his power more sweetly." This sounds like a rich description
of worship—treasuring and savoring Christ. He goes on to explain what he
hopes people will have in worship:

> An experience of such power—of such awakening—that it
> persists and endures, settling deep into the heart and the con-
> science of a believer that is carried through all emotional highs
> and lows. And yet, again, this is not a second conversion experi-
> ence, as it were, but rather a deeper and fuller appreciation of
> the first and only necessary conversion, a greater vision of what
> we perhaps only barely and minimally perceived upon salvation
> (comparatively speaking).[39]

In Wilson's chapter entitled "Wakened Worship" he confesses that
his original description of gospel wakefulness of "treasuring Christ more
greatly and savoring his power more sweetly" really is just a "long way of
writing *worship*."[40] To experience the gospel is to treasure Christ, which is
to worship.

---

38. In *A Treatise Concerning Religious Affections*, Jonathan Edwards refers to the
gospel as "the true saint's superstructure." In contrast he refers to the gospel as having been merely "the hypocrite's foundation." While the hypocrite loves to hear of "the
wonderful things of the gospel, of God's great love in sending His Son, of Christ's dying
love to sinners, and the great things Christ has purchased, and promised to the saints
. . . if their joy be examined, it will be found to have no other foundation than this,
that they look upon these things as theirs, all this exalts them." Edwards' conclusion is
that their joy "is really a joy in themselves, and not in God." While the true saints find
similar joy in the gospel's truth, and in hearing "the wonderful things of the gospel,"
their "first spring of joy" is that they delight in God (Edwards, *Religious Affections*, 251).

39. Wilson, *Gospel Wakefulness*, 24–25.

40. Wilson, *Gospel Wakefulness*, 77; emphasis Wilson's. This is similar to Edward's
description of the gospel's effect (see n38 above). See also Piper, *Desiring God*.

> In baptism, preaching, and the Eucharist we act out a story. The
> story has to do with what God has done for us and our response
> to God's work. Therefore, when the worship is acted out in faith,
> the believer experiences again the refreshment of his or her re-
> lationship to God and he or she spontaneously experiences the
> joy of salvation.[53]

Webber and Cherry both (among many others) advocate worship's
structure as historically organized around four movements: the Gathering,
Word, Sacrament, the Sending (based upon the encounter with the risen
Lord on the road to Emmaus in Luke 24:13–35 and Acts 2:42).[54] The gathering aspect was to demonstrate that when God's people worship, they do so
by gathering in a local church around traditional Christian symbols and liturgy. This is true wherever the gospel has gone. The revelation and response
aspects of their model are found in the Word and Sacraments portions of
the four movements. The Word is a revelation of God's character and work
and the Table is man's response to that revelation. The Sending is a reminder
that believers are to go and live differently in the world because of what they
have experienced in worship, demonstrating the transformation that should
occur in worship. Webber shows the gospel shape by connecting the movements to the Plan of Salvation, as shown in figure 3.[55]

This model has been embraced as the historical model of worship in
the early church and has continued in many traditions until today.[56] The
shape can be clearly seen in the Catholic Mass with the Service of the Word
(e.g., the synaxis) and the Service of the Table (e.g., the eucharist). The recent Liturgical Renewal has brought it to popularity once again and many
Protestant churches have sought to employ the model for the first time since
the Reformation. Much work has been done to establish it as a viable option
for worship renewal among Protestant churches. However, the weakness of
this pattern for the nonliturgical, Baptist tradition that has arisen in the last
two centuries is at least twofold: (1) Many churches today do not celebrate
the Table every week (even in the midst of a Liturgical Renewal movement
in which more are doing so and encouraging others to do so), which leaves
one to wonder where and how the worshipers' response should be in this
model; (2) An increased emphasis on the worship elements that precede the

---

53. Webber, *Worship Old and New*, 73.

54. Schmit, *Sent and Gathered*, 24.

55. Cherry, *Worship Architect*, 49.

56. See also Dix, *Shape of the Liturgy*. Dix is often cited as the first to recognize and
document this historic shape in worship's liturgy. His classic scholarly work was first
published in 1945 and is seen as the fundamental historical study of the church's *ordo*.

Word seems to be weightier than simply gathering for worship. Is there not also a sense of dynamic and recurring revelation and response during this time that the fourfold model simply calls "gathering?"[57]

Plan of Salvation	Parallels	Worship Order
God acts first; God seeks us, call us; God desires to be in fellowship with humanity; God initiates an awakening through the power of the Holy Spirit; God comes to us.	↔	The Gathering
Because our relationship with God is fractured through the fall, he sends his Son to restore the relationship; Christ, the living Word, is freely given to the world through his life, death, and resurrection; Christ is God's revealed truth.	↔	The Word
Such revelation demands a response; We are offered an invitation to repent and believe the gospel; we come to Christ in faith and respond to God's plan of salvation by saying "yes;" we lay our sins on Jesus, accept his forgiveness, and resolve to take up our cross daily and follow him in true discipleship.	↔	The Table
Becoming followers involves being sent; God intends for his people to be active representatives in his world; the message of Christ is now our message.	↔	The Sending

Figure 3. Robert Webber, The Fourfold Pattern of Worship

57. Cherry addresses this sense by writing, "The movement of the gathering is from the general to the specific, from fragmented thoughts to focused thoughts that prepare us for the Word" (Cherry, *Worship Architect*, 56). However this minimizes what many of those in the free church tradition wish to accomplish during this time. Especially in light of the influence of the worship practices of the Charismatic/Pentecostal movement, and many other non-charismatic movements that are modeling protracted singing/prayer worship times after their example.

Felde writes, "It has been suggested that Christian worship everywhere should look sufficiently the same so that even a foreign Christian would recognize it . . . the Gospel, the story of Jesus and the word of the apostles, must be the normative proclamation in every gathering, for 'my thoughts are not your thoughts, declares the Lord' (Isa 55:8)."[58] Since there are similarities in all of these models due to their adherence and intention to be shaped by the biblical gospel, perhaps there is a different pattern for the Baptist tradition to employ that still adheres to the gospel shape, while still leaving room for the variety and flexibility that is common to Baptist worship planning and practice.

A Proposed Model for Baptist Worship

In each of the models presented above (Chapel, Leafblad, and the Fourfold Model represented by Webber/Cherry/Dix), the three broad aspects of the "gospel shape" can be seen—Revelation, Mediation, and Exhortation. Admittedly, they are broad categories, and they represent God's portion of the dialogue only. However, when man's response in worship is added, a very similar structure emerges to that of these models. Due to the fact that worship is the expression of a relationship between God and his people, a pattern for worship should encompass both sides of this relationship (e.g., the "revelation and response" pattern). Gary A. Parrett writes, "Worship involves a rhythm of revelation and response: God graciously reveals himself to us and we faithfully respond—all the elements must help worshipers participate in this rhythm."[59] By adding man's responses to the pattern, the rhythm of revelation and response can be clearly seen, as shown in figure 4.[60]

God		Man
Revelation	↔	Response
Mediation	↔	Response

58. Felde, "Truly Vernacular Worship," 44–45.

59. Parrett, "9.5 Theses on Christian Worship," 40.

60. Timothy Keller wrote of Calvin's view, "Calvin saw the entire service, not as a performance for God by the celebrants, but as a rhythm of receiving God's word of grace and then responding in grateful praise. . . . For Calvin, then, each service reenacted the reception of the gospel" (Keller, "Reformed Worship in the Global City," in Carson, *Worship by the Book*, 215). Calvin's Genevan liturgy included three cycles: (1) "Isaianic" cycle which approximates Isaiah 6; (2) "Mosaic" cycle which seeks to experience the knowledge of his glory as Moses did at the burning bush; and (3) "Emmaus" cycle in which Jesus becomes known in the breaking of bread. Keller concludes, "The goal is entering the presence of God, in our amazement at God's grace (cf. Exod 33:18)" (217).

Exhortation   ↔   Response

Figure 4. A proposed gospel-shaped model for Baptist worship

The response side should include those worship response elements suggested by Chapell and Leafblad above (e.g., Adoration, Confession, Thanksgiving, Dedication, Supplication, etc.). Those are certainly the most natural responses to God's actions in the gospel-shape of worship. However, it seems freer to allow room for the worshiper to respond to God's actions in worship as each is prompted to do. Worship is dynamic—one worshiper may be responding with adoration while another with confession to the same element of worship. Still another may be compelled to give thanks while yet another turns to supplication. By simply listing "response," the pattern seems to better represent the dynamic element of worship and is less rigidly scripted for worship planning and design. This type of interchange is less linear than the visual graphic can portray. Worship encounters can have a hundred different exchanges going on individually. Corporately, however, the pattern should be somewhat uniform as the body of Christ is led through worship in a unified manner. The myriads of microscopic exchanges are just beneath the surface of a macroscopic dialogue that is taking place corporately between heaven and earth.

Methodology

The primary question this study seeks to answer is, "How did Baptists in North America take the gospel initially brought from England and *re-present* it in worship for successive generations of Baptist worship?" This will require both the identification of a stream of prominent Baptist churches in North America as well as a methodology for studying the information that describes their worship. The study of prominent Baptist churches should be reflective of the major streams of historic Baptist worship.

This study is predominantly an effort in historical research. It has required the identification and research of primary source materials to learn the story of Baptist worship in North America. Due to the necessity of primary and accurate secondary source material, a certain amount of delimitation has already taken place by virtue of the information available for study. Very little has been written about the vast majority of Baptist churches in North America, especially the oldest churches. Many have ceased to exist with little record of their existence. Of what is written, very little is ever said in them about a church's worship form or gospel content.

Of those churches covered in this study, some are included partially because there is information about them to study. However, the churches selected are also considered due to their prominence in North American Baptist history and in particular, the historic thread that this effort is seeking to identify. Other than some figures and movements that had initial influence on English Baptists, all historical figures and churches included in this study are Baptist.

The following criteria were used for determination of inclusion in this study and in this order of priority:

1. Prominence of influence upon Baptist worship

2. Prominence of influence upon Baptist church life in other areas

3. Representation of a chronological period of Baptist history not already covered

4. Availability of information to be studied

Pennepek Baptist Church and the Philadelphia Association are an essential component as one of the first Baptist churches in America and the first association of Baptists. They serve as a starting point for the North American Baptist worship story. Also, First Baptist Church of Charleston ("Charleston Tradition") and Sandy Creek Baptist Church ("Sandy Creek Tradition") are requirements for such a study on Baptist worship due to their influence in worship style and tradition. After surveying the early Baptist migration from England to the new world in chapter 2, these three churches form the foundations of Baptist worship established in the eighteenth century in chapters 3, 4, and 5. In some cases, a church may be chosen for study due to the prominence of the pastor at the time such as Siloam Baptist Church in Marion, Alabama,[61] which has historical significance to Southern Baptists in particular and is covered in chapter 6. It also has personal significance to me, as it is the church where my mother and grandparents were members. Jarvis Street Baptist Church in chapter 7 is the Canadian Baptist representative and is from outside the Southern Baptist Convention. It represents evangelical strength in the north. I also have personal interest in Walnut Street Baptist Church in Louisville, Kentucky, because of its proximity to, and relationship with, the Southern Baptist Theological Seminary. This church is covered in chapter 8. These last three churches provide

---

61. Siloam Baptist Church had a prominent role among Baptists by helping to establish Judson College in 1838, Howard College in 1841 (which became Samford College), the *Alabama Baptist* in 1843, and the Southern Baptist Domestic Board of Missions in 1845 (became the Home Mission Board and now the North American Mission Board) which was housed in Marion until 1882 (see Flynt, *Alabama Baptists*, xix).

examples of the worship synthesis of the nineteenth and early twentieth centuries. The last representative of the Baptist worship story is also found in Louisville. Sojourn Community Church is a multisite church that is covered in chapter 9 and brings the story to a close in the twenty-first century.

Few robust historical accounts of Baptist churches exist,[62] especially from two and three hundred years ago. The historical accounts that exist rarely mention the order or content of their worship services.[63] However, some interesting volumes have been written about the most prominent Baptist churches. There are also some historical accounts of Baptist Associations[64] and State Conventions[65] that contain helpful information. Biographies and dissertations on prominent Baptist figures and the topic of worship have been written that are within the purview of this study. A wealth of information has been left in the prefaces to hymnals as well as studies done on the most popular hymns and hymnals utilized in each time period.[66] Finally, a variety of other sources have been found in historic journal articles, diary entries, letters, church minutes and records, and newspaper accounts to provide the information necessary to conduct this study. Other historians,

---

62. FBC Charleston has a significant history by Baker et al., *History of the First Baptist Church of Charleston, South Carolina, 1682–2007*; FBC Providence has several, but a most significant one has just been published in the Baptists in Early North America Series, Lemons, *First Baptist, Providence*. There are other rather substantial efforts on the history of FBC Boston and FBC Philadelphia, and numerous forthcoming volumes from the Baptists in Early North America series. All of these serve this research effort.

63. According to Ted Rivera, who wrote a single volume of devoted work to the topic of Jonathan Edwards on worship, "The oldest extant order of worship in North America is found handwritten in the front pages of *The Psalms of David* (Boston, 1801), a double volume that also includes *Hymns and Spiritual Songs*. Both of these volumes are by [Isaac] Watts, and printed by Samuel Hall." This was the pulpit hymnal of the church in Hubbardston, Massachusetts, and is an example of Puritan worship, though not specifically Baptist worship. Since this dates no earlier than 1801, if Rivera is correct, there is no other example of a recorded order of worship from a church of any kind from the eighteenth century or earlier (see Rivera, *Jonathan Edwards on Worship*, 9). Horton Davies has done some work on this topic of early American worship order and content in his *Worship of the American Puritans*.

64. For example, Barnett L. Williams Jr. wrote his dissertation on Baptist worship from 1620–1850 and Amy Lee Mears wrote her dissertation on the worship of Charleston Baptist Association churches.

65. For example, Flynt, *Alabama Baptists*, is over 700 pages about the history of Alabama Baptists.

66. For example, see Platt, "Hymnological Contributions," in which he describes Manly's preface to *Baptist Chorals* (1859) as "a pulpit from which to articulate his philosophy of congregational song" (71). See also Murrell, "Examination of Southern Ante-Bellum Baptist Hymnals," and Gregory, "Southern Baptist Hymnals."

for different purposes, have identified and addressed some of the materials helpful to this study, while other information waits to be discovered.

The methodology of this study is patterned after the approach used by Christopher Ellis to perform a similar study of English Baptists in *Gathering: A Theology and Spirituality of Worship in Free Church Tradition*. His work is founded upon the approaches of French liturgist Louis Bouyer and Alexander Schmemann in the field of liturgical theology. The relationship between *lex orandi* and *lex credendi* is a complex consideration, especially in Baptist worship. Schmemann argued in his work,

> Liturgical theology . . . is based upon the recognition that the liturgy in its totality is not only an 'object' of theology, but above all its source, and this by virtue of the liturgy's essential ecclesial function: i.e., that of revealing by the means which are proper to it (and which belong only to it) the faith of the church; in other words, of being that *lex orandi* in which the *lex credendi* finds its principal criterion and standard.[67]

Schmemann's claim was that "historically, as well as theologically, worship comes before theology" and quoted *lex orandi, lex credendi* to support this.[68] This belief that theology flows "from" worship is a critical clarification for Schmemann and other liturgiologists to contend for the use of formal liturgy as the preferred approach to worship. In response Ellis warns,

> Using Baptist worship as a case study for doing liturgical theology in a Free Church context will enable us to see some of the difficulties of giving uncritical authority to the theology embodied in worship. The free nature of that worship requires that there be norms and guidelines which will ensure that the worship indeed expresses what the Christian community believes.[69]

Ellis provides a four-stage methodology that he has founded upon Schmemann's work, but adjusted for the unique aspects of Baptist (e.g., "free") worship.[70]

1. Establish the liturgical facts ("What happened in historical worship?").

---

67. Schmemann, "Liturgical Theology," 137–38.

68. Ellis, *Gathering*, 17.

69. Ellis, *Gathering*, 19.

70. Ellis, *Gathering*, 23–24. The first three steps of this methodology are from Alexander Schmemann whereas Ellis adds the fourth step as an adjustment specifically for Baptist (e.g., "free") worship.

2. A theological analysis of those liturgical facts ("What impact does the order of the elements of worship have?").[71]

3. A synthesis of the inherent theological meaning from the witness of the *epiphany* itself ("What was the exposition of faith as a result of worship?").

4. An analysis of the exposition of faith of the worshipping community under a broader theological scrutiny ("Does what worship seemed to align itself with what other sources of theology plainly teach?").[72]

This is the methodology that will be employed for the study of the Baptist churches representative of Baptist worship in North America. It will be the process that will be used to discern the function and relationship of the gospel to worship among Baptists.

Conclusion

This study will show that a prominent thread of gospel faithfulness in worship is identifiable that connects seventeenth-century England with twenty-first-century America. In the conclusion, final observations of historic Baptist worship will be drawn from the study and summarized in order to demonstrate that gospel-centered worship design is not only historically verifiable in Baptist history, but also is preferable for worship service design today. Where the gospel has been maintained in worship, the churches have grown, at least in maturity, if not also numerically. Sometimes it appears that this gospel content in worship is seemingly accidental, but as Chapell has said, "the gospel controls its forms." Adherence to the gospel doctrine provides the only opportunity it needs to shape worship to itself. This is the work of the Holy Spirit through the word of God. Where the gospel is preached faithfully, believed desperately, and applied correctly, Christ is

---

71. Schmemann's contention here is that worship is "undergirded by an *ordo*, or pattern, and this *ordo* is manifested through the way in which the individual components interact . . . an item in worship, though outwardly unchanged, may have a different theological meaning when placed at different points in a service" (Ellis, *Gathering*, 23–24).

72. Ellis explains, "The exposition of the third stage is, as we have seen, essentially descriptive. But if we are going to arrive at a point where it can have an authoritative status for guiding the Church in its believing and in its worship, then it will be necessary to engage with other theological expressions of faith within the Christian community, such as creeds, confessions of faith, analytical theology and especially, Scripture. While worship embodies a theology which we will attempt to identify, clarify and expound, that theology also needs to bear the same scrutiny which any other theological endeavours may properly face" (Ellis, *Gathering*, 24).

exalted and he draws men to himself as they are conformed to his image. The result of the gospel's effect is to sanctify the worshiper, thus making him into the image of the one in view—that of Jesus Christ who is both the pattern and provider of sanctification. This is the effect of the distinct grace of the gospel's sanctifying effect in worship. Its shape and content in a worship service habituates the worshiper to its application in a life of worship. This is the story of how Baptists have sat beneath the gospel's joyful sound in corporate worship Sunday after Sunday for three and a half centuries; and how Christ has been revealed as supreme among them as a result.

PART ONE

Worship Foundations

2

The First Baptists in North America

Introduction: English Beginnings

JEREMIAH BURROUGHS PREACHED A series of sermons in the mid-1640s on the subject of worship. This was during the period in which the Westminster Assembly convened (1643–c. 1649) and the First Baptist London Confession (1644) had just been drafted and distributed. These sermons were published posthumously under the title *Gospel Worship*, going through multiple printings beginning in 1648. His work is significant because it represents both the ethos and the argument for the priority of authentic worship among the Congregationalists, and like-minded groups such as the Baptists. It was easy to be unified against the inventions of man found in Catholic and Anglican services for something as critical as worship. However, as will be discussed below, it was much more challenging for Congregationalists and Baptists to be unified regarding what corrections should be made in worship. Though not a Baptist, Burroughs represents the common viewpoint of the use of the regulative principle among Baptists: "In God's worship, there must be nothing offered up to God but what he has commanded. Whatsoever we meddle with in the worship of God must be what we have a warrant for out of the Word of God."[1]

William Kiffin (1616–1701) is one of fifteen signatories—representing the first seven Particular Baptist Churches—of the London Confession of 1644. He was also a prolific debater and author in the dialogue that shaped the early days of Baptist church thought, especially regarding worship.

---

1. Burroughs, *Gospel Worship*, 11.

Kiffin cited Burroughs often in his arguments and leaned heavily upon Burroughs in what Matthew Ward calls "one of the greatest Baptist treatises ever written about worship—*A Sober Discourse of Right to Church-Communion.*" In this treatise Kiffin reflects a similar concern for worship as Burroughs:[2]

> I have no other design, but the preserving of the Ordinances of Christ, in their purity and Order as they are left unto us in the holy *Scriptures* of Truth; and to warn the Churches *To keep close to the Rule*, lest they being found not to Worship the Lord according to his prescrib'd Order he make a *Breach* among them.[3]

This desire to get worship right was revealed initially in the debate between Kiffin and John Bunyan (1628–1688) over the connection between believer's baptism and communion. If there was any ordinance that Baptists were determined to get right, it was this one. Bunyan had determined that baptism was an individual's decision, rather than that of the church. In doing so, he advocated open-communion—those who had been baptized only as an infant were welcome at the table at Bunyan's church at Bedford and as a member of the church. This was highly controversial for Kiffin and most other Baptists who believed that this matter was foundational to pure worship[4] and gospel order. How could someone worship at the Lord's Table if they had not followed him in this fundamental example of submitting to his lordship in obedience? Worship for Baptists was the "right and Orderly Administration of Ceremonies," and by that Kiffin clearly is referring to the ordinances—the first of these in the matter of gospel order in worship was baptism.[5]

---

2. Ward, *Pure Worship*, 102.

3. Kiffin, *Sober Discourse*, loc. 68; emphasis Kiffin's. This was a written response to John Bunyan (1628–1688) and his open-communion position of allowing those who had not been baptized by believer's baptism to the table. In this response, Kiffin cites Burroughs' *Gospel Worship* as he establishes "Gospel Order," or the "rule of the Gospel" with regard to worship. Kiffin heard Burroughs preach in the 1630s and was convinced of nonconformist views regarding Anglican ceremonies as a result. Later, Kiffin sought out Burroughs and his friends in 1644 for counsel regarding the relationship between Baptists and Congregationalists, which served "to maintain communion between their churches." See Simpson, *Life of Gospel Peace*, 226.

4. Matthew Ward uses this term to describe the early English Baptists' "fundamental desire to worship God purely." He breaks his discussion into three main components: free worship (e.g., no formal liturgy and free to worship according to the Scriptures), true worship (e.g., the regulative principle), and gospel worship (e.g., gospel as a liturgical hermeneutic).

5. Kiffin, *Sober Discourse*, loc. 664. The term "worship" at the time was used consistently to describe the church's corporate actions. It should not be reduced to "singing" as is often the modern context. See Ward, *Pure Worship*, 186.

The proper application of the regulative principle was also demonstrated in the contentious debate over congregational singing that also involved Kiffin, but placed Benjamin Keach at the center of a debilitating controversy. Matthew Ward writes, "The hymn-singing controversy should be recognized as a key event defining the end of the early Particular Baptist vision and a valuable tool for understanding their opinions on complex theological matters."[6] The key figures of the discourse were, William Kiffin, Isaac Marlow, and Benjamin Keach. While the Baptists had seen numerical growth during the persecution that followed the Act of Uniformity of 1662, not long after the Act of Toleration of 1689 they began to lament the state of their devotion in worship. In their self-evaluation recorded in the *Narrative of the Proceedings of the General Assembly* (1689), they lamented a "want of holy Zeal for God." They feared "the Power of Godliness being greatly decayed" and that "the Lord's Day is no more religiously and carefully observed."[7] Benjamin Keach served as secretary of the Assembly. As mentioned above, he desired to raise the issue of congregational singing as a potential solution to the current spiritual malaise in worship, but this was not allowed due to the contentious nature of the issue. However, his conviction of the necessity of singing in worship explains the title of his famous treatise soon after the Assembly: *The Breach Repaired in God's Worship.*[8] It was his view that those who did not allow their congregations to sing were not worshiping God properly (e.g., according to Scripture). Keach writes,

> I am perswaded, for several reasons, since this is so clear an Ordinance in God's Word, that the Baptized Churches, who lie short of the Practice of singing Psalms, etc. will never thrive to such a degree as our Souls long to see them, to the Honour of the Holy God, and Credit of our sacred Profession, and Joy and Comfort of those who are truly spiritual among us: for tho many things, as the Causes of our sad witherings, have been inquired into; yet I fear this, and the neglect of the Ministry, are the two chief, which are both holy Ordinances of Jesus Christ; and yet our People, (that is, some of them) do not love to hear of either of them.[9]

6. Ward, *Pure Worship*, 184.

7. *Narrative of the Proceedings of the General Assembly*, 4–5. The decline that began with the recognition of these observations did not seem to be truly corrected until the Second Great Awakening of the late eighteenth century and early nineteenth century.

8. Keach, *Breach Repaired*. The title plays on the same word in Kiffin's quote above. It was a common expression of the time to refer to a violation or transgression of God's command, in this case related to worship.

9. Keach, *Breach Repaired*, 99. Also quoted in Ward, *Pure Worship*, 186.

Keach had led his church to vote in favor of regular congregational singing on January 1, 1691, after more than a decade of singing a hymn after the celebration of the Lord's Supper. This treatise, published later the same year, seems to indicate that his church at Horsleydown was experiencing the benefits of congregational singing for which he was advocating.

Both the debate over open-communion, and the controversy regarding congregational singing, demonstrate the struggles that early Baptist worship encountered. The Second London Confession and Assembly of 1689 avoided both controversies and the issues were not resolved. Both sides of these debates argued from the regulative principle to their conclusion, and both felt the word of God positively supported their position against the other.[10] The true area of dispute was over the matter of what constituted *adiaphora*, or the things indifferent in worship. There were hermeneutical issues at the heart of the disagreement. How should the Old Testament worship practices be considered in relation to their New Covenant fulfillment? What difference does the closing of the biblical canon make with regard to the role of the Spirit and his gifts in worship? What is the true nature of the primitive (Apostolic) church's practice and what should be emulated and what should be considered unique to the apostolic age? These were among the interpretive areas that led to disagreement and strife. Added to this were the disagreements over "conjoined" worship (e.g., believers and unbelievers singing together), the nature of what are truly Christ's ordinances for worship, and what constitutes a form of worship (e.g., ceremonialism) versus simple worship preparation (e.g., sermon notes, written hymns, etc.). Ward concludes, "The Bible did not answer every question in the form Englishmen asked. The hymn-singing controversy forced Keach to acknowledge that on behalf of all Baptists, and not all Baptists appreciated the revelation."[11]

The Gospel as Liturgical Hermeneutic

According to Ward, "One of the most important contributions Baptists made to the overall understanding of worship was the relationship between worship and the gospel."[12] Their pursuit of gospel order and the regulative

10. See Ward, *Pure Worship*, for a detailed analysis of these debates over the Baptist application of the regulative principle. Ward's premise is that the pursuit of "pure worship" was the defining distinctive of the Early English Particular Baptists and all other matters of significance were tied to this. His familiarity with the primary source material regarding worship during this time period is impressive, though his main argument has failed to persuade some.

11. Ward, *Pure Worship*, 202.

12. Ward, *Pure Worship*, 204. Ward refers to this as utilizing the gospel as a liturgical

principle were rooted in the concern that Anglican ceremonialism had no biblical sanction and as a result, obscured the gospel. Baptists had a compelling desire that the gospel be clearly portrayed in worship, which required adhering to Scripture as closely as possible. Believer's baptism is a primary case in point, which was Kiffin's concern with Bunyan's view. Infant baptism did not accurately portray the gospel. Only the baptism of a professing individual could truly demonstrate the gospel power of an individual's faith in Christ. Believer's baptism was Christ's ordinance to show that the believer was "dead and buried with him" and "raised to walk in newness of life with him," and was now following him in this first step of obedience in a transformed life (Rom 6; Luke 9:23, etc.). This not only reinforced the faith of the individual being baptized, but it also accurately communicated the gospel to all of those present to observe the ordinance. Infant baptism could not do either of these things.[13] Kiffin felt similarly about close-communion and its requirement for baptism in his debate with Bunyan. While Bunyan saw both ordinances as teaching tools of the gospel, Kiffin saw in Bunyan's practice an unacceptable distortion of the same message.[14]

Early Baptists did not restrict the ordinances to these two, however. While they could not agree which ordinances could be celebrated in a mixed assembly (e.g., the practice of congregational singing), they saw all ordinances, including preaching, prayer, and reading God's Word, as the primary if not only means by which evangelism occurred. Hanserd Knollys wrote, "Jesus Christ hath instituted and ordained the Ministry of the Gospel, *Eph.* 4. 11, 12, 13, and all Gospel-Ordinances for the salvation of sinners, to the Glory of God the Father."[15] However, the greater clarity in these ordinances was enjoyed by the believer—"The Ordinances of the Gospel give a more clear vision of Christ, than those under the Law."[16] Keach was adamant regarding this view, especially with his aforementioned conviction

---

hermeneutic. He writes, "On the one hand, a liturgical hermeneutic is the principle by which a worshiper understands and shapes worship; on the other hand, it is also a principle by which a worshiper interprets his or her own faith. . . . To call the gospel a liturgical hermeneutic simply means that Baptists considered and intended their worship to communicate and embody the gospel of Jesus Christ" (145).

13. See Spilsbury, *Treatise Concerning the Lawfull Subject of Baptisme.*

14. Bunyan wrote regarding the ordinances of baptism and the table: "Both which are excellent to the Church, in this world; they being to us representations of the death, and resurrection of Christ, and are as God shall make them, helps to our faith therein" (*Confession of My Faith*, 65, quoted in Ward, *Pure Worship*, 149).

15. Knollys, *World That Now Is*, 10.

16. Knollys, *Exposition*, 190, quoted in Ward, *Pure Worship*, 149. Ward also points out that the First London Confession "declared preaching as the ordinary means of begetting faith" (149; see also *First London Confession* [1644], article 24).

regarding congregational singing. He also advocated a Calvinistic view of Christ's real presence at table rather than the Zwinglian (e.g., symbolic) view held by many of his Baptist brethren. Matthew Ward writes of him:

> When Benjamin Keach stated that God appointed [the Ordinances of the Gospel] "for the begetting of Faith," it was not by causing regeneration, but by putting one's self in a place where God's Spirit was known to work. Keach was not esoterically claiming that God's Spirit moved where God's people celebrated God's ordinances to the potential spiritual benefit of non-Christians present; he was very strict about those who could receive the Lord's Supper at Horseleydown. But God communicated saving truth through the ordinances. Even Baptism was more than a ceremony for the saved but a kind of wordless sermon ("analogical proposition") that presented the facts of the gospel, acknowledging Christ as Messiah and trusting in Him for forgiveness of sin, for all to hear and see. The more elaborate the setting or ceremony, the more obscured this basic truth became. In their worship, the Baptists wanted to celebrate the purity of the gospel, and they were willing to reevaluate much about their churches in the process.[17]

For Baptists, the worship service needed to be a simple, interactive presentation of the gospel. They were concerned that formal liturgy and ceremonialism would take the place of worship in word and spirit. Therefore they rejected formal worship for a more flexible, if not spontaneous form. Hanserd Knollys similarly believed "pure worship could only be performed by the Word of God and the Gifts of the Spirit, and he desired pure worship far above respectable worship."[18]

It is from this concern that some of the controversy over the practice of singing was generated. At what point were the preset forms of lyrics set to prearranged music—or even sermon notes for that matter—neglecting a proper reliance upon the Spirit? While they had long ago rejected the Anabaptist practice of putting aside all books in worship, they were uncertain how far to go in preparing for worship. At what point might proper preparation for worship lead them to the slippery slope of liturgical forms that might usher them right back into Anglicanism? They did not want the gospel obscured by ceremonialism. Yet, they had confidence that the Holy Spirit would not only form the gospel in their midst, but point them

17. Ward, *Pure Worship*, 149–150. See also Keach, *Golden Mine Opened*.

18. Ward, *Pure Worship*, 178. Ward references Keach, *Breach Repaired*, 136; Tombes, *Jehovah Jireh*, 5; and Knollys, *Parable of the Kingdom*, 15.

to Christ and his glory through it. They only needed to discover and adhere to pure, gospel worship. Scripture's role here, and the regulative principle, was critical because God promised to use Scripture in the revelation of the gospel. This is why Ward claims that the London Particular Baptists "used the gospel as a liturgical hermeneutic even if they may not have been fully intentional about (or even aware of) such a practice. They took very seriously the form and presentation of the gospel in their worship services in more than just their preaching."[19] Their adherence to the word in worship was adherence for the sake of gospel clarity. This driving conviction, among others, led many to forsake England for the New World to find a place where they could worship according to their convictions about Scripture.

Foundational Studies of the English Baptists

Christopher Ellis in *Gathering* presents an analysis of the theology and spirituality of worship among English Baptists.[20] His study seeks to identify the heart of Baptist worship from its inception until modern day. His conclusion is that the confession "Jesus is Lord" is the "presiding conviction" in Baptist worship. Of this he writes, "Christian prayers usually end with the formula, 'through Jesus Christ our Lord', or variations on it. This is not a magical incantation guaranteed to provide petitionary success, but a kerygmatic affirmation that Christian worship is through the mediatorial service of Jesus Christ and that the liturgical assembly is an assembly which

---

19. Ward, *Pure Worship*, 143. Ward summarizes chap. 5, "Gospel Worship and a New Purpose of the Gathering" this way: "In summary, the commitment to gospel worship took London Particular Baptists in very different directions from other Protestants. They believed that worship was for Christ, to celebrate His salvation and His Lordship over them. The message of salvation, combined with their understanding of election, led to a very intentional and unique (if seemingly haphazard) worship service. Their commitment to the gospel led them to eliminate all ceremonies that detracted from Christ in any way, including infant baptism, sacraments that confused the nature of salvation, and all external forms that distracted the senses. They desired a simple and austere worship that hearkened to some types of Puritan worship, but they used the ordinances to communicate the message of salvation, which was why they believed Christ instituted them in the first place. The purpose of their gatherings was not a base mental edification; worship was for God who communicated spiritual blessings through the encounter. Preaching was not just to teach doctrine but also to stir emotion, to call for a response, and to invite outsiders to Christ. Though Baptists shared many principles with their Protestant brethren, outsiders found their worship services irregular and irreverent; by this they meant that Baptists did not follow a careful liturgy or employ strict ceremony. Baptists believed that the Spirit participated in pure worship, and He was not predictable any more than salvation was predictable" (182).

20. See Ellis, *Gathering*.

bears his character."[21] In other words, it has been the Baptist conviction in worship that it is by the gospel that sinners are called out of darkness to be joined to the body of Christ. It is therefore by the gospel that the church can gather for worship. This makes the worship gathering both a celebration and expression of the gospel. It is in the ordinances and elements of worship that the gospel is rehearsed and its effects of grace applied. This is the paradigm of worship that the Baptists brought to, and sought to practice in, America.

Matthew Ward studies a smaller cross-section of Ellis' broader scope, but he does so in great depth and detail. He studies the earliest congregations of Baptists from which Ellis' study builds, and from which the subjects of this study originate. He also sees the centrality of Christ and the gospel in English Baptist worship. He notes the critical emphasis of the word of God and the reliance upon the Spirit. In many ways, he performs a similar type of study to Ellis, but rather than looking at the worship services, he assimilates the primary source material behind the worship services by combing the writings of the worship leaders (e.g., pastors). He highlights as elements of worship those identified by the Second London Confession—prayer, reading Scripture, preaching and hearing the Word of God, teaching and admonishing one another in psalms, hymns and spiritual songs, baptism and the Lord's Supper, with the last two being the two ordinances.[22] His conclusions regarding the nature of Baptist worship are predictably very similar to those of Ellis.

Ellis, on the other hand, arrives at his conclusion by observing and evaluating examples of Baptist worship services. Based upon the principles of the field of liturgical theology[23] he writes, "If worship embodies theology, then we have to recognize that it is particular, concrete examples of worship which need to be examined."[24] However, because Baptist churches practice free worship, the nature of this task can become quite interesting. Ellis describes freedom in worship in this manner:

> This freedom is the freedom of local congregations to order their own gathering for worship; it is the freedom of spontaneity which is open to the extempore guidance of the Holy Spirit; and it is the freedom of a particular worshipping community to

21. Ellis, *Gathering*, 231.

22. Ward, *Pure Worship*, 117. This is essentially a reprinting of the list from the Westminster Confession of Faith.

23. Ellis cites the work of Alexander Schmemann, Geoffrey Wainwright, Paul F. Bradshaw, and Kevin Irwin. He also provides the methodology based upon Schmemann's work that is utilized in this work.

24. Ellis, *Gathering*, 7.

respond to the reading and preaching of Scripture addressed to them as God's living Word.[25]

Given this description, it is hard to imagine an example of historic worship that more aptly fits this model than that of Baptists, save maybe the Quakers who exalted the Spirit at the expense of Scripture. This requires an adjusted research approach from the model typically used for a similar study of the worship practices in a liturgical tradition. Ellis warns,

> Using Baptist worship as a case study for doing liturgical theology in a Free Church context will enable us to see some of the difficulties of giving uncritical authority to the theology embodied in worship. The free nature of that worship requires that there be norms and guidelines which will ensure that the worship indeed expresses what the Christian community believes.[26]

In some ways, Ward's study provides some of those "norms and guidelines" that Ellis sought for the first chronological cross-section of his study. Additionally, given that their findings agree, their conclusions are helpful as a proper foundation for this study. It is from their English Baptist foundation that Baptist worship in North America is derived. The priority of the word of God, the active presence of the Holy Spirit, and worship in Jesus' name (i.e., through the gospel) are key distinctives of Baptist worship. Towards that end, the approved elements for worship are prayer, reading Scripture, preaching, and praising God in psalms, hymns and spiritual songs. Christ's ordinances are baptism and communion.

Liturgical theology of any worshiping group requires an evaluation of the worship texts. This requires looking at the words spoken and sung in worship services, as well as the descriptions of worship when available. Due to the unique nature of Baptist worship, some attention must also be given to the goals and priorities of what is valued in worship. Therefore, just as in Ellis' study, "commentaries and reflections on worship in the Baptist community" will be included in this study.[27] In view of this, Ellis provides a four-stage methodology that he has founded upon Schmemann's work, but adjusted for the unique aspects of Baptist (e.g., "free") worship.[28] This process requires, (1) establishing the liturgical facts; (2) analyzing those facts;

25. Ellis, *Gathering*, 27.

26. Ellis, *Gathering*, 19.

27. Ellis, *Gathering*, 30.

28. Ellis, *Gathering*, 23–24. The first three steps of this methodology are from Alexander Schmemann whereas Ellis adds the fourth step as an adjustment specifically for Baptist (e.g., "free") worship.

(3) synthesizing the meaning of the worship services; and (4) determining if the worship meaning is aligned with the broader theological convictions of Baptists. Due to the fact that Baptist worship is free worship this last step is especially important to ensure that what is conveyed in worship is authentic to Baptist belief.

Given the major studies on English Baptist worship already referenced above, their findings serve as the foundation of liturgical theology for this study. Ellis' conclusion that the heart of Baptist worship is the confession "Jesus is Lord" as a kerygmatic affirmation, and Ward's conclusion that they likewise employed the gospel as a liturgical hermeneutic for worship, essentially define the expected findings of these British emigrants. Once again, the question under consideration is, "How did the Baptists in North America re-present the gospel in worship that they brought from England?"

In summary, historic Baptist worship will be evaluated for three components that will serve to identify the presence of gospel form and content:

1. Is Christ central to worship?

2. Is the gospel content present in terms of historic narrative and effects in the believer's life?

3. Is the gospel faithfully "re-presented" according to the proposed "shape?"[29]

Baptists in North America

Some claim that the Baptist story on English soil began in America. Isaac Backus (1724–1806), prominent Baptist historian and leading Baptist preacher during the American Revolution, is one such advocate. He claims that the results of Roger Williams' (1603–1683) baptism and subsequent baptizing of his small gathering in Providence was "the first immersionist church in the entire English world."[30] Whether or not this claim is accurate,

---

29. This question is evaluated in a less stringent manner than Chapell did with formal liturgy (see Chapell, *Christ-Centered Worship*). In a Baptist model, the representation of seven or eight conversational elements is unlikely to be identifiable. However, the presence of elements that characterize God's initiative and man's response are much more likely. Also, the presence of elements that represent the central work of the cross and the sending of the church in its "vocation" as a result of worship are also likely to be present. This "shape" is represented by a simplified threefold model for evaluation: revelation and response; mediation and response; and exhortation and response.

30. Grenz, *Isaac Backus*, 45. If Backus' date of 1639 for Williams' baptism is correct, his claim is inaccurate given the accepted date of 1638 for John Spilsbury's Particular Baptist congregation in London. However, J. Stanley Lemons, the leading historian

it certainly is the first Baptist church in the New World as this group began meeting in Williams' house in 1638. Williams' religious journey was from Anglican priest trained at Cambridge, to Puritan, to Separatist, to Baptist. After four months he left the first Baptist church to become a "seeker." J. Stanley Lemons explains that soon after his departure, the church began to flounder. Some became Quakers while others began to cheat the Indians of their land and to sell them liquor and gunpowder. "Some even betrayed Providence Plantations by registering their property deeds in Massachusetts, giving the Bay Colony an excuse to assert authority over part of Williams' colony." Under the leadership of Chad Brown and Thomas Olney, The congregation soon evolved into a General Six-Principle Baptist Church[31] in the 1640s—making it the first General Six-Principle Baptist church in the American colonies as well.[32] There are no written records for the church prior to 1755, but dispute and division seem to mark its early history.

According to Lemons, it was not until James Manning (1738–1791) became pastor in 1771 that the church stabilized, "leaving what eventually became a sidetrack in the Baptist movement in America [the General Six-Principle Baptist Association] for the mainline, the Regular Baptists."[33]

---

on the Providence Baptist story claims a date of 1638 for this initial gathering of the Calvinistic Baptist church, which is the more commonly accepted date now. Thomas Helwys' Anabaptist church was gathered at Spitalfields in London about 1612. See Lemons, *First Baptist, Providence*, xiii–xiv.

31. General Six Principle Baptists are based upon the six principles outlined in Heb 6:1–2: repentance, faith, baptism, laying on of hands, resurrection of the dead, and final judgment. The most controversial of which is "going under hands" which is required for membership and participation in the Lord's Supper. One of their historians claims a lineage that dates back to "About sixty years after our Lord ascended to glory, his kingdom came into our land; which of the messengers of his grace was first sent to prepare his way in the region, is not now certainly known, but it is generally believed that Paul and his associates first preached the gospel to the Britons" (Knight, *History of the General or Six Principle Baptists*, 2). Their activity in the New World was centered in Rhode Island during the Colonial Period of American history. David Benedict writes that at Providence, "It is probable that singing was first laid aside in times of persecution, on account of the danger of practicing it, and afterwards it was difficult to revive everywhere a due sense of its worth as a divine appointment" (Benedict, *General History*, 454). This seems to indicate that they may have sung at some point in their early history but likely laid it aside when they embraced Six-Principle Baptist tenets in 1652. David Music and Paul Richardson write, "The congregation remained songless for nearly 120 years, singing not being reintroduced until 1771 by pastor James Manning" (Music and Richardson, *"I Will Sing the Wondrous Story,"* 72).

32. Lemons, *First Baptist, Providence*, xiv–v.

33. Lemons, *First Baptist, Providence*, xxiii. "All of the pastors between Roger Williams (1639) and James Manning (1771) were laymen chosen from within the congregation and ordained as Elders. . . . The coming of James Manning to the pulpit of the Providence church brought with it that developing network of churches, ministers,

Manning was from the Philadelphia Baptist Association, the influence of which will be discussed in detail in chapter 3. Not much is known about Providence worship in their earliest years. "They did not preach from a prepared text, but exhorted as they were inspired by God. They did not use prayer books, hymnals or psalters in their worship. Like the Quakers, they banned congregational singing. The only written text was the Bible itself; all else was extemporaneous."[34] This all changed with the arrival of Manning, as Lemons explains:

> The coming of James Manning to Rhode Island, the founding of the first Baptist college [Rhode Island College which became Brown University], and the organization of the Warren Association were all consequences of the efforts of the [Philadelphia Baptist Association]. The transformation of the Baptist church in Providence came with James Manning who brought the entire agenda of the Philadelphia Baptist Association with him, including Calvinist theology, a paid, educated ministry, congregational singing, the relaxation of the requirement for laying on of hands, and greater order and decorum, including the silencing of women in the meetings.[35]

---

education institutions, and aspirations of the Regular Baptists" (xxiii–xxiv).

34. Lemons, *First Baptist, Providence*, xxvii.

35. Lemons, *First Baptist, Providence*, xxvi. Lemons writes, "One of the most contentious issues for First Baptist was Manning's introduction of congregational singing to a church that had not sung a song for over a century because the General Six-Principle Baptists banished singing from their services. Elder Samuel Winsor declared that such singing was 'very disgustful' and was one of the causes of the rupture in 1771. It took decades to establish congregational singing, and an organ was not installed until 1834." When the church inquired about the non-attendance of one member—Arthur Fenner—in January 1778, he said he "abstained from Communion with this church in consequence of their practice of promiscuous Singing in Public worship, which he could not fellowship." Fenner was one of the remaining Six Principle Baptists after nearly ninety of them split in 1771. He eventually left the church to join the General Six-Principle Church in Johnston, which was then pastored by the aforementioned Samuel Winsor. The church records from 1797 refer to a letter from Mr. Alpheus Billings that "his declining state of health would prevent his conducting the singing at Publick worship." Mr. John Newman was to be solicited as a replacement, recorded Thursday evening, July 27, 1797 (156). A report from Thursday evening, September 27, 1798, reads: the committee "appointed at our last Meeting to Consult on the best mode of performing sacred musick at the usual Time of Divine Service report as their opinion, that a number of the Members of the Church Qualified to Conduct the Musick should Convene in the Choristers Seat in order to take the lead and that such of the Congregation are inclined to join the same and that in order to promote this design a Meeting of the Church should be held once a week in the room below to improve themselves in singing, that the Congregation be inform'd of the same from the Pulpit and invited to attend the Meetings for instruction, and to unite Publickly in the performance of a

John Clarke established the second Baptist church in America at New-port, Rhode Island in 1644.[36] The third Baptist church was Second Baptist Newport, established in 1656. First Baptist Church of Swansea, Massachusetts was established in 1663.

First Baptist Church of Boston was established in 1665 as the fifth Baptist church in America and one of the most influential in New England. A Baptist church in the heart of the Puritan Commonwealth was a prime target for persecution. Its founding pastor, Thomas Goold (1619–1675), attempted to stay in his Congregationalist church at Charlestown for many years after refusing to have his infant daughter baptized in 1655. He was eventually censured and put out. In 1663, a group of Baptist sympathizers began having worship services in his home. Some of these Baptists had recently fled England due to the harsh Clarendon Code of the 1660s and 1670s. When Goold was told that he should not have separated from the Charlestown Church because it was "God's temple," Goold answered, "Christ dwelleth in no temple, but in the heart of the believer."[37] Goold felt that he had been put out of the Congregationalist church and had no option but to separate and suffer the consequences. He was arrested multiple times as a "schismatic" and subsequently imprisoned at least twice (in 1666 and 1668).

The church covenant of First Baptist Church of Boston, recorded March 28, 1665, expressed the Baptist commitment to word and Spirit:

> The 28 of the 3rd mo. 1665 in Charlestowne, Massachusetts, the Churche of Christe, commonly (though falsely) called Ana-baptiste were gathered together And entered into fellowship & communion each with other, Ingaigeing to walke togather in all the appointments of there Lord & Master the Lord Jesus Christ as farre as hee should bee pleased to make known his mind & will unto them by his word & Spirit, And then were Baptized.[38]

A description of their worship gathering is recorded from July–August 1665. It reads, "The Anabaptists gathered yms into a church, prophesied one by one, & some one amongst ym administered ye Lords Supper [Thomas Goold]. . . . They also set up a lecture at Drinkers house once a fortnight.

---

branch of Divine Worship so pleasing, solemn & Edifying" (161–62). Additionally, the first inquiry regarding the cost of an organ was in 1817. It took seventeen years for an organ to be acquired finally in 1834 (xxvi).

36. Some date this church earlier but apparently they were not a "baptizing" church until at least 1644 (Lemons, *First Baptist, Providence*, xviii).

37. Weaver, *In Search of the New Testament Church*, 44–45.

38. Wood, *First Baptist Church*, 56.

They were admonished by ye court of Assista."[39] Their "Confession of Faith"—one of the oldest in North America—also records their guidelines for worship: "When the church is mett together they may all propesie one by one that all may all learne & all may be comforted [1 Cor 14:23, 24, 25, 31] & they ought to meete together the first day of the weeke to attend upon the Lord in all his holy ordinances continuing in the Apostles doctrine and fellowship & breaking bread & praise [Acts 20:7, 1 Cor 16:2, Acts 2:42]."[40]

On March 6, 1689, the constables of Charlestown were sent to Goold's house to see who was meeting there and to report back. After a list of about twenty names, the report records the following:

> When we came into the hous John Johnson was exorting the pepell: After he had don Thomas Goold spack from that place in first of the canticells the second vers let him kis me with the kisis of his mouth & then went to prayer & so ended. They said it was att 2 of ye clock when they went thither to Th: Goolds hous.[41]

There was no singing in worship at this time. Nathan Wood, the early historian of this group, seems surprised by this and indicated that the reason was, "perhaps lest it should attract too much attention, and yet they made no secret of their meeting together." He continues, "One or two of them exhorted from the Scriptures, a prayer or two was offered, and they separated."[42] It also is recorded that the church observed the Lord's Supper once every month, which was the practice also at the time of the writing of Wood's history of the church (1899).[43] According to Horton Davies, a typical Puritan order of worship in Boston in the late seventeenth century is set forth in figure 5.[44]

---

39. Wood, *First Baptist Church*, 64.

40. Wood, *First Baptist Church*, 66.

41. Wood, *First Baptist Church*, 90.

42. Wood, *First Baptist Church*, 91. Wood also points out that they were not dependent on the presence of a minister. "They believed that every individual should have liberty of utterance in their social gatherings. They had an elder who usually preached and administered the ordinances in an orderly way, but if the elder were necessarily absent, some lay brother was called on to preach or exhort in his place." He concludes, "It is probable that the very simplicity and flexibility of the organization preserved it from utter destruction. It did not depend on any one man. Any one might expound the Scriptures to the others. Any one might pray in their assembly. Whoever of their number might be in prison, or absent for other cause, there was always some one present and ready to lead their service of worship."

43. Wood, *First Baptist Church*, 136.

44. Davies, *Worship of the American Puritans*, 8.

Opening Prayer of Intercession and Thanksgiving

Reading and exposition of a chapter of the Bible

Psalm singing

Sermon

Psalm singing

Prayer

Blessing

Figure 5. Horton Davies, Typical Puritan order of worship in Boston

This order is reconcilable with the account of First Baptist Church of Boston above. Often, persecuted churches did not sing, especially if they knew constables were watching. Their presence might also have affected the freedom of these Baptists to worship as normal. It is likely that the structure Davies suggests is very similar to Baptist practice, especially since this structure seems to be embedded in most Baptist worship service orders that follow. Communion, when celebrated, would likely have followed the sermon. After meeting in private homes (most often in that of Goold) for its early existence, a meetinghouse was finally built in 1679 for its growing congregation.

It is not certain when they began singing in worship, but the early practice was fraught with logistical challenges and a lack of congregational skill. At the Baptist Church at Newport, John Comer first introduced congregational singing in 1726.[45] There was a close connection between the Baptist churches at Newport and Boston, so it is possible that singing began in Boston around the same time, if not before since Comer came from Boston. However, during the time of Elisha Callendar (ca. 1688–1738, ordained in 1718) as pastor, there is evidence of the church singing in worship. One of the most enlightening and humorous descriptions of singing in early Baptist worship comes from this congregation. Wood describes an entry into the Church Record in 1728:

> At a church meeting Sep 8 1728. Voted that our Brother Skinner Russell be desired from that time forward to "Set the Psalm in Publick." The singing in public worship of that time was wonderful in its variety and lack of harmony. There were no

---

45. Wood, *First Baptist Church*, 220. Comer was saved in 1721 and became an elder at First Baptist Church, Boston before becoming pastor at First Baptist Church, Newport. As a Reformed, Six-Principle Baptist who advocated singing, Comer is an unusual mixture (Weaver, *In Search of the New Testament Church*, 52). Elisha Callendar's grandson later became the pastor at Newport (Wood, *First Baptist Church*, 220).

instruments of music. The Psalms, distorted into something which was strangely supposed to be metre, were sung. The irregularity of the metre made it impossible to fit any regular tune to a psalm. Sometimes, when the psalm was long, the singing would occupy a half-hour, during which the congregation stood, and each one sang a tune which seemed to have little connection with the tune of any other singer. The result was a singular babel of sounds in which harmony was not the most noticeable feature. The one hundred and thirty-third Psalm furnishes illustration of the irregularity of the metre:

How good and sweet to see
   It's for brethren to dwell
      together in unitee;

Its like choise oyle that fell
   the head upon
   that down did flow
   the beard unto
   beard of Aron
   the skirts of his garment
   that unto them went down;

Like Hermons due descent
   Sions mountains upon
   for there to bee
   the Lords blessing
   life aye lasting
   commandeth hee.[46]

The awkward rhythm of the metrical psalm, and the lack of enough psalters for everyone to read along, made singing in unison nearly impossible. Wood explains, somewhat humorously, "The singers had no notes before them and each one sang pretty much at his own pleasure. It cannot be denied that they enjoyed their own singing and entered into it with peculiar zest. Perhaps the very defiance of all the rules of music gave them a sense of unconstraint, which was the chief element of their delight."

A new technique referred to as "lining out the psalm" was being practiced in an effort to get the congregation into some semblance of order and to improve their singing. However, as most musical innovations in the church tend to do, this divided the congregation and some preferred the old way. "The new way seemed an encroachment upon liberty." The "liners" eventually won out, but the new method really did not prove to be any

46. Eliot et al., "Psalm 133," in *Bay Psalm Book*.

great improvement over the old. According to Wood, "No method could make psalms metred after the fashion of 'The Bay Psalm Book,' to be sung well." Brother Russell was supposed to "set the tune" at this time, but there is no evidence that the church fully employed the method of lining out at this time, though later they did. Reading the Scriptures to the congregation was not a common practice at this time in Baptist or Congregationalists churches.[47]

On July 7, 1740, "The Church voted to sing that Version of the Psalms done by Dr. Brady & Mr. Tate, so long as no objections should be offered against it."[48] It appears that there were none and the church began using *Tate and Brady* at this time. The worship order was simply the following: "One psalm was sung without instrumental accompaniment, a prayer and the sermon followed. The service would not be overlong even if the sermon were longer than at present."[49] In 1771, the church adopted Watts' collection of Psalms, Hymns and Spiritual Song to replace *Tate and Brady*. In 1791, the congregation decided to use the London Baptist pastor John Rippon's *Selection of Hymns* "at baptism and communion seasons, as a supplement to Dr. Watt's hymns."[50] These two examples at Providence and Boston in New England represent the earliest beginnings of Baptist worship, but not the most influential; that came from the Middle and Southern Colonies.

47. Wood, *First Baptist Church*, 218–20. Wood explains that Brattle Street—a Congregationalist church—was organized in 1699 "because of the dissent from the custom of not reading the Scriptures in public worship and the requiring of experience as a prerequisite to admission to the Lord's table." At the Second Church (another Congregationalists church) they were not read until 1729.

48. Wood, *First Baptist Church*, 220.

49. Wood, *First Baptist Church*, 220.

50. Music and Richardson, *"I Will Sing the Wondrous Story,"* 82.

3

The First Baptists in Philadelphia
(1688–1746)

Introduction

THE FIRST HISTORIC EXAMPLE of worship under consideration in this study is that of the Baptists in Philadelphia. There are three reasons for beginning this study with the Baptists at Philadelphia: (1) the connection here with the founding influence from Baptists' roots in England is clear; (2) persecution did not hinder the free growth and development of the movement; and (3) the influence from this group upon other Baptist churches is unparalleled. Tom Nettles writes, "The Philadelphia Association serves as a bridge . . . between much of the Baptist life and self-conscious identity taken on by English Baptists and that which defined the growth of Baptists in America."[1] The founding members of these early churches were primarily Baptists from England and Wales. They embraced Baptist theology and practices in the motherland of the British Isles while under the persecution of the Act of Uniformity and the Clarendon Code. They subsequently came to the New World to freely express the Baptist faith and advance it. The freedom of religious opinion, instituted by the Quaker William Penn (1644–1718), is a leading reason why so many came to Pennsylvania. Here they were free to assemble, practice, and propagate a Baptistic identity to a degree that was not possible in New England.

---

1. Nettles, *Baptists*, 75.

While they are not the first Baptists in America, they are the first major influencers of Baptists in America.[2] In a century that began with no more than twenty Baptist churches but ended with almost a thousand, it is important to consider the substantial influence that this group had in the eighteenth Century. James L. Clark writes,

> This was the first Baptist association organized in the New World and it remained the only body of its kind in the colonies for forty-four years. During this period the Baptists in all parts of the country looked to it for advice and assistance. It, therefore, became the model for the other early associations and retained this distinction long after those associations began to appear in the colonies."[3]

The Particular Baptist tradition of England became known as the "Regular" Baptist tradition in America. Additionally, Regular Baptist life in the eighteenth century is typically viewed with the Philadelphia Baptist Association as the epicenter of its activity. According to Weaver, "Scholars call it the most important Baptist entity of the century and thus refer to its influence as the 'Philadelphia tradition.'"[4] As with so many other aspects of church life, what happened in Philadelphia with regards to Baptist worship became a model and influence for other Baptist churches around the country to emulate.

A Brief History

Many of the Baptists in Philadelphia were Welsh Baptists. David Spencer writes in his nineteenth-century history of this group, "The Welsh Baptist historian (J. Davis) claims that 'Wales is to be considered as the parent of the Baptist denomination in Pennsylvania.'"[5] Upon the restoration of Charles II and the Act of Uniformity, persecution in Wales had intensified greatly. After years of meeting in secret and experiencing fines, arrests, and whippings,

2. James L. Clark writes, "The Pennepek congregation was the mother church for Baptists in the Middle Atlantic States of Pennsylvania, New Jersey, New York and Delaware much like the First Baptist Church of Providence was in the New England States" (*Set Them in Order*, 370).

3. Clark, *Set Them in Order*, 2.

4. Weaver, *In Search of the New Testament Church*, 52. "Before the First Great Awakening, there were actually more Six-Principle Baptists in New England, especially in the cradle of early Baptist life, Rhode Island. Most, but not all, Six-Principle Baptists affirmed Arminian theology. After 1750 and the First Great Awakening, the majority of Baptists were 'Five-Principle,' Calvinistic, and practiced 'closed communion.'"

5. Spencer, *Early Baptists of Philadelphia*, 18.

several members of the Baptist Church of Dolau in Radnorshire, Wales, sailed for America. They arrived in Philadelphia in 1686 and settled on the banks of Pennepek Creek.[6] Other Baptists in this area of Pennsylvania came from Rhode Island including a pastor. Rev. Thomas Dungan, originally from London, had previously been a member of the First Baptist Church of Newport where he had studied for the ministry.[7] Dungan settled in this area in 1684 and started a church at Cold Spring that was the first Baptist church in the area. Upon the death of Dungan in 1687, members of the church began trickling into the Pennepek church until it finally disbanded in 1702. Many of the Cold Spring members ultimately joined the Baptist church at Pennepek.

In 1687, Elias Keach arrived in Philadelphia. As the son of the celebrated Baptist minister in London, Benjamin Keach, he came dressed as a minister himself—in black with a band—as a ruse to cover what is reported to have been a "gay, wild, [and] thoughtless" life.[8] He was asked to preach and many people came to hear the son of the famous Baptist preacher. This was his first sermon and likely preached one of his father's sermons. Of this event Morgan Edwards (1722–1795), later a prominent pastor of FBC Philadelphia and historian writes,

> He performed well enough till he had advanced pretty far in the sermon. Then, stopping short, he looked like a man astonished. The audience concluded he had been seized with a sudden disorder; but on asking what the matter was, received from him a confession of the imposture, with tears in his eyes, and much trembling.[9]

He was subsequently baptized by Thomas Dungan and ordained, counting that moment as his conversion.

6. Spencer, *Early Baptists of Philadelphia*, 21. Pennepek is also spelled "Pennypek," "Pennypack," "Pennypeka," "Pennepeck," and "Pennypeck." The church later became known as Lower Dublin Baptist Church.

7. While FBC Providence was a non-singing congregation, FBC Newport seems to have been a singing congregation in its early days. In 1656 a group of members withdrew to form the Second Baptist Church, in part because of First Church's use of psalmody. It abandoned the practice some time before 1725 as it is reported at that time that they were a non-singing congregation (Music and Richardson, "I Will Sing the Wondrous Story," 72–73). It is not clear if Thomas Dungan advocated singing but it is possible and if so, this possibility contributes to the potential early singing date of the Pennepek Church, though Elias Keach's influence alone is sufficient to establish this possibility.

8. Jones, *Historical Sketch*, 5.

9. Spencer, *Early Baptists of Philadelphia*, 23.

The Pennepek church was constituted in January 1688, with twelve members and the recently converted Keach as their pastor. This was the seventh Baptist church in America. It became the hub of vibrant gospel activity around the Philadelphia area. From there, Keach traveled and preached the gospel to any who would listen. Spencer writes, "Mr. Keach extended his ministerial labors into New Jersey, to Trenton, Burlington, Middletown, Cohansey and Salem. He also frequently preached in Philadelphia, Chester, and other places. At that time all the Baptists of Philadelphia and New Jersey were regarded as general members of [the Pennepek] church."[10] They gathered quarterly for the ordinance of communion, in a different location each quarter, to accommodate distant members. A cooperative work began to evolve as these locales began forming churches: Middletown in 1688, Piscataway in 1689, Cohansey in 1690, and Philadelphia in 1698. First Baptist Philadelphia became the eleventh Baptist church in America though it was considered an extension of Pennepek for almost fifty years.

David Benedict, the renowned nineteenth-century Baptist historian, writes of Keach: "He may be considered as the chief apostle among the Baptists in these parts of America."[11] However, doctrinal disputes such as the matter of laying on of hands, among others, became contentious enough that Keach felt it best to free himself to continue traveling and preaching. Keach resigned his pastorate and moved to New Jersey where much of the growth was occurring at this time (the three newest churches after Pennepek were in New Jersey). John Watts (1661–1702) assumed the pastorate vacated by Keach in 1690. Watts was from Kent County, England, but had been baptized at Pennepek by Keach. Keach eventually returned to London in 1692 to a very successful pastoral ministry there where he served until his death. Watts preached at Pennepek and, beginning in 1698, also preached twice a month at Philadelphia until his death in 1702. This process of sharing pastors between the two churches continued until 1746. Philadelphia was considered a branch of Pennepek during that time. Evan Morgan (served 1706–1709), Samuel Jones (served 1706–c. 1722), Joseph Wood (served 1708–c. 1747), Abel Morgan (served 1711–c. 1722), and Jenkin Jones (served 1725–1746) all preached at both churches under a similar organization. FBC Philadelphia was formally constituted on May 15, 1746, as the center of activity had shifted away from Pennepek to the First Church in Philadelphia. Jones continued with them exclusively as their pastor until 1760, and was then succeeded by the dynamic and eventful tenure of

10. Spencer, *Early Baptists of Philadelphia*, 24.
11. Benedict, *General History*, 597.

Morgan Edwards, also a Welsh Baptist. Edwards had been recommended to the church by the famous English Baptist pastor, John Gill (1697–1771).

The Theology in Practice

As has been mentioned, the majority of the founding and influential members of this group were largely of Welsh Baptist descent, committed to Particular Baptist principles. This group of churches became a bastion of Regular Baptist theology with the prevailing view of the atonement as being Calvinistic. They were also evangelistic as their history demonstrates. Douglas Weaver cites a response by the Association in 1724 to a query from one of its churches in which they refer to "a confession 'owned' by the association."[12] Given that the founding pastor of the Pennepek church was Elias Keach—son of the secretary of the 1689 Second London Confession—and the orientation of the Baptist movement, as well as the colonies as whole, was to London; it is certain that this was the confession in view. This is further confirmed by the ratification of the same confession less than twenty years later as the Philadelphia Baptist Confession (1742). This version contained the addition of two new sections—one on the laying on of hands after baptism and one on the singing of hymns in worship.[13] The influence of the elder Keach through his son seems apparent here, as both of these were also present in the 1697 personal confession of Benjamin Keach. Weaver explains, "The strong Calvinism of the Philadelphia Confession made that theological persuasion dominant in much of American Baptist theology during the eighteenth and nineteenth centuries."[14] This fact points to the remarkable influence this group had upon Baptists in America. This also demonstrates their early commitment to sound doctrine and adherence to the word of God. Clark writes, "The Philadelphia Association had no sympathy whatsoever with that which it considered to be false doctrine."[15]

12. Weaver, *In Search of the New Testament Church*, 53. Tom Nettles confirms that it was the Second London Confession in view here, which they considered a "standard of orthodoxy among Baptists" (Nettles, *Baptists*, 76). Bill Leonard writes, "Known in the colonies as 'Keach's Confession,' it was used in 1712 to resolve a doctrinal dispute in the Baptist church at Middletown, New Jersey" (Leonard, *Baptists in America*, 84).

13. James Clark believes the Welsh Tract Church was instrumental in the other Baptist churches adopting these two additional articles (Clark, *Set Them in Order*, 11).

14. Weaver, *In Search of the New Testament Church*, 53. David McCollum writes, "The Calvinistic Philadelphia Baptists emphasized evangelism because of their Welsh roots, which help them accept the [Great] Awakening. Philadelphia's influence spread until most American Baptists accepted evangelistic moderate Calvinism" ("Study of Evangelicals," 193).

15. Clark, *Set Them in Order*, 88. "Those who had strayed from the doctrines which

The minutes of the Association are filled with examples of this conviction as the leaders respond to doctrinal questions (e.g., queries from the churches), handle matters of doctrinal disputes (e.g., "laying on of hands"), and give instruction through circular letters. The crowning effort in this regard is the ratifying of the first Baptist confession in America—The Philadelphia Baptist Confession of 1742. Weaver writes, "Baptists in the Philadelphia Baptist Association affirmed the final authority of the Bible in Religious matters. Nevertheless, they used a confession of faith as a doctrinal guideline and standard for orthodoxy. Doctrinal agreement was a condition for associational membership."[16] They were confessional Baptists and they continued this inherited practice in the New World.

The Practice in Worship

As with any group that worshiped over three hundred years ago, reconstructing their regular practice of worship is a significant challenge. However, certain undeniable pieces can be assembled and then propositions may be suggested based upon other primary source material. It is certain that the earliest Baptists in Philadelphia maintained the practice of "the reading of the Scriptures, Preaching, and hearing the word of God" in worship, as prescribed by the Second London Confession. As described above, this included the application of the regulative principle in worship and the effort to discern "the acceptable way of worshipping God." This called into question for some the practice of congregational singing. The confession states that worship should include, "teaching and admonishing one another in Psalms, Hymns, and Spiritual songs, singing with grace in our Hearts to the Lord."[17] The disagreement ensued over whether singing in the heart should also afford the public expression with the voice, or should it be merely internal. Additional concerns regarding "conjoined" singing with unbelievers and the authenticity of the expression; the presence of fixed forms such as a psalter or hymn book in worship; and the appropriate matter for singing (e.g., Psalms or hymns of human composure?); makes this a highly contentious matter in both the New World and Old. Benjamin Keach is at the

---

had been delivered 'once for all to the saints' were first approached on the subject and given opportunity to reconsider and then if they saw fit to repudiate the erroneous doctrine they were forgiven. But, if they decided to maintain the new doctrine they were immediately excluded from the membership of their church by its members."

16. Weaver, *In Search of the New Testament Church*, 53.

17. Lumpkin, *Baptist Confessions of Faith*, 281. Chapter 12, "Of Religious Worship, and the Sabbath Day."

center of the controversy among London Baptists and it appears that his son also may have played an influential role in Philadelphia, which will be discussed below.

The Philadelphia Baptists also gathered in a variety of regional locales to celebrate communion at least twice a year, especially as the influence of the church widened in its geographical circle with the travel and preaching of Elias Keach and before local churches were established. This created a sense of cooperation and uniformity even before the Philadelphia Baptist Association was formed in 1707. Gavin Morton Walker, in a historical address in 1932 celebrating the 225th anniversary of the Association, describes the early worship of the churches:

> In early days [of worship] fixed forms were objected to because they did not give room for individual expression. Any Baptist might take part in his meeting. Hymn-singing was suspected by many because unscriptural persons might take part insincerely. It took about a century in America for congregational singing to become a regular practice among Baptists; but the Welsh element led to its adoption here earlier. A clerk led the singing from a place in front of the pulpit. Psalm- and hymn-books were at first procured in Britain, and later prepared here. Choirs appeared in the gallery, and a little over a century ago an organ was sanctioned in the First Church, without expense to the congregation.... Gradually ritual has grown in our churches, the more so where the building is of the more appropriate type, and now our churches generally have forms of service which include, in varying degree, all that is acceptable in evangelical churches. (The writer has had for years, during Lord's Day morning worship, a period of silent prayer, when the congregation is asked to make confession, return thanks, offer petition and intercession, and renew their dedication to the Saviour). More and more the fact of worship is being stressed and its enrichment sought. The danger now is that the values of expression in worship may be missed; none of our meetings are conserving this sufficiently.[18]

Of communion he writes, "Development . . . has been in the introduction of individual cups and of unfermented wine, while close communion has given place to open." This infers that the original practice was that of a common cup of wine and close communion—allowing only baptized believers who were church members to participate. This ensured that those who came to the table were known by the church as having expressed authentically a profession of faith both in public affirmation and symbolic

18. Walker, *Philadelphia Baptist Development*, 10.

witness through baptism. Baptism was required for church membership and in some places laying on of hands was required as well. This led to baptisms and communion being held at a separate time, for church members only, and was not open as was public worship on Sunday.

Walker continues, "For these two centuries and more there has not been the slightest inclination on the part of any of our churches toward belief in any magical change in the elements of the Lord's Supper." Of Baptism he writes, "In Philadelphia baptisms were on week-days in the Schuylkill, and at the place of the baptisterion a two-story brick building was erected for us on such occasions." Finally—"Our churches have never christened children, and have never wanted to; but the idea of dedicating children to the Lord in a suitable ceremony has found favor in many of our churches. In early records we find that it was considered irregular to baptize a person who wished to commune elsewhere, and baptism by one not baptized himself was null and void."[19] Walker also believes that the Baptists of Philadelphia were "very strict about the laying on of hands on the reception of members, at the setting apart of deacons, elders, and ministers." The role of this practice was especially stringent with regard to ministers. "A minister not ordained by the laying on of hands could not administer baptism and the Supper. One ordained by the laying on of hands for a Ruling Elder must be ordained again by the laying on of hands when called to the Word and doctrine."[20] While the matter of laying on of hands was one of the added sections to the Philadelphia Confession (1742), the church records indicate that this matter was one of great contention from the earliest days and was not widely held elsewhere. This was one of the early disputes that led to Keach's decision to resign from the pastorate at Pennepek, and most likely the predominant one, as it is the one most often referenced.[21]

There is little doubt that one of the other matters in dispute included the practice of congregational singing and hymns. Keach was a proponent of singing hymns as added to the Philadelphia Confession in 1742 from the "Keach Confession." However, at this early date—some fifty years before—these were still highly contentious matters as in other parts of the colonies and in England. The minutes of the Pennepek church reveal that Keach

19. Walker, *Philadelphia Baptist Development*, 10.

20. Walker, *Philadelphia Baptist Development*, 11.

21. Spencer lists only this matter specifically among "other matters of doctrine and practice" (Spencer, *Early Baptists of Philadelphia*, 25). Horatio Jones mentions the matter of "predestination" in addition to laying on of hands (Jones, *Historical Sketch*, 10). Morgan Edwards lists the issues as being "absolute predestination, laying on of hands, distributing the elements, singing Psalms, seventh-day Sabbath, etc., which through [sic] the body ecclesiastic into a fever" (Edwards, *Materials Towards a History*, 9).

"'usually concluded' the Lord's Supper 'with singing of a hymn of praise composed for that purpose.' Before preaching, he also 'commonly used to sing a Psalm or part of a psalm.'"[22] After Keach's return to London in the spring of 1692, he organized a church there where congregational singing was practiced regularly. In 1696 he published a collection of one hundred hymns for use in worship, entitled *A Banquetting-House Full of Spiritual Delights; or, Hymns and Spiritual Songs on Several Occasions*. In 1697 he published *The Glory and Ornament of a True Gospel-Constituted Church*, in which he outlined the principles of a true gospel church, including his thoughts on worship. These two works provide some insight into the early perspective that Keach might have brought to the early Baptist worship experience near Philadelphia.

On the title page of the hymn collection Keach lists Ephesians 5:19 to endorse the command from Scripture for singing. He then lists three reasons for such a collection in the "Epistle Dedicatory": (1) the personal benefit of recalling sermons for private meditation; (2) the family benefit of hymns and spiritual songs to sing at home; and (3) "for the better and more orderly performance of this part of divine worship in the publick assembly; for my premeditation you will be capable conjointly to sing with more judgment and understanding and make the sweeter harmony in the ears of the God of order."[23] These three reasons demonstrate the connection he saw between corporate worship and worship in the rest of life. He then expresses in no small detail his intention of keeping these hymns simple and accessible to all. He mentions the ongoing public debate regarding singing but feels that Richard Allen's *An Essay to Prove Singing of Psalms with Conjoined Voices a Christian Duty* (1696) has settled the matter and that he could not improve on it. However, he then includes a paragraph arguing for congregational singing anyway. His final benedictory remarks in the "Epistle Dedicatory" give a sense of the gospel theme of the collection:

> And the God of peace, that brought again from the dead our
> Lord Jesus, that great Shepherd of the Sheep, through the blood
> of the Everlasting Covenant, make you perfect in every good
> work, to do his will, working in you that which is well-pleasing

---

22. *Minutes from Olde Pennepack Record Books*, 126, quoted in Music and Richardson, "*I Will Sing the Wondrous Story*," 76. "The wording suggests that Elias may have been the author of the communion hymns. It is also possible that these texts were written by his father, Benjamin, who had first introduced hymn singing in connection with the Lord's table. If the hymns were by Elias, they may be among those published in London, in 1696, following his return there."

23. Keach, *Banquetting-House*, 18.

in his sight through Jesus Christ; to whom be glory forever and
ever, Amen.

The collection is essentially a collection of gospel-centered songs. He
included songs for baptism, which became a common section in subsequent
Baptist hymnbooks because no other groups besides Baptists were writing
these. He also included several communion hymns that reflect a sense of the
real presence of Christ at the table.[24] According to David Music and Paul
Richardson, "A prominent theme in his hymns is that of covenant."[25] Many
of them emphasize the keeping power of Christ, the benefits of the gospel to
the believer, and the praiseworthiness of Christ.

In *The Glory and Ornament of a True Gospel-Constituted Church*, Keach makes some very compelling and robust observations regarding worship. Given that much of his teaching in Philadelphia was while traveling
to assembled groups that became churches, his influence could have spread
quite widely and strategically. Keach believed that it is in gathered worship
that the church has access to "divine Presence with them: or when the Glory
of God fills his temple (Exod. 24.24. Mat. 18.20)."[26] Because of this, he believes public worship should be preferred before private, though he advocated private and family worship as was mentioned above.[27] While anyone
could attend the general worship service, "the Lord's Supper, holy discipline,
and days of prayer and fasting" were to be shared as "the Church of Old" in
"separat[ing] themselves from all Strangers (Neh. 1.2.)." The "publick Ordinances" of the church were "publick prayer, reading and preaching the Word,
and in singing God's praises, as hath formerly been proved." At this point
in his discourse he chastises those who might join the church in prayer but
"not praise God with us."[28] His definition of praising God certainly includes
singing and he takes the next portion of the treatise to outline the benefits
for the believer of participating in public worship, including singing. Much

24. He subtitles many of these as "A Sacramental Hymn" and they generally include
language provoking the active image of Christ on the cross before the participant: "Be-
hold! (saith Christ) look up, and see | your bleeding, dying Lord; O look! | Come hither,
view me on the Tree! | And by my dear Father forsook. | Behold my wounds, darlings
'tis I | See here my bleeding hands and feet? | Draw near unto Mount Calvary, and at the
cross your Savior greet (Keach, *Banquetting-House*, 3). It is quite possible that some of
these hymns were composed and sung while in Philadelphia.

25. Music and Richardson, *"I Will Sing the Wondrous Story,"* 17.

26. Keach, *Glory and Ornament*, 18.

27. The concept of private and family worship at least in part, was to prepare oneself
for public worship. Early Baptists placed some emphasis on the need to prepare oneself
spiritually to come to worship. It was never to be entered glibly or without serious
consideration of its importance.

28. Keach, *Glory and Ornament*, 21.

as his father pleaded in 1689 for singing as a solution to the acknowledged spiritual decline and zeal in Baptist worship, Keach advances the church's prioritization of worship as a whole, to include singing. It is in the worship service that the church responds to God's command and preference for his people to gather to praise him. He gives four reasons for doing so:

> (1) Since God prefers it thus: Or has so great esteem of his pub-lick worship. (2) Because he is said to dwell in Sion; It is his Habitation for ever. The place where his Honour dwells. (Psal. 132.13. Psal. 25.9.) (3) Here God is most glorified. In his temple everyone speaks of his glory; My praise shall be in the great congregation. (Psal. 29.2). (4) Here is most of God's gracious presence (as one observes it.)[29]

The first three points being a matter of obedience, the fourth engen-ders extended support. Keach adds several supporting points regarding the manifest presence of God in worship as his primary argument for the ben-efit of the worshiper. This is perhaps the most compelling part of his treatise to this study as he outlines the effects of transformation upon the worshiper:

> His effectual Presence, in all Places; Where I record my Name, thither will I come; and there will I bless thee. (Exod. 20.24.) Here is More of his intimate presence: Where two or three are gathered together in my Name, there am I in the midst of them. He walks in the midst of seven Golden Candlesticks. (Mat. 18.20. Rev. 1.13.) Here are the clearest manifestations of God's Beauty, which made holy David desire to dwell there forever. See the ap-pearance of Christ to the Churches, Rev. 2. chap. 3. (Psal. 27.4.) In that it is said, that those that should be Saved, in the Apostles days, God added unto the Church. (Acts 2.47.) Here is most Spiritual Advantage to be got: Here the Dews of Hermon fall, they descend upon the Mountain of Sion. Here God commands the Blessing, even Life for evermore. I will abundantly bless her Provision, and satisfie her Poor with Bread. Here David's Doubt was resolved. (Psal. 132.3. Psal.130.15. Psal. 73.16, 17.) Here you received your first Spiritual Breath, or Life, many Souls are daily Born to Christ. That good which is most Diffusive, is to be Pre-ferred; but that good which most partake of, is most Diffusive; O magnify the Lord with me! Let us exalt his Name together. Live Coals separated, soon die. (Psal. 87.5. Psal. 34.3.) Brethren (as a worthy Divine observes) the Church in her publick Worship is the nearest Resemblance of Heaven, especially in Singing God's Praises. What Esteem also had God's Worthies of old, for God's

29. Keach, *Glory and Ornament*, 21.

publick Worship? My Soul longeth, yay, even, fainteth for the
Courts of the Lord. How amiable are thy Tabernacles, O Lord
of Hosts! (Psal. 84.1, 2.) See how the Promises of God run to
Sion, or to his Church: He will bless thee out of Sion. O let nothing discourage you in your waiting at the Posts of Christ's Door.
David desired Rather to be a Door-Keeper in the House of God,
than to Dwell in the Tents of Wickedness. Yet nevertheless do
not neglect, for the Lord's sake, private Devotion; viz. Secret,
and Family-Prayer: O pray to be fitted for publick Worship![30]

He concludes this section by emphasizing the way that private, family, and corporate prayer and devotion work together as a threefold cord.
However, priority is given to the public worship of God in the gathered assembly. Worship flows from the private prayer closet to the family hearth to
the church's gathering. The worship gathering then sends one back to live a
transformed life in the other circles of life.

For Keach, the fundamental elements of public worship are prayer,
Scripture reading, preaching and praising God. In a letter written on behalf
of the Pennepek congregation in 1698, these same elements are listed: "We
agree in the public worship of God and common duties of religion, as in
prayer, preaching, praising God, reading and hearing the word."[31] There is
at least one other reason that the element of "praising God" included singing for the Pennepek congregation. Morgan Edwards explains that in 1701,
an entire church of sixteen members arrived in Philadelphia that had been
constituted in Pembrokeshire, South Wales. The Baptists in the region welcomed them and encouraged them to settle in the vicinity of Pennepek as
they had many principles in common. They stayed for almost two years
and added twenty-one new members before relocating to Delaware due to
tension over their insistence upon the practice of laying on of hands.[32] In

30. Keach, *Glory and Ornament*, 21–22.

31. Spencer, *Early Baptists of Philadelphia*, 33. This letter was written to a congregation of Presbyterians who were sharing a building in Philadelphia (known as the
Barbados storehouse) with the Baptists for worship. Their new pastor was from New
England where Baptists were actively being persecuted and he did not possess a positive
attitude toward the Baptists in Philadelphia. He was attempting to drive them out of the
building where the two churches had shared occupation for over three years. This letter
from John Watts, Samuel Jones, and three others representing the Lower Dublin branch
of Baptists meeting in Philadelphia was a courteous and cordial attempt to make peace.
After two subsequent attempts to meet face to face with the Presbyterian minister to
no avail (he never showed up at either appointed time that he set), the Baptists found
another building to meet in—Anthony Morris' Brewhouse.

32. Spencer explains that the Lower Dublin church practiced this at first but afterwards grew indifferent to the practice. It was practiced in other churches as well and
was originally required as a term of communion. Eventually, it was agreed that the

Delaware they purchased a tract of land and became known as the Welsh Tract Baptist Church. Edwards explains, "They were the first to receive the *Century Confession* which was subscribed by 122 of them in 1716 with addition of article xxiii and xxxi. It has been translated for their use by Mr. Abel Morgan."[33] Spencer cites Edwards in the following manner, "[The Welsh Tract Church] was the principle, if not sole, means of introducing singing, imposition of hands, church covenants, etc., among the Baptists in the Middle States. Singing psalms met with opposition, especially at Cohansey."[34] This quote referenced a time period around 1706. If Spencer's citation is correct, some Baptists were singing in worship near the turn of the century, even after Keach had departed. This would make them likely one of the earliest groups of Baptists to sing regularly in public worship. By the middle of the century, most Baptist churches sang corporately in worship.[35]

One other reference is particularly noteworthy to the study of this time period. Spencer records a query made to the Association from the church at Brandywine. The Association, convened on September 23, 1723, was asked how the church "might improve their vacant days of worship, when they have no minister among them to carry on the public work?" The Association responded,

> Solution—We conceive it expedient that the church do meet together as often as conveniency will admit; and when they have none to carry on the work of preaching, that they read a chapter, sing a psalm, and go to prayer and beg of God to increase their grace and comfort, and have due regard to order and decency in the exercise of those gifted at all times, and not to suffer any to exercise their gifts in a mixed multitude until tried and approved of first by the church. Agreed that the proposal drawn by the several ministers, and signed by many others, in reference to the examination of all gifted brethren and ministers that come

"practice or disuse of the ordinance should not be a bar to communion" (Spencer, *Early Baptists of Philadelphia*, 40–41).

33. Edwards, *Materials Towards a History*, 20. The Century Confession was the Keach Confession (e.g., Second London Confession with the addition of the two articles on singing hymns and laying on of hands).

34. Spencer, *Early Baptists of Philadelphia*, 41. The Edwards citation either was different in another place or Spencer has elaborated on it. The citation in question is the one above. The early influences for singing at Pennepek could have come from Thomas Dungan's group or Elias Keach, or both, before the founders of the Welsh Tract Baptist Church arrived in 1701.

35. Music and Richardson, *"I Will Sing the Wondrous Story,"* 78. "A major influence on the adoption of singing by many Baptists was the Great Awakening that occurred in the colonies during the second quarter of the eighteenth century."

in here from other places, be duly put in practice, we having
found the evil of neglecting a true and previous scrutiny in
those affairs.[36]

In this response, the Philadelphia Baptist Association essentially codified their approach to worship decorum and order. The word of God is central to worship and the preaching of the word by a man approved to do so is
the central act of hearing from God in worship. If such an equipped man is
not present, the church is cautioned against allowing unproven and untest-
ed men to attempt to exercise this gift. This had apparently caused serious
problems elsewhere. They encouraged the churches to practice a rhythm of
Scripture, singing a psalm, and prayer. This simple *ordo* is a demonstration
of an early Baptist sense of dialogue with God in worship (e.g., revelation
and response). The word of God is the revelation of God; the psalm is an
expression of praise in response to God; and prayer is invoking his aid to
"increase their grace and comfort," to which they anticipate his response
in instructing and empowering them. Given the overt gospel content expressed above, it is not a stretch to imagine that the nature of the mediation
of Christ is consistently represented in some manner in these gatherings

36. Spencer, *Early Baptists of Philadelphia*, 57. It is not clear that the churches were
practicing prophesying (e.g., the reading of Scripture with interspersed comments) at
this time, as was done in Baptist worship elsewhere. Perhaps they were and that is what
this concern was related to. There was a sense that worship needed to take on more decorum at the time of this request. The response seems to demonstrate that this practice,
if practiced earlier, has become less prevalent and possibly may be completely replaced
with the prepared sermon by the called minister. This is likely as a result of the general
desire of the Association to guard against false doctrine. Spencer writes of the time
around 1700, "The varieties and phases of theological opinion prevalent [Quakers, Kei-
thians, Seventh-Day Baptists, Presbyterians, Socinians, Anglicans, Sabellians, etc.], led
the Baptists to feel the need of proper instruction in the true faith for their children and
the church members" (Spencer, *Early Baptists of Philadelphia*, 29). Spencer also reveals
a meeting at another time of the week that was held early in the history of Pennepek in
which men met to pray and read and interpret the Scriptures. It is from these gatherings that future pastors and elders were identified. Some of these men would preach
and lead in prayer on Sunday's "meetings for Conference" when Keach was traveling
so that "the church enabled always to have within her own fold those upon whom she
should depend in the absence of her pastor" (25). This practice continued well into
the eighteenth century. "The meetings for conference sustained by the Lower Dublin
Church developed the talents of their young men, and kept up a constant supply of
preachers for their pulpit. These young men, too, were under the constant supervision
and encouragement of the pastor, and acted as his assistants" (43). Given the early problems experienced with doctrinal disagreement from alternative and erroneous strands
of theology, and the impressionability of young converts in young churches, it seems
likely that the Sunday services quickly became more regulated. The instruction from
the Association given here seems to confirm that was the case, at least in the absence of
a preacher, if not at other times as well.

as well. These early Baptists were gospel-centered people and they came to worship expecting to hear the gospel and with the anticipation that unsaved people would also be present and likewise in need of the gospel. The question of singing being answered, the content of the singing is the next matter of inquiry.

Early Baptists who sang were psalm singers, as were Congregationalists and other Separatists. Louis F. Benson theorizes, "If the earliest New England Baptists practiced psalm singing at all, they probably, like their neighbors, lined the psalms out of *The Bay Psalm Book* (1640)."[37] William Reynolds disagrees, noting that this was unlikely "at least until many decades had erased from Baptist minds the memories of the persecution they had suffered at the hands of Boston divines, some of whom were responsible for this psalter."[38] This likely meant they instead sang from the Sternhold and Hopkins *Psalter* (1562), the Ainsworth *Psalter* (1612), or one of the editions of the *Anglo-Genevan Psalter* (1556). Nahum Tate and Nicholas Brady's *A New Version of the Psalms* (1696), and Isaac Watts' *Hymns and Spiritual Songs* (1707) and *The Psalms of David Imitated in the Language of the New Testament* (1719) became options at the turn of, and early in, the eighteenth century. A common progression for churches in this century was to sing *Sternhold and Hopkins* ("the old version"), *Tate and Brady* ("the new version") and then Watts' psalms and hymns or Rippon's *Selection*. There must have been some demand in Philadelphia for Watts because Benjamin Franklin issued a reprint of Watts potentially as early as 1733.[39] The progression among Philadelphia Baptists began with psalm singing and a hymn at communion, but at Pennepek probably expanded more quickly. Whether or not they used *Sternhold and Hopkins* is unclear, but the progression to hymns from Watts and Rippon seems certain. This is not just a progression toward hymnody, but toward gospel-centered hymnody. The metrical psalmody of *Sternhold and Hopkins* and *Tate and Brady* were from the biblical psalms in Old Testament language. These were replaced in some churches by Watts' *Psalms of David Imitated in the Language of the New Testament*. It was a means of maintaining psalm singing with Christ-centered texts. Watts' psalms are quite prevalent by mid-century and his hymns soon after as the desire for gospel-centered language in congregational singing grows along with the acceptance of congregational singing. In 1782, the growing acceptance of Watts among Baptists led the Philadelphia Association to

37. Benson, *English Hymn*, 196.

38. Reynolds, "Baptist Hymnody in America," 31–32.

39. Benson, *English Hymn*, 197. Franklin actually printed Watts' *Psalms of David* in 1729. It was the first book that he printed at his own risk.

recommend to its constituent churches an edition of Watts' psalms published by printer Robert Aitkin in the city during the previous year.[40]

In 1789, the Association determined that a Baptist Hymn Book should be prepared for the churches. The Minutes state,

> Our brethren Samuel Jones, David Jones, and Burgiss Allison are appointed a committee to prepare a collection of Psalms and Hymns for the use of the Associated churches, and the churches of this and of our sister Associations are requested to conclude how many of said collection they will take, sending information to Brother Ustick, with all convenient dispatch.[41]

Samuel Jones, pastor of the Pennepek (e.g., Lower Dublin) church served as the chairman of this committee. *Selection of Psalms and Hymns Done under the Appointment of the Philadelphian Association* went through several editions and contained nearly four hundred hymns.[42] It appears to have been in wide use among the churches. All of the psalm versifications are from Watts' *Psalms of David.* Several of Watts' hymns are also included as are hymns by Benjamin Beddome, Anne Steele, Charles Wesley, William Cowper, Samuel Davies, Philip Doddridge, Benjamin Francis, Joseph Hart, John Ryland, and John Newton. Jones references the *Rippon Collection* in the preface and part of the intent with this collection seems to have been to make a less expensive but comparable collection available to Baptist churches in America. Given that two pastors in the Association personally selected the hymns, it can safely be assumed that some of these were hymns in active use at the time, and potentially for some time before.

Additionally, the hymnbook also reveals something of the placement of hymnody in the Baptist worship service of the eighteenth century. The hymns are divided into three functions related to their placement in the service: (1) to open the service, (2) before the sermon, and (3) after the sermon. Jones explains, "It is thought, however, that no material inconvenience will follow, except that sometimes it may be difficult to find an hymn after the sermon, that will accord with the subject of the discourse: but the hymns under the word Dismission, in the Index, which are of general import, will

---

40. Gillette, *Minutes of the Philadelphia Baptist,* 1880–1881. Songs from Watts' *Psalms of David* and his *Hymns and Spiritual Songs* are utilized in the 1763 ordination of Samuel Jones in Philadelphia (Music and Richardson, "I Will Sing the Wondrous Song," 84).

41. Spencer, *Early Baptists of Philadelphia,* 142.

42. It was reprinted in 1801, 1807, and 1819 according to Clarke (*Set Them in Order,* 17).

in good degree remedy the defect."[43] It is clear that it had become common practice to have a closing hymn that related to the sermon.[44] This gave the congregation a vehicle to respond to the sermon text and a memory aid to recall the main points of the message upon their departure. In this way, they left the service singing the main points or theme of the sermon set to a tune. The organization of this hymnal also demonstrated a pattern of congregational singing at the start of the service and then both before and after the sermon. Prayer and Scripture reading (if practiced) likely occurred between the opening hymn and the hymn before the sermon, where prophesying used to occur. More will be said about this below.

As to theme, hymns in the section entitled "At the Opening of Public Worship" are generally hymns of gathering and entreaty, whether calling people's attention to God in worship or calling upon the Holy Spirit to inhabit and help them in their praise. Anne Steele's "The Savior's Invitation," Watts' "Come We that Love the Lord," and Wesley's "O For a Thousand Tongues to Sing" are among those found in this section. A poignant example of an opening hymn is Benjamin Beddome's "Sprinkled with Reconciling Blood I Dare Approach Thy Throne, O God." Each of the twenty-five "opening hymns" suggested is reflected by gospel content and as a whole are representative of a general sense of approaching worship on the basis of Christ's completed work of atonement. While the Steele and Beddome hymns were relatively recent to this 1790 publication, the hymns of the earlier British hymn writers (e.g., Watts, Wesley, Cowper, Newton, etc.) had been around for decades. It is possible that some of these hymns had been being sung for half a century before this hymnbook was printed.[45]

Hymns in the section entitled "Before the Sermon" are clear expressions of consecration and invocation. This had been a practice with Keach as well. Here the intent seems to be for the church to call upon the Lord to help them by preparing them for the sermon they are about to hear. Anne Steele's "Father of Mercies, In Thy Word What Endless Glories Shines?"

43. Jones and Allison, *Selection of Psalms and Hymns*, iv.

44. It was the practice of John Newton at Olney to sing a hymn before the sermon, and to write a hymn each week that fit the theme of the sermon in order to sing one afterwards as well. (See Phipps, *Amazing Grace in John Newton*, 118.)

45. See Edwards, *Customs of Primitive Churches*. Edwards cites the use of Watts in "a narrative of proceedings at the constitution of one Baptist church in the year 1732" (7). He notes that the congregation and Watts' version of Psalm 132 (10–11) and describes the singing of Watts hymns and psalms—noting the texts and accompanying tunes for each—at the occasions of ministerial ordinations and installations, rebuking of backslidden members, readmission of excluded members, the Lord's Supper, laying on of hands, and burial of the dead (23, 31, 52, 71, 79, 83, 89, 98). Also quoted in Music and Richardson, *"I Will Sing the Wondrous Song,"* 85.

Wesley's "O For an Heart to Love my God," and Watts, "Come, Holy Spirit, Heav'nly Dove" exemplify the intended ethos of this section. Interestingly, there are also numerous hymns in this section that call the congregation to reflect on the gospel as they prepare to hear the word of God. Several Watts' hymns such as "Sweet is the Memory of Thy Grace," "What Shall I Render to my God for All His Kindness Shown," "Father, I Sing Thy Wondrous Grace, I Bless My Savior's Name," and "Let Our Lives and Lips Profess the Holy Gospel We Profess" are examples of this. There appears to have been a sense at this point in the service that the gospel had been reviewed, and the heart softened, before hearing the word of God. It is only by the gospel's converting power that the worshiper could have ears to hear and eyes to see the beauty and truth of God's word. By the same transforming power, the truth could change them. There are thirty-four hymns in this section; almost half reflect specific gospel content and the rest gospel effect.

Hymns in the section entitled "After the Sermon" are varied. Some are intentionally gospel-focused such as Watts' "Blest Are the Souls That Hear and Know the Gospel's Joyful Sound," and "Out of the Deeps of Long Distress," and the anonymous text "Rich Grace, Free Grace Most Sweetly Calls," are chief examples of the invitation hymn calling the unsaved who are present to respond to Christ for salvation. Others are songs of benediction such as Joseph Hart's "Father Before We Hence Depart" and one by Thomas Gibbons from *Rippon's Selection.* In this hymn both the anticipation of sanctification and ultimate glorification in eschatological hope are evident:

Now may the God of peace and love,
Who from the imprisoning grave,
Restored the shepherd of the sheep,
Omnipotent to save.

Thro' the rich merits of that blood,
Which he on Calvary spilt,
To make the eternal covenant sure,
On which our hopes are built.

Perfect our souls in every grace,
To accomplish all his will,
And all that's pleasing in his sight,
Inspire us to fulfill.

For the great Mediator's sake,
We for these blessings pray:
With glory let his name be crown'd,

Thro' Heaven's eternal day![46]

While these are merely a handful of examples of almost four hundred hymns, the sampling demonstrates at least two aspects of eighteenth-century Baptist worship. First, there was a desire for intentional gospel content throughout the service. Examples of gospel content are found in opening hymns, hymns before the sermon, and hymns after the sermon. Second, there is a sense of dialogue inherent in the delineation of hymn placement among other elements of worship. Opening hymns tend to orient the worshiper to God (e.g., revelation). Hymns before the sermons are varied, but many reflect on the gospel as the basis for hearing and responding to the word about to be preached. Others simply aim to give the worshipers words to prepare their hearts to be changed. Finally, hymns after the sermon were intended to correlate with the sermon's discourse. There is an intentional effort to send the people out with a better sense of how they should now live in light of what they have heard from God's word and experienced in worship that day. A spoken benediction also seems to have been a common practice in worship at this time in addition to the closing hymn.[47]

Summary

There is no example of a bulletin or order of Baptist worship from the late seventeenth or early eighteenth century. They do not exist now because they did not exist then. There also does not appear to be a thorough description of any single worship service from which one could be derived.[48] At best there are broad summary descriptions such as have been discussed above. However, in piecing together some of the historic accounts, instructions from pastors and the Association, and reflections of the leaders in worship, a sketch of early Baptist worship in Philadelphia may be derived. The

46. Gibbons, "Now May the God of Peace and Love," in Jones and Allison, *Selections of Psalms and Hymns*, lxxi.

47. Morgan Edwards demonstrates this in his example from 1732 with use of the Num 6 Aaronic blessing. See *Customs of Primitive Churches*, 11.

48. The only exception to this seems to be Morgan Edwards' *Customs of Primitive Churches* (1768) who elucidates almost every word spoken in the services he represents. Many of these are unique types of services rather than a typical public worship service. The work is intended to be an account of how each of these services (e.g., ordination, Lord's Supper, laying on of hands, burial of the dead, etc.) was performed in a particular church, in order to serve as a model for other churches. However, the Philadelphia Baptist Association never adopted the work for use in its churches and the Association spoke out in 1771 when it had been assumed that they had done so. See Gillette, *Minutes of the Philadelphia Baptist Association*, 141.

elements of worship included prayer, Scripture reading, singing (e.g., praising), and preaching. Communion and baptism were often held at different
times than public worship to ensure that only truly converted church members were present. Specific songs were written for these events, especially
since Baptists were the only ones who needed songs for believer's baptism.
The gospel was the central message of public worship. This provided the
opportunity for unbelievers to hear and respond to it in saving faith; and
believers to rejoice in, reapply, and renew their commitment through it for
sanctifying faith. The migration from metrical psalms to Watts' Psalms in
New Testament language to hymns with intentional gospel content demonstrates this expanding emphasis in congregational singing.

Christ is central to the worship gathering and his manifested presence
through the Holy Spirit is expected. Therefore, Baptist worship is unapolo-
getically Trinitarian. The main element of worship is preaching. If prophesying was practiced in the earliest days, it has either been suppressed or
eliminated by the early eighteenth century in Philadelphia. This was likely
due to the concern over maintaining sound doctrine, which was a deep concern for this group. The gifts of those in the congregation were to be proven
first, and then employed in public worship. One of the earliest suggested
forms of worship shape (e.g., *ordo*) includes Scripture reading, a psalm,
and prayer for aid, when there was no one to preach. This demonstrates
the rhythm of dialogue in early Baptist worship. God speaks through the
Scripture reading; man speaks in response through the psalm; and man asks
for God's help in prayer. This help would presumably come in the sermon
through which God would again speak and to which man could again respond. Though the information derived from the 1790 Baptist hymnbook is
after the time period under consideration, it likely reflects a pattern that had
developed, or was developing during this time period among the churches.
The hymnal is organized with the anticipation that the recipients would
understand and agree to the need for hymns in these places of the worship
service, without any explanation in the hymnal as to why this should be
done. Jones and Allison presume this is (or should be) the practice wherever
this hymnal is used. Morgan Edwards in *The Customs of Primitive Churches*,
writes in 1768, "This is plain, public worship should begin in prayer, [1 Tim
11:1], and end with a benediction, [1 Cor 14:16], and that the [rest] should
be decently ordered, [1 Cor 14:40]." While he states that what comes between the opening prayer and closing benediction has to change at times
for different purposes, he provides what he considers a standard order for
worship: "short prayer suitably prefaced; reading a portion of Scripture; a
longer prayer; singing; preaching; a third prayer; singing a second time;
administering the Lord's supper; collecting for the necessities of the saints; a

benediction."[49] Reconciling the two sources provides an expanded potential *ordo* of Baptist Worship in Philadelphia, as shown in figure 6.

Opening Prayer

Opening Hymn*

Scripture Reading*

Prayer*

Hymn before the sermon

Sermon closed with prayer

Lord's Supper (when celebrated)

Collection for the saints

Closing Hymn

Benediction

*The order of these elements may have varied according to Edwards

Figure 6. Potential order of worship at Philadelphia (early eighteenth century)

Regarding the model proposed in this study, there are clear aspects of the presence of each gospel movement (e.g., revelation and response; mediation and response; exhortation and response). God's revelation is either represented by the opening hymn or responded to in the same. There is uncertainty regarding how the prayer and Scripture time might be used, but many of the examples of hymns to precede the sermon reflected on the gospel as an impetus to hear him speak or the effects of the gospel that compel one to listen. The sermon was doctrinal, but rooted in a declaration of the gospel for all.[50] This is poignantly demonstrated by a sermon delivered by Samuel Jones at the century anniversary of the founding of the Philadelphia Baptist Association.

The sermon was read—for which he apologized—and it contained a historical review of the first one hundred years of the Association. However, the general theme was the advancement of the gospel. Finally, at the end of

---

49. Edwards, *Customs of Primitive Churches*, 100.

50. There are four of Elias Keach's sermons available to modern readers. They are sermons preached in London in 1693, but very likely represent the style and typical content of the type of sermon he preached in Philadelphia a year or two earlier. The four sermons are all based on Rom 3:24 and are a systematic discourse on the topic of justification preached on four consecutive Sundays in September of that year. The form of the sermons appears to be in the Puritan pattern of doctrine, reason, and use. The weightiest aspect of the sermon is the doctrine section, which occupies the vast majority of the sermon. See Keach, *Plain and Familiar Discourse*.

the sermon, after his apologies for the unusual content of his sermon, he delivered the gospel:

> To speak of the deplorable state of man under the wrath of God, and the sentence of condemnation; to display the unsearchable riches of the grace and love of God in the way of recovery and salvation through Jesus Christ; to describe the work of the Spirit in taking the things of Christ and showing them unto us, his work of conversion and sanctification; to paint the awful process in the great day, and finally the irrevocable perdition of the ungodly, and the glory and felicity of the righteous; these are subjects that will admit, and even call for animation. Here the preacher may well glow with ardor, and the hearer feel an interest. These subjects, when accompanied with divine power, will melt the affections, bow the will, and mend the heart.[51]

This is Jones' way of delivering the expected message in a sermon and exhorting other preachers to do the same. Whatever the doctrine of the morning, it should be tethered to the gospel. The service was concluded with a hymn that often correlated with the sermon, followed by a spoken benediction. It does not take too much imagination to see a revelation and response, mediation and response, and exhortation and response pattern fitting into this form. There is little question that the worship service intended to point worshipers to God initially and provide the means of response throughout the service. There is also little question that the sermon is a means of exhortation with the concluding hymn, benediction, and manner of life that follows serving as a response to that. This is two-thirds of the model. The theology for mediation and response was inherent in many elements, especially the hymns, but the *ordo* may not have been specific to the model. Did Baptists have a means in the middle service elements of prayers, Scripture reading, and the hymn that preceded the sermon of pointing worshipers to the need for confession and then to the cross for provision of forgiveness? The intentional gospel content throughout may have provided that through the hymns and sermon, or the expectation of preparation before coming to worship may have intended that.

---

51. Jones, *Century Sermon*, 25. There is an advertisement on the back of this sermon pamphlet for two hymnals: A new edition of *Dr. Watts Psalms and Hymns Adapted to the Baptist Churches* and the third edition of the *Selection of Psalms and Hymns of the Philadelphia Baptist Association*.

4

The First Baptist Church of Charleston
(1750–1800)

Introduction

ON DECEMBER 20, 1746, the Baptist Church at Southampton, Pennsylvania licensed a young man named Oliver Hart (1723–1795) to preach the gospel. During the next three years Hart was married, had his first child, and he was ordained. He is listed among the ministers of the Philadelphia Association in 1749, though he certainly attended these meetings earlier.[1] Upon receiving an urgent call from the Baptist Church in Charleston, which was in dire need of a pastor, Hart responded immediately: "I embarked at Philadelphia on board the ship St. Andrew, James Abercrombie Commander, for Charles Town, South Carolina, on ye 13th day of November 1749 and arrived at Charles Town the 2nd day of December following, out 19 days."[2] Hart served that church for the next thirty years. Tom Nettles describes Hart's influence in this manner, "Hart's Christian worldview and zeal for the church and the truth had long-term impact for the influence of Christianity, particularly Baptist life, in America."[3]

---

1. Gillette, *Minutes of the Philadelphia Baptist Association,* 59. Hart's name is listed in the Associational minutes from September 19, 1749, alongside Jenkin Jones, the pastor who had baptized him after his conversion in 1741. Jones was the pastor of the Pennepek and Philadelphia congregations at the time of Hart's baptism. In 1749 he was solely the pastor of the First Baptist Church of Philadelphia.

2. Hart, *Diary.*

3. Nettles, *Baptists,* 77.

Loulie Latimer Owens, prominent Charleston Baptist historian, has stated, "It would be inaccurate to refer to a 'Charleston Tradition' before the pastorate of Oliver Hart."[4] One of the documents bearing Hart's name in Philadelphia was an essay entitled "The Power of the Association" (1749). By 1751, he was responsible for the formation of the second association of Baptist churches in America. In Ward Furman's history of the Charleston Association, he describes the providential arrival of Hart: "The settlement of Mr. Hart in Charleston is an important event in the annals of these churches. His unexpected arrival while the church was destitute of a supply, and immediately after the death of the excellent man [Isaac Chandler or Chanler] who had occasionally officiated for them, was believed to have been directed by a special providence in their favor."[5] His work at the Charleston Church was providential for Baptist worship also.

While the Philadelphia Tradition is synonymous with associational cooperation among a group of churches, the Charleston Tradition is synonymous with a distinctive approach to worship that was founded in Philadelphia. This approach was established and defined by Oliver Hart and refined by Richard Furman (1755–1825). This was a tradition with roots that reached back to the Puritan tradition of the English Particular Baptists, with at least one significant source connecting through the Baptists of Philadelphia and the other being the group that founded the church out of New England. Both of these influences had a deeply historical perspective. Walter Shurden writes, "At the heart of [Puritanism] were two central affirmations which were bequeathed to Charleston. One was the centrality of the religious experience; the second was the sole authority of Holy Scripture.[6] Amy Lee Mears' dissertation is a helpful survey of the worship during this time period. She affirms Philadelphia's imprint: "The worship patterns of the Philadelphia churches were reflected in Charleston worship."[7] Mears also highlights the connection to English Baptists through the Kittery transplant. These Baptists came from FBC Boston, which she considers, "one step removed from the British Baptists who were the progenitors of the faith tradition."[8]

If there is one word to describe the Charleston Tradition, especially against its counterpart in Baptist life in the Sandy Creek Tradition, it is the word "order." Shurden categorizes this worship order in four respects:

4. Mears, "Worship in Selected Churches," 100.

5. Furman, *History of the Charleston*, 8.

6. Shurden, *Not an Easy Journey*, 202.

7. Mears, "Worship in Selected Churches," 56.

8. Mears, "Worship in Selected Churches," 57.

(1) theological order, (2) ecclesiastical order, (3) liturgical order and (4)
ministerial order.[9] Theological order is represented by the Charleston Association's adoption of the Philadelphia Confession in 1767 as *The Charleston
Confession*. Ecclesiastical order is demonstrated by the practice of church
discipline learned in Philadelphia and codified in Charleston through its
publication of "A Summary of Church Discipline."[10] Of the liturgical order
Shurden explains,

> It represented a style in public worship that was ordered and
> stately, though pulsating with evangelical warmth. The ordi-
> nances were more important to those eighteenth-century Bap-
> tists than to many of their successors. Worship appeared to be
> neither spontaneously charismatic nor primarily revivalistic. It
> was directed toward heaven, not earth. The object was to praise
> God, not entertain people.[11]

With regard to ministerial order, the vision of Hart precipitated a legacy of support and funding for ministerial education. The first educational
fund ever promoted and supported by a group of Baptists in America was by
Charleston Baptists in 1755. At least five colleges can trace their founding to
the active work of these same Baptists and the roots of the first seminary for
Southern Baptists also reach back to Charleston Baptists.[12] Their inclusion
in this study of worship is for three reasons: (1) The Charleston Tradition
is one of the defining styles of worship among Baptists; (2) The extraordinary influence of the Charleston Baptist Association is similar to that of the
Philadelphia Baptist Association;[13] and (3) Its influence through training
ministers makes its model highly influential as the worship of the "Mother
Church of Southern Baptists" is propagated through the ministerial training
process and the ministry of the ministers trained by it.

9. Shurden, *Not an Easy Journey*, 202–3.

10. Charleston Baptist Association, *Summary of Church Discipline*. A copy of this is
available in Garrett, *Baptist Church Discipline*.

11. Shurden, *Not an Easy Journey*, 203. Shurden's description of Sandy Creek as reflecting ardor rather than order seems to downplay his description here of Charleston's
"evangelical warmth."

12. Furman, Georgetown, Richmond, Wake Forest, and Mississippi College, as well
as the Southern Baptist Theological Seminary are "clearly traced to the Charleston Tradition" (Shurden, *Not an Easy Journey*, 203).

13. Shurden writes: "In the eighteenth century Charleston was to the Baptists of the
Southern Colonies what Philadelphia was to the Middle Colonies—the hub of Baptist
Activity" (*Not an Easy Journey*, 202).

A Brief History

Though the distinctive characteristics of Charleston order have as their codifying influence an eighteenth-century Baptist from Philadelphia, the foundation of this congregation came from New England Baptists in the seventeenth century. William Screven (1629–1713) was ordained for gospel ministry by the First Baptist Church of Boston. Screven traveled regularly by horseback from Kittery, Maine to Boston in order to attend the church. The church planting effort began simply enough as Screven and his wife, along with a man named Humphrey Churchwood,[14] were baptized on June 21, 1681. That Screven was well known and proven to the Boston church is demonstrated by the fact that he was licensed, ordained, and the church planted by September 25, 1682, just fifteen months later.[15] Screven had already known persecution in Boston as he had been arrested and imprisoned earlier in 1682. This persecution seems to have continued initially in Kittery, but whether it was due to persecution or other reasons, the Kittery church relocated to Charleston, South Carolina in 1696.[16]

That this was the total relocation of the church is demonstrated by the fact that the church remained as constituted in Charleston, and that there is no record of a Baptist church in Kittery after Screven and his group departed. There were other Baptists in Charleston who eventually joined with the Kittery group. Basil Manly Sr. (1798–1868), one of the subsequent pastors of the church, and prominent Southern Baptist statesman, noted in the Charleston Association minutes that most of the early Charleston church consisted of the migrants from Maine.[17] They built their first house of worship by 1701. These were Regular or Particular Baptists for the most

14. Churchwood wrote the letter, dated January 3, 1682, requesting of the Boston church, "to have a gospel church planted here in this place; and in order hereunto, we think it meet that our beloved brother, William Screven, who is, through free grace, gifted and endued, with the spirit of veterans, to preach the gospel" (Baker et al., *First Baptist Church*, 50–51).

15. Wood, *First Baptist Boston*, 179–181. Humphrey Churchwood is listed as the church's only deacon on the church covenant, along with the names of eight men—all of whom were baptized in Boston—representing the founding families of the church that became FBC Charleston. Wood believes this is the first Baptist covenant among English speaking people (182).

16. Baker and Craven believe persecution by the Puritan theocracy in Massachusetts had ceased by 1684. Indian raids during King William's War; the harsh climate of Maine winters; the presence of plentiful timber in South Carolina for the ship's masts; and the possibility of contacts (including Baptists) in South Carolina, are suggested as contributing factors for the church's relocation (Baker et al., *First Baptist Church*, 68).

17. Baker et al., *First Baptist Church*, 81. Manly prepared a historical address for the church in honor of its 150th anniversary of the church.

part, though some disputes would arise early in the church's history from General Baptists in the church. While there were some General Baptists in the minority, Screven seems to have been able to unite both Particular and General Baptists in one Baptist congregation. However, a schism began to grow and Screven urged the church to secure promptly a Particular Baptist as pastor to follow him. Manly quotes Morgan Edwards on Screven's request: "Had they attended to this counsel, the distractions, and almost destruction of the Church, which happened twenty-six years after, would have been prevented."[18]

The decades between William Screven's death in 1713, and the arrival of Oliver Hart in 1749 were marked with suffering and harassment for all of the inhabitants of the city. Hurricanes, fever, Indian raids, Queen Anne's War, and the tyranny of pirates delivered wave upon wave of devastation for the people of Charleston and the surrounding region. While the church records from this time period were destroyed by a hurricane on September 15, 1752, Robert Baker and Paul Craven, leading historians on the Charleston church, have been able to piece together enough details to formulate the following summary of "the darkest days of the Charleston Church":

> The internal history of the church was just as tumultuous as conditions were on the outside. The principal problems involved the difficulty of securing stable pastoral leadership, the loss of many leaders by death and removal, a diminishing membership because of the formation of separate churches by some of the arms or branches of the original church, doctrinal controversy and schism, conflict over George Whitefield and the First Great Awakening, a deep rift in the membership over the dismissal of the pastor, and a lengthy period of litigation over the church property.[19]

Manly referred to this time period in his historical account as "a mournful pause in the hopes of the church."[20]

---

18. Manly, *Mercy and Judgment*, 16. The event Manly references as having occurred "twenty-six years later" is the schism of November 25, 1736, when General Baptists and Particular Baptist formally separated. The General Baptists withdrew on this date and formed the General Baptist church at Stono. Screven's request was made in 1710, three years before his death (Baker et al., *First Baptist Church*, 109).

19. Baker et al., *First Baptist Church*, 101. It is especially difficult to determine the names and dates of the pastors during this time. They all were likely part-time or lay ministers. Isaac Chanler (also Chandler), pastor of the Ashley River church helped out about once a month, but he died unexpectedly on November 30, 1749, leaving what Manly referred to as a "famine of hearing the words of the Lord" (121).

20. Manly, *Mercy and Judgment*, 29.

When Hart responded to the desperate request from Charleston, he found a broken body of believers. Strife and controversy had battered the group now in desperate need of strong and stable pastoral leadership. They had not had a dedicated pastor since 1744. Isaac Chandler, that pastor of the Ashley River church, had been preaching for the Charleston Church once a month as their only source of true preaching. He died in 1749, leaving them with no source of sound preaching. Manly describes the event of Hart's arrival in typical sermonic flair:

> But, while God's dispensations are mysterious, they are all wise; and while it is the rule of his administration to interpose with seasonable aid in the hour of his people's extremity, he sometimes brings them into the greatest straits, that they may better appreciate and improve the blessings he bestows. The Lord had provided an instrument by which he designed greatly to promote the cause of truth and piety in the province, in the person of the Rev. Oliver Hart; and having selected the Charleston Church as the honored receptacle of such a gift, he prepared them to value it by quenching the only lamp that gleamed through the dark wilderness around. The feelings of the more reflecting part of the church, therefore, can be better imagined than described, when they discovered that *on the very day* on which "devout men carried" Mr. Chanler "to his burial, and made great lamentation over him," *Mr. Hart arrived in the city.*[21]

Hart's grandfather has been active in the Pennepek Baptist Church in its earliest years. Hart, who was raised in the Pennepek congregation himself, became a leader in the Southhampton branch of that congregation that officially formed as an independent church in 1746. The 1740s were the revival years of the Great Awakening. Hart had heard the preaching of Jonathan Edwards, George Whitefield (1714–1771), and Gilbert Tennent (1703–1764). He had also heard great Baptist preachers such as Abel Morgan (1673–1722) and Benjamin Miller (1715–1781). His presence at the center of the active and vibrant Philadelphia Baptist Association, under the tutelage of Jenkin Jones (1690–1761), had prepared him well for this daunting task.[22] The letter from the Charleston Church was read at

21. Manly, *Mercy and Judgment*, 11; emphasis Manly's.

22. Baker and Craven: "His preparation, however, had been more complete than appears at first glance. The normal method of training for the ministry in that day was through an intensive internship program. Often the young novitiate would move into the home of his pastor, accompany him in his daily ministry, read his books, watch him observe the ordinances, and perhaps even copy his style of sermon preparation and preaching. It is quite probable that this kind of internship was practiced by young Hart

the Philadelphia Association meeting of September 19, 1749—the first time Hart had attended as a messenger. Baker and Craven write, "Oliver Hart was especially fitted to wrestle with the very problems that he would meet at Charleston."[23]

Hart possessed a deep spirituality and an energetic spirit for pastoral work. His preaching schedule in Charleston included regular preaching services on Sunday mornings and afternoons at the meetinghouse; a Sunday evening lecture in one of the church member's homes on some aspect of doctrine; three weekly evening lectures (Monday, Wednesday and Friday) to the Religious Society organized in 1755; and a Wednesday afternoon lecture that he lamented was poorly attended. Regarding spiritual zeal, he may have been unparalleled among the ministers in the city. When Edmund Botsford found himself under the conviction of sin in 1766, he went from one place of worship to another to find a preacher who could speak to his needs. At the time he was staying with a family of very wicked people and one of the boarders, a scoffer, told him: "There is but one minister in this place, who can be of any service to you, but he, I am told, is a Baptist; all the rest of the ministers deserve not the name. I would advise you to go and hear him."[24] Botsford did so and was soon after converted and became a member of the church.

The controversy between Regular and General Baptists had resulted in such a contentious division, that litigation was required to determine legal ownership of the original church building on lot 62 of Church Street. Even though the church erected another building at the south end of Church Street, (later called the Mariner's Church), the congregation met alternately in both buildings. After Hart arrived, an agreement was reached whereby the General Baptists were given sole use of the old building while sole use of the parsonage on the same property, and the new building belonged to Hart's congregation. Baker and Craven conclude, "This seems to have ended the continuing confrontation between the two groups, and there is no indication of any further friction between them during the remainder of Hart's

---

between 1741 and 1748 when he married. He was quite close to Jenkin Jones, his pastor, until 1746. This kind of internship would provide him with a considerable amount of spiritual and functional preparation that could never have been found in a classroom" (Baker et al., *First Baptist Church*, 127).

23. Baker et al., *First Baptist Church*, 127. Hart would not only have to deal with the significant problems in the church, but the extraordinary affluence in the town with its related pitfalls; multiple destructive hurricanes; and two major wars impacted his ministry efforts while there.

24. Mallory, *Memoirs of Elder Edmond Botsford*, 28–30.

ministry in Charleston."[25] This spirit of cooperation was extended also to Separate Baptists as that movement expanded into the area. Even Joseph Pilmoor (1739–1825), one of the first Methodist missionaries (e.g., Arminian in theology) sent to America by Wesley, was welcomed by Hart who allowed him to preach twice to large crowds at his church.[26] This cooperative spirit, coupled with visionary leadership skills, enabled him to become a prominent fixture in the Charleston Baptist Association and among Baptists in the South. As many Baptist pastors often did during his day, he not only carried on his pastoral and preaching responsibilities admirably, but "lead broad foundations for a cooperative denominationalism in South Carolina." Baker and Craven describe his denominational role:

> He was the pioneer denominational leader in the South and vitally concerned with the growth and development of other Baptist churches. He sensed that in winning people to Christ he had fulfilled only part of the Great Commission. Baptists as a denomination should share the responsibility of "teaching them to observe all things" after they had become disciples and been baptized.[27]

Theology in Practice

As mentioned above, the Philadelphia Confession was adopted in Charleston in 1767 under Hart's leadership. That confession was the original Second London Confession of 1689, with the two articles added from the Keach Confession regarding the laying on of hands and congregational singing. The Charleston Association dropped the article regarding laying on of hands, though they did prescribe the practice for the ordination of a

---

25. Baker et al., *First Baptist Church*, 133.

26. Baker and Craven relate the following story when Hart was fleeing from the British in 1780: "This friendly attitude toward other denominations did not mean that Hart was not totally Baptist in his doctrinal views. . . . Two Presbyterian elders [in Mossy Brick, Virginia] were impressed by his biblical preaching and invited him to speak for them at their Stone Meeting House on the following Sunday. . . . Hart said in his diary that after his companion Edmund Botsford had preached, he arose and took the text from Mark 16:16 'from which Text I endeavored to prove that Believers are the only proper Subjects of Baptism, and that Dipping is the Mode of Administration'" (Hart, *Diary*, 14). Subsequently, "all invitations to the Baptist ministers to preach there had been canceled" as "the Presbyterians did not want a Baptist preaching in their churches any more" (Baker et al., *First Baptist Church*, 135).

27. Baker et al., *First Baptist Church*, 147.

minister.[28] The doctrinal and theological convictions in Charleston were very similar to those of the Baptists in Philadelphia. The conviction regarding the atonement was decidedly Calvinistic, though the presence of General Baptists in the church, and the history of strife with this group, certainly resulted in a softening to the Calvinistic edge. The rigor to guard the doctrine in Philadelphia seems slightly more vigilant than in Charleston, though the same principles of church discipline were put in place. In fact, the manual for church discipline was written in Charleston.[29] It seems unlikely however, that the Baptists in Philadelphia would have allowed a professed Arminian Methodist sent from John Wesley himself, to preach at the Pennepek church where Hart grew up. Hart was vigilant to warn against false doctrine and in the circular letter found in the minutes of 1774, he says as much: "Strictly guard against all heretical principles and men; keep a close communion with God; endeavor to inculcate by instruction and promote by example the fear of God in your families."[30] He was seemingly able to do this while extending the opportunity for others to preach in his pulpit on occasion.

Richard Furman called Hart "a fixed Calvinist, and a consistent, liberal Baptist." To this he added, "Christ Jesus, and Him crucified, in the perfection of his righteousness, the merit of his death, the prevalence of his intercession, and efficacy of his grace, was the foundation of his hope, the source of his joy, and the delightful theme of his preaching."[31]

Baker and Craven write of Hart, "The Charleston church heard pungent and powerful preaching when her pastor was in the pulpit."[32] While he did not receive formal training himself, he was diligent in his study. This diligence was both to ensure that he had interpreted the text rightly, and that he had sufficient application for his hearers. Furman described Hart's preaching thus, "His sermons were peculiarly serious, containing a happy assemblage of doctrinal and practical truths, set in an engaging light, and enforced with convincing arguments." His use of Scripture revealed "an intimate acquaintance with the Sacred Scriptures, and an extensive reading of the most valuable, both of ancient and modern authors." As to delivery, Furman describes him in this way, "His eloquence, at least in the middle stages of life, was not of the most popular kind, but perspicuous, manly and

---

28. Charleston Baptist Association, *Minutes*, February 6, 1775, 2. "A Minister is to be set apart by the laying on of hands after prayer and fasting" (2).

29. See Charleston Baptist Association, *Summary of Church Discipline*.

30. Charleston Baptist Association, *Minutes*, February 7, 1774, 4.

31. Sprague, *Annals of the American Baptist Pulpit*, 7:49.

32. Baker et al., *First Baptist Church*, 136.

flowing—such as afforded pleasure to persons of true taste, and edification to the serious hearer."[33]

Finally, the Calvinistic theology of Hart and his church was equally evangelistic, just as it was in Philadelphia. Basil Manly describes Hart's example and practice: "While his great end in life was the glory of God, he viewed the salvation of sinners as a principal means of promoting it. He longed for the souls of men; and was jealous over them and himself, with a godly jealousy, lest by any means he should run in vain."[34] The desire to make disciples of Christ also translated into a concerted effort to identify and train up other men to send out for the gospel's sake. A strategic effort to contend for the faith, which was once delivered to the saints was mounted through the formal education of ministers. The efforts of the Association having been mentioned above, Hart's impassioned appeal on their behalf is represented in the minutes in 1774: "Brethren lift up your hearts for success on the word preached, and that God would raise up many faithful Ministers of the Gospel: look out among your young men for such as have pioneering abilities, and encourage them to improve their talents for the service of the sanctuary."[35]

The Practice of Worship

Hart's ministry in Charleston was cut short when he had to leave abruptly, fleeing from the British in 1780. He was never able to return to his position in Charleston. Soon thereafter, he found himself back in the Philadelphia Baptist Association as pastor of the Hopewell Baptist Church in New Jersey where he served until his death in 1796. Unlike his previous tenure in the Philadelphia Association—as a young, aspiring minister—he was now a seasoned pastor with much valuable experience. Having been asked to preach to the Association in 1783, he prepared a message from Haggai 2:4, entitled "An Humble Attempt to Repair the Christian Temple." This message provides a starting point for discerning his theology of worship practice. His concern was that "lukewarmness and indifference in religion" remained a chief concern among the Baptist churches.[36] This was reflected in a number

33. Sprague, *Annals of the American Baptist Pulpit*, 7:49.

34. Manly, *Mercy and Judgment*, 33–34.

35. Charleston Baptist Association, *Minutes*, February 7, 1774, 4. Speaking of the College in Providence, Rhode Island, Hart writes: "In this seminary several pious young men already have been, and no doubt many more will be educated, who may be able defenders of gospel doctrines and ordinances, against the errors which are continually propagated, by the energies of gospel truths."

36. Hart, *Humble Attempt*, 3.

of ways, but attendance at worship was a clear one. In outlining the responsibilities of various offices in the church (e.g., civil magistrates, pastors,
deacons and church members), his charge to the church members was "they
should constantly attend the word and ordinances, in their own church. The
shameful negligence of too many professors, in this respect, is one grand
cause of the decay of religion among us."[37] The benefits of attending worship
are numerous, but they center on the gospel and the presence of Christ that
it reveals to the worshiper.

Hart tells the pastors that their primary duty is to preach the gospel
(Mark 16:15). He elucidates what preaching the gospel means and in doing
so provides the shape and content of the gospel in worship:

> Preaching the gospel will lead to an explanation of what the
> apostle calls *the form of sound words* [2 Tim 1:3]. Which may
> include the following and sublime and important doctrines,
> viz. the being of a God—A trinity of persons in the godhead—
> the fall of Adam, and the imputation of his sin to his poster-
> ity—The corruption of human nature, and impotence of men
> to that which is spiritually, or morally good—The everlasting
> love of God to his people—The eternal election of a definite
> number of the human race to grace and glory—The covenant
> of grace—Particular redemption—Justification by the imputed
> righteousness of Christ—Pardon and reconciliation by his
> blood—Regeneration and sanctification by the influences and
> operations of the holy Spirit—The final perseverance of the
> saints in grace—The resurrection of the dead and eternal judg-
> ment. This is the epitome of *the faith which was once delivered
> to the saints*, which ministers are to preach, and for which they
> should *earnestly contend* [Jude 1:3].[38]

Using the terminology introduced in this study—revelation and response, mediation and response, and exhortation and response—Hart has
broadly described the gospel, with its eschatological hope. In a sermon two
years earlier to the same body in 1781, he was more explicit in his explanation of how the gospel functions in worship. This gospel-themed and Christ-
centered focus in worship was inherited from Philadelphia. However, it was
instilled in Charleston in a very intentional and well-developed manner.
His 1781 message to the Association is a treatise on worship and represents
a seasoned maturity and understanding of the topic. What he was exhorting

---

37. Hart, *Humble Attempt*, 28.

38. Hart, *Humble Attempt*, 14–15; emphasis Hart's.

the ministers in Philadelphia to now do in worship, he had developed in Charleston for the previous thirty years.

This sermon based upon 2 Chronicles 29:35, is entitled "A Gospel Church Portrayed and Her Orderly Service Pointed Out." His intention was to show how the gospel orders a church, and in so doing, its worship. Using the reference point of Hezekiah and the rebuilding of the temple, he established his motive: "So the service of the house of the Lord was set in order." Hart applies the old covenant concept of rebuilding the ceremonial rituals to the new covenant reality of worship through Christ. "The *service* of this house comprehends the whole of social, publick, gospel worship, as pointed out in the holy Bible. Good *order* is essentially necessary to an acceptable discharge of this service."[39] Clearly the recent attraction of the more emotional and spontaneous Separate Baptist worship is fixed as the backdrop to his corrective exhortation: "It is a mere burlesque on religious worship, to attend on it, in a confused, clamorous, frantick manner, as some do; insomuch that the house of God among them, seems to be metamorphosed into a bedlam." He concludes his introductory remarks with a citation from 1 Cor 14:40: "Let all things be done decently and in order."[40]

Hart then begins to assemble the order of the analogous *house* of new covenant worship. The foundation of worship is the church built upon the Lord Jesus Christ. The building materials are "only those persons who are regenerated, converted, and sanctified."[41] They become the house of God through the gospel. Hart explains,

> They become a gospel church, therefore, by consideration, or mutual compact; in which, "they give themselves up to the Lord," "and to one another, by the will of God;" covenanting by grace divine, to discharge all the duties incumbent upon them, in this gospel relation; and to walk in all of the commandments and "ordinances of the Lord blameless." Thus they become a body corporate under Christ the head.[42]

The door to the house is Christ, the shepherd of the sheep (John 10:9). There are windows in the house that represent the ordinances of Christ:

> These ordinances, therefore are the windows of the church; and being exceedingly lucid, let in the most refulgent rays, emitted from the glorious Sun of righteousness; to the great comfort

---

39. Hart, *Gospel Church*, 7; emphasis Hart's.

40. Hart, *Gospel Church*, 7.

41. Hart, *Gospel Church*, 9–10.

42. Hart, *Gospel Church*, 12. Citations are from Col 2:19ff.

and inexpressible joy of all who are so happy as to dwell in this house, which often causes them to say, "It is good for us to be here."[43]

Inside the door of the church is a pavement of tightly fixed stones, which are the saints of God in close fellowship with one another. Though they consider themselves the meanest on earth and are often trampled upon by the world, "they are polished by the gracious influences of the Spirit of God." The pillars of the church are the ministers who stand tall both in the "outward deportment," but also "with regard to the doctrines of the gospel."

Using the analogy of a king in a gallery, he encourages the audience to consider an example of the splendid gallery that houses a great king:

> How splendid! How well decorated! How finely finished! Incapable of any additional elegance or beauty, from the nicest touches of the finest pencil! —Those galleries must have been intended to accommodate persons of high rank. The grandest monarch might, in character, reside there. —But here is the inscription, in capitals—*the king is held in his galleries*.[44]

He reveals the greater reality in the following words, "These things will appear more conspicuous if we scrutinize the figure before us. These galleries are the ordinances of the gospel. —The king who is said to be held in them, is King Jesus—The King of Glory—the king of the saints." The ordinances serve as galleries, which serve to afford communion and delight of the saints with their king. "In these ordinances he is held with the cords of love, grace, and promise. Here is his abode—here he delights to dwell, and hold fellowship with his saints."[45] He then quotes John Gill on Song of Solomon 7:5:

> Here Christ and his people walk and converse together; here he discloses the secrets of his heart to them, leads them into a further acquaintance with his covenant, and the blessings and promises of it; and here they have delightful views of his person and fullness; see the king in his beauty, and behold the good land which is far off.[46]

---

43. Hart, *Gospel Church*, 14. Citation is from Peter on the Mount of Transfiguration (Matt 17:4).

44. Hart, *Gospel Church*, 17; emphasis Hart's.

45. Hart, *Gospel Church*, 17.

46. Hart, *Gospel Church*, 17–18. The citation is from John Gill's *Exposition on the Whole Bible: Canticles* vii.5.

In worship, the worshiper is drawn to the roof, which are "all the perfections of the deity." It is the roof that "claims our principal attention."[47] This is the house of worship built on the gospel plan. While the saints are this gospel-built house of living stones, its builder is "the triune Jehovah" and worship should draw their attention to Him.[48]

The second part of his sermon is the manner in which the service of this house may be built in order. This requires the proper roles of the officers of the church. In particular, the ministers, whose work lies chiefly in "preaching the gospel, administering ordinances, leading and governing the church." Hart lists the elements of worship as preaching the gospel, prayer, singing the praises of God, and the ordinances of baptism and communion. This list is right out of the historic Baptist confessions. Hart also references church discipline as a necessary part of gospel worship.

Hart calls preaching "the most important service that ever demanded the attention of man." In preaching, the preacher "stands between the living and the dead—the living God and dead sinners." Referencing the gravity of the act, Hart exhorts preachers: "They should preach the pure gospel, and not a mere system of morality. Cautious should they be of blending law and gospel, grace and works. They should preach salvation, through Christ, in a way of free, rich, and sovereign grace." He continues, "Their language should be plain, yet masculine; their reasoning clear, yet nervous; their countenance open and free; their action easy and graceful."[49] Mears writes, "Even when other purposes existed, [sermons] functioned as vehicles by which men and women were brought to the knowledge of God in Christ. Regardless of the calendar or liturgical setting, the prevailing concern of the preacher was to present salvation through Christ to the hearers."[50] In

47. Hart, *Gospel Church*, 18.

48. Hart, *Gospel Church*, 19.

49. Hart, *Gospel Church*, 23. Amy Lee Mears writes, "The preaching of Oliver Hart was probably the strongest influencing factor on preaching styles among South Carolina Baptists in the eighteenth century" (Mears, "Worship in Selected Churches," 100). When speaking to two young men who aspired to gospel ministry, Hart gave this advice: "You cannot be qualified to deal with wounded spirits, unless you have been sensible of your own wounds. It is not possible you should, in a suitable Manner, direct Sinners to Christ, without an actual Closure with him yourselves" (Baker et al., *First Baptist Church of Charleston*, 140). Today this practice has been characterized as "Preaching the gospel to yourself every day" (Bridges, *Discipline of Grace*).

50. Mears, "Worship in Selected Churches," 90. Mears also points out the inherent connection here between "Charlestonians" and "the moderate Calvinism of their Philadelphia counterparts." This is not to say that other doctrines were not taught. "Sermons for adults taught doctrine, Scripture, and godly living. Oliver Hart's 'Christian Temple' sermon lists fourteen doctrinal matters that lend themselves easily to preaching. The nature of God, the Trinity, the fall of humanity, human depravity, God's love, election,

early Baptist history, services were likely to have two or three sermons on a Sunday. When the Association gathered their first two days were spent "in public exercises of devoting" before handling the Associational business for two days.[51] This generally consisted of a sermon in the morning, one in the afternoon, and one in the evening, with the last sermon of the second day following by communion. The structure of preaching should also represent order. This taught the worshiper how to listen to the message. One approach seemed best to Hart as his sermons followed a predictable structure. He introduced the text, exegeting the passage. He then proceeded to number and explain the points under consideration—a process called "proving." He closed with application where he drew conclusions for each group of hearers.[52] This pattern is the essentially the doctrine, reason, use pattern he learned in Philadelphia.

Prayer is the "very material part of the house of the service of the house of the Lord." Hart muses, "But there could be no propriety in terming the Lord's house, a house of prayer, if prayer were not a considerable part of the service of that house." Just as King Solomon dedicated the temple "by a most excellent prayer," in like manner, "the gospel church is an house of prayer." Hart described the relationship of three venues of prayer and worship in a circular letter to the Charleston Association in 1775:

> *First*, be careful to maintain the Life and Power of Godliness in your Souls; in order to which, keep close to God in Prayer; the Neglect of which tends to Coldness in Religion, and renders the Soul more unfit for Communion with God. *Secondly*, Maintain the Worship of God in your Families, pray with and for them, instruct them in the Principles of Religion, and enforce your Precepts by the best Examples. *Thirdly*, Keep your Places in the House of God, and neglect not the assembling of yourselves together, as the Manner of some is; but keep close to the Ordinances of God's House; attend to all publick and private Meetings of the Church to which you belong.[53]

Here he references the preparation for worship in private prayer that is a common practice in the spirituality of the day. He also shows the

---

grace, redemption, justification, reconciliation, sanctification, perseverance of the saints, resurrection of the dead, and eternal judgment are included among the important doctrines that should be 'delivered to the saints'" (95).

51. Charleston Baptist Association, *Minutes*, November 15, 1791, 1.

52. Mears, "Worship in Selected Churches," 113.

53. Charleston Baptist Association, *Minutes*, February 8, 1775, 4; emphasis original.

concentric circles of private prayer, leading to family prayer, which usher the family into the corporate gathering of worship.

There does not seem to be any recorded controversy regarding singing in Charleston.[54] If there was one, it occurred before Hart arrived. In his sermon, Hart refers to "Harmoniously singing the praises of God, with united voices." His estimation of singing in worship is very high. He writes in the 1781 sermon, "No part of the divine service so resembles heaven as [singing]. The angels, we are sure, make it part of their service." While the church at Charleston had been singing in worship, his support for singing is certainly made in the context of a debate that still lingered over the matter:

> The light of nature directs us to the performance of this service. It is of a moral nature, binding upon all rational intelligences, and has ever been in practice, from the earliest ages, not only among those who have had the advantage of divine revelation, but also among the heathen. The "sweet psalmist of Israel," who was a man after God's own heart, advanced psalmody to a high pitch of glory [2 Sam 23:1]. In his opinion, this service was more pleasing to God than offerings and sacrifices; and he was anxious that all the inhabitants of the earth should join in this service. Good king Hezekiah, when restoring the worship of God, was careful to set this service in order; so that, "when the burnt offering began, the song of the Lord began also." [2 Chron 29:27] Neither was this glorious part of divine worship omitted in the gospel church. At the institution of the Lord's Supper, the solemnity was concluded by singing an hymn. [Mark 14:26] A divine precedent this—sanctioned by the direction of Christ, who, no doubt, joined in chorus with his disciples. The apostle Paul, in two distinct epistles, exhorts the churches to the practice of speaking to themselves, or "teaching and admonishing one another, in psalms and hymns and spiritual songs, singing and making melody, with grace in their hearts, to the Lord." [Eph 5:19; Col 3:16] Now the apostle might have saved himself this labour, had it not been the duty of the churches to sing praise to God, with united voices. I would ask for what purpose the Almighty has endowed us with organical powers of melodious symphony, or a concordant harmony of voices, if not publickly to sound forth his praise? Methinks the winged choristers of the grove, which sing among the branches, reproach the silence of

---

54. The *Summary of Church Discipline* (1772) that Hart helped assemble included singing as a component of ordination (Charleston Baptist Association, *Summary of Church Discipline*, 9).

those people, who do not make singing praises of God, an important branch of the service of the house of the Lord.[55]

Edmund Botsford's description below from 1766 references the act of congregational singing in worship at First Baptist Charleston in passing, as if a forgone conclusion. The next year in 1767, the Charleston Baptist Association adopted the Philadelphia Confession, taking care to exclude the article on the laying on of hands, but to include the article on congregational singing. A church covenant of the Cashaway Baptist Church, part of the Charleston Baptist Association stated, "We believe, that singing of Psalms, Hymns, and Spiritual Songs vocally is an Ordinance of ye Gospel to be performed by Believers and that every one ought to be left to their liberty in using it."[56]

It is certain that by the turn of the century, singing in the Charleston Tradition was in full bloom. Leah Townsend cites the city newspaper in Charleston regarding a service led by Richard Furman on the death of Alexander Hamilton in 1804: "Hymns and anthems sung by the choir accompanied these and other services. It was thus with music and fine oratory and influential leadership that the First Church of Charleston entered the new century."[57] The style of singing in the Charleston Tradition is generally considered to be more orderly or restrained when contrasting it with the Separate Baptists' Sandy Creek Tradition. The worship at FBC Charleston "made fuller use of standard psalm and hymn texts and tunes sung in a more restrained manner."[58] It is likely that the ordinary progression from psalmody to hymnody occurred in Charleston just as it did in Philadelphia. Given that singing had already been accepted, and hymn singing at

55. Hart, *Gospel Church*, 25–26.

56. Townsend, *South Carolina Baptists*, 88–89. Townsend notes, "The article is almost identical to one promulgated by the British Baptist pastor John Gill in 1729." She also references the diary of "Mr. Pugh" who attended singing school in 1765 and who "made a hand copy of *The Cashaway Psalmody*." Cashaway was originally a branch of the Welsh Tract Baptist Church in Delaware that relocated from the Pennepek area and were strong proponents of congregational singing there. Cashaway was a part of the Charleston Baptist Association and the Associational meetings were hosted there for a few years after 1758 to accommodate the distance for them and certain North Carolina churches in the Association (112).

57. Townsend, *South Carolina Baptists*, 31. While most choirs at this time were seated in the balcony at the rear of the sanctuary, in Charleston the choir was seated at the foot of the pulpit, "around the font," according to Tupper (Tupper, *Two Centuries*, 297). The Furman-era building included the church's first "indoor baptistry at the base of the pulpit" (Baker et al., *First Baptist Church of Charleston*, 284). The purpose of the choir would have most likely been to support and provide leadership for the congregational singing (Music, "Congregational Song Practices in Southern Baptist Churches," 13).

58. Music and Richardson, *"I Will Sing the Wondrous Story,"* 79.

that, one expects that Watts, and later Rippon, were the main psalm and hymn collections in use during Hart's tenure and the beginning of Furman's pastorate.[59] Watts was introduced largely by Whitefield through the Great Awakening. Rippon's *Selection* introduced American Baptists to the great Baptist hymn writers of England.[60] Additionally, the choir probably was not a regular fixture until the nineteenth century. Reminiscences by Eliza Yoer Tupper observed that it was during the pastorate of Richard Furman (served 1787–1825) that the choir at Charleston's First Church would commence "some familiar old-fashioned tune."[61] The presence of an organ probably did not occur until after Furman, probably by 1831.[62]

The only existing description of a worship service under Hart's leadership is from Edmund Botsford, who visited on the last Sunday of August 1766:

> Presently the minister came; though I did not like his dress, there was something in his countenance which pleased me. He

59. Mears believes that the version of Watt's psalms and hymns arranged by John Rippon was popular in South Carolina, as it was already in use in New England when printed in 1792. It had been printed in London in 1787. Rippon's *Selection* was also in use in South Carolina after its English publication in 1787. "As Joseph Cook, pastor of the Euhaw church was dying in 1790, he asked a friend to read to him from Rippon's *Selection*, Hymn 324. 'Thus far my God hath led me on,' a hymn of John Fawcett." In 1994, a copy of Rippon's *Watts* was discovered on a shelf with various old hymnals in the history room of the Welsh Neck church ("Worship of Selected Churches," 136). Henry S. Burrage believes that *Psalms and Hymns of Dr. Watts, Arranged by Dr. Rippon; with Dr. Rippon's Selection* (1820) was popular in the Middle Atlantic States. "The [2nd ed.] was recommended by several Baptist pastors in Philadelphia to 'all Baptist churches throughout the country,' as the 'best book of Psalms, Hymns and Spiritual Songs in use among Christians.'" (See *Baptists Hymn Writers*, 648.)

60. Richard Rose writes: "This volume brought to America the works of important English Baptist hymn writers. Appearing first in 1787 in England, Rippon's *Selection* contained 599 hymns with a heavy representation of Baptist authors" (see "'Psalmist,'" 26). R. D. Roberts adds, "Because of the universal acceptance of Rippon's hymnal, he is responsible, more than any single person, for launching the prominent eighteenth century Baptist authors into the main stream of English hymnody. Through the Rippon collection the works of Beddome, Fawcett, Fellows, Needham, Ryland, Steele, and Samuel Stennett became well-known to all Protestant congregations in both England and America" (see "John Rippon's 'Selection of Hymns' and its Contributions," 35–36).

61. Tupper, *Two Centuries*, 297.

62. Tupper, *Two Centuries*, 107. Tupper cites the treasurer's account book for that year [1831]: "Paid Organ Committee. [$] 1210." That organ was subsequently destroyed during the Civil War. Music and Richardson write, "In 1829, the First Baptist Church of Philadelphia, in a close vote, granted permission to have an organ installed at no expense to the Church." They also cite the Methodist, Francis Asbury writing in his journal: "[The Baptists in Georgetown, South Carolina] have built an elegant church, planned for a steeple and organ" (*"I Will Sing the Wondrous Story,"* 106–7).

began worship by prayer; I was pleased with it. After singing, the venerable man of God took his text from Acts xiii.26; "Men and brethren, children of the stock of Abraham, and whosoever among you feareth God; to you is the word of this salvation sent." To describe the exercise of my mind under this sermon would be impossible. However, upon the whole, I concluded it was possible there might be salvation for me, even for me. I then determined, that, in future, I would attend worship in this place. I do not remember, that, when able to go, I ever once omitted attending, while I lived in Charleston. Indeed, I would not have omitted one sermon for all the riches in the world.[63]

There were no kneeling benches or altars for people to come kneel and pray. Mears cites an unpublished essay by Edmund Botsford in which he "made an effort to explain the Baptist disapproval of bowing and kneeling, particularly during the administration of the Lord's Supper."[64] The original floor plan for the 1775 building included a center aisle. This design was controversial due to the associations with the processionals of the Anglican and Catholic traditions. The plans had to be redrawn with two aisles, and other South Carolina churches followed the same pattern. The only real movement in Baptist worship was the journey to the river for the baptism before the advent of the interior baptistry. "After a protracted time of worship and baptism, 'the audience sang with great energy and harmony up to the house,' where the recently baptized members had changed clothes and joined the congregation for further worship."[65] Baptisms always concluded with the observance of communion during this time.[66]

It is not clear how the Lord's Table was fenced rather than celebrating communion at a different time and place, as was done in the early days at Pennepek. Morgan Edwards seemed to indicate that this had changed by the time of his pastorate in Philadelphia in the mid-eighteenth century. He lists that element as part of the Sunday order of worship, when celebrated. This may have been the practice Hart observed growing up, though he might have observed the earlier practice of a separate meeting. In Charleston, communion was either a part of the baptism service as noted above, or the regular Sunday worship service as Edwards describes. Unbelievers would have been present if the latter. In *The Gospel Church*, Hart states that the

63. Mallory, *Memoirs of Elder Edmund Botsford*, 30. His reference to Hart's dress is that of the black minister's gown and white band that Hart regularly wore.

64. Mears, "Worship in Selected Churches," 71.

65. Mears, "Worship in Selected Churches," 74. Mears cites Johnson, "Reminiscences of William B. Johnson," 23.

66. Baker et al., *First Baptist Church*, 284.

proper participant of communion was one "in a church state"—the baptized believer. Those who were not members in good standing were not eligible to participate. He so emphasized the ordinance that he stated, "It is of so much importance that there cannot be an orderly gospel church without it."[67] According to Mears, most churches in the Charleston Baptist Association celebrated the Lord's Supper on a quarterly basis. It was a common practice for churches to meet on the Saturday before communion "in order to prepare for the ordinance" in which a "preparation sermon" was preached.[68] Hart's sermon in 1781 designates aspects of Zwinglian symbolism, but he also cites John Gill and the Song of Solomon in his section regarding the ordinances that reflects Calvin's real presence.

With the close connections between Charleston and Philadelphia, it is likely that the order of worship was similar. Mears explains, "Though there have been discovered no detailed, prescriptive worship orders for the Charleston church, the patterns [described] . . . contain similarities to those of the Philadelphia congregation." She continues, "The interspersed prayers, the reading of Scripture, singing, the sermon, and the collection were elements shared by churches of both regions."[69]

Summary

Don Hustad suggests that the reason that there is no recorded worship patterns for Charleston Baptists is that their "separatist and nonconformist heritage caused them to be hesitant to prescribe any worship order."[70] In all of the research done on this historic church and its prominent model for Baptist worship, there does not appear to be a single worship order recorded. The closest is the Botsford summary above, which is stark and possibly oversimplified. He also was emphasizing the preaching of Hart in his journal so he seemed to single that part of the service out. What can

67. Hart, *Gospel Church*, 27–28. The *Summary of Church Discipline* included instruction regarding who many participate in communion and the process of restoration. Edmund Botsford issued tickets for communion as was Morgan Edwards practice in Philadelphia (Mears, "Worship of Selected Churches," 175).

68. Mears, "Worship in Selected Churches," 173–74. This aspect of preparation for the table is demonstrated by the decision by the Association to maintain their two-day schedule of public devotion that culminated with the Lord's Supper. The minutes record the following in response to the request to adjust the schedule: "It is proper and necessary that the exercises of the Saturday should be preparatory to the sacred transaction of approaching the table [on Sunday]" (Charleston Baptist Association, *Minutes*, November 5, 1808, 3).

69. Mears, "Worship in Selected Churches," 185.

70. Hustad, "Baptist Worship Forms," 31.

be discerned for this account is that Hart opened the service with prayer, as Morgan Edwards described. Also, singing preceded the sermon, as the *Selection of Psalms and Hymns Done under the Appointment of the Philadelphian Association* (1789) indicated was the practice. However, given the overlap of Morgan Edwards historical research and the "golden years" of the Charleston Tradition under the Furman pastorate, the worship services may have eventually looked similar to what Edwards reported from Philadelphia. Hustad suggests that may have been the case. A potential order of worship for Charleston is shown in figure 7.[71] This certainly fits Botsford's account. Hustad also points out that Edwards insisted upon a congregational "amen" at the end of prayers, which may or may not have been at practice in Charleston. The ecclesiastical gown and band seem to have been the practice in both places as Botsford commented on in his journal. Hart likely brought that practice from Philadelphia.

A short prayer, suitably prefaced

Reading of Scripture

A longer prayer

Singing (congregational)

Sermon

A third prayer

Singing

The Lord's Supper (on appointed Sundays)

Collecting for the necessities of saints

Benediction[72]

Figure 7. Potential order of worship at Charleston (mid-eighteenth century)

One other note regarding worship content (e.g., the words spoken/sung in worship) should be made here. In Barnet Williams' study, "An Investigation of Baptist Worship from 1620–1850," he cites the practice of singing a hymn at Baptism by the First Baptist Church at Charleston. The specific hymn he mentions is John Ryland's (1753–1825), "Baptismal Hymn" from the *Watts and Rippon Hymn Book*. He believes this practice "began about the middle of the eighteenth century."[73] The practice may have begun at this time (during the Hart pastorate) but the hymn he references was not

71. Hustad, "Baptist Worship Forms," 32.

72. Edwards, *Customs of Primitive Churches*, 100.

73. Williams, "Investigation of Baptist Worship," 38–39.

published until 1791.[74] Additionally, *The Psalms and Hymns of Dr. Watts, Arranged by Dr. Rippon*, was not published until 1827. *Rippon's Selection* was first published in 1787, which included Watts' hymns but not the one in question by Ryland.[75] While it is likely true that they sang a hymn at baptismal services in the mid-eighteenth century as was referenced above, it was not the Ryland hymn and it was not from Rippon's collection of Watts. However, this does reflect the pervasive use of Watts and Rippon in the church. This reflects strongly upon the gospel content of hymns sung in the worship that became known as the Charleston Tradition.

There are two important conclusions regarding Charleston worship, given that an order of worship cannot be derived other than what as already been established in Philadelphia. The first conclusion is the penchant for order. Though some Separatist flexibility in worship order is potentially maintained before the sermon, the emergence of the Separate Baptists and the Sandy Creek tradition out of the Great Awakening serve to *push* the Charleston tradition towards more order. Later examples of the Charleston Tradition are very fixed. However, this is more than *ordo*. In fact, it may be truer regarding hymn selection and focus in the service as the following study of the Sandy Creek Tradition will reveal. The content of hymnody practiced, and the general focus of the service are different in the two traditions. This serves to highlight the second important conclusion regarding worship in Charleston. It is decidedly Christ-focused and gospel-themed. Recalling Furman's quote evaluating Hart's preaching: "Christ Jesus, and Him crucified, in the perfection of his righteousness, the merit of his death, the prevalence of his intercession, and efficacy of his grace, was the foundation of his hope, the source of his joy, and the delightful theme of his preaching."[76]

The overall service—including the increasing presence of Watts' psalms and hymns, and later Rippon's Selection—was gospel-themed throughout. The heart message of the service was the birth, life, death, burial, and resurrection of Jesus Christ, and man's response to that. This is why Edmund Botsford found at First Baptist, Charleston, and only First Baptist, the message of the gospel he so badly needed to hear.

74. John Ryland, "When Abraham's Servant to Procure," also known as a "Baptismal Hymn," first appeared in *The Christian's Duty, Exhibited, in a Series of Hymns* (Germantown, PA: Peter Leibert, 1791), No. 314, p. 284. This hymnal was printed by the German Baptist Brethren. (See "Christian's Duty, Exhibited, in a Series of Hymns.")

75. Music and Richardson, *"I Will Sing the Wondrous Story,"* 52.

76. Sprague, *Annals of the American Baptist Pulpit*, 7:49.

5

The Baptists at Sandy Creek, North Carolina (1755–1800)

Introduction

THE GREAT AWAKENING OF the second quarter of the eighteenth century is considered such because it impacted people from New England to Georgia and involved multiple denominational groups.[1] The result was religious growth throughout the colonies. At times, the growing pains of the Awakening precipitated theological strife and splits within denominations. Weaver describes this aspect of the Awakening: "Baptists were generally opposed to the revival. The Arminian churches in New England disliked the Calvinism of the revival leaders. Many Baptists were wary of the episodes of wild emotionalism that characterized some of the conversions. Most of the conversions were among Congregationalists." Ironically, the first Great Awakening still proved to be a major factor in Baptist growth as the Congregationalists split. "Many 'New Lights'—those who advocated revival methods—left the Congregationalist fold after abandoning their commitment to infant baptism in favor of believer's baptism."[2] Many of these "Separates" became Baptists, establishing their identity as "Separate Baptists."

1. Weaver, *In Search of the New Testament Church*, 60. See also Kidd, *Great Awakening*.

2. Weaver, *In Search of the New Testament Church*, 60. It is of this movement from the Congregationalists to the Baptists that George Whitefield reportedly said, "My chickens have turned to ducks" (60–61).

Isaac Backus and Shubal Stearns (1706–1771) were Congregationalist converts from New England. Their similar spiritual journeys from Congregationalist to Awakening convert to Baptist are illustrative of the journeys of countless others during this time period. Additionally, the majority of the Baptist churches in New England became Calvinistic Baptist churches as a result of the influence of the Awakening. This change allowed the Associations at Philadelphia and later Charleston to become cooperative partners with a wider circle of influence in the gospel effort. Backus became the pastor of the Separate Baptist Church at Middleborough, Massachusetts in 1756, a church he started. Closed communion and itinerant evangelism marked this church, much as the practice had been in Philadelphia and Charleston. He published the earliest history of Baptists in America; a three-volume work entitled *A History of New England with Particular Reference to the Denomination of Christians Called Baptists* (1777, 1784, 1796).[3]

Shubal Stearns' journey began similarly, but his path within the Baptist faith took a different direction geographically. Converted under the preaching of George Whitefield, he initially became the preacher of a new Separate Congregationalist church in rural Connecticut. The church eventually split over the matter of baptism and he took a group first to Virginia, and ultimately the group settled at Sandy Creek, North Carolina. Joined by his sister and brother-in-law, Martha (1726–1754) and Daniel Marshall (1706–1784), Stearns became the undisputed leader of the Separate Baptists movement in the colonial South. Separate Baptists grew so rapidly that by the time of the American Revolution they were the largest dissenting group in the South.[4]

Many of this group having experienced spiritual birth as a result of the Great Awakening amidst its dramatic experiences and spiritual exercises,[5] they sought the same dynamic quality for their worship services. Hustad writes, "Strongly influenced by the George Whitefield renewal movement in the colonies, they practiced a charismatic variety of worship whose central purpose was evangelism."[6] John F. Loftis describes the typical worship service of the Sandy Creek Tradition:

3. Weaver, *In Search of the New Testament Church*, 61.

4. Weaver, *In Search of the New Testament Church*, 62.

5. David McCollum defines these "exercises," or "bodily exercises," as "Revival phenomena which engaged the psyche and/or the body were called among other things 'experiences,' 'enthusiasms,' 'extravagant affections,' and 'bodily agitations.' 'Exercises' is a general descriptor that signified the means of grace and religious experience. This usage of 'exercises' spanned the period . . . 1730–1805." He adds, "These behaviors were not confined to the religious gatherings popularly called camp meetings. They occurred at church services, riverside baptisms, Bible studies, prayer meetings and in the workplace" (McCollum, "Study of Evangelicals," 1).

6. Hustad, "Baptist Worship Forms," 32.

In general, worship among Separate Baptists was characterized by informality, noise and disorder. Separate preachers exhibited an energetic, passionate, and loud proclamation style.
Congregations were often moved to tears, screaming, and even
rendered prostrate. Members of the congregation entered spontaneously into the service with prayers and exhortations. Even
young converts and women were encouraged to respond to the
movement of the Spirit.[7]

Often characterized as the worship of the fiery, frontier folk of the
day, this movement was the counterpart to the comparatively refined
Charleston Tradition. Shurden writes, "The second word in the Southern
Baptist synthesis is *ardor*." This comes from the Sandy Creek Tradition.
Where the Charleston Tradition generally connotes the word "order" in
worship, this movement has been perceived as people given to ardor. And
this was expressed in "individualism, congregationalism, biblicism, and
egalitarianism."[8] To this, Shurden adds four characteristics of Separate Baptist worship as expressed in the Sandy Creek Tradition.

First, their worship was evangelistic. "They had one value: winning
people to Jesus Christ and to an emotionally identifiable experience. Faith
was feeling and every Sunday was a camp meeting." Second, their ministry was charismatic. Just like the conversion experience, the call of God to
preach "was internal and experiential, never a professional choice. Ministerial education was not encouraged, it was discouraged." It was deemed a

7. Loftis, "Factors in Southern Baptist Identity," 89–90.

8. Shurden, *Not an Easy Journey*, 204; emphasis Shurden's. Shurden is credited with
having made popular the phrases "Charleston Tradition" and "Sandy Creek Tradition"
that have become shorthand for defining these distinctive Baptist worship styles. One
weakness of such a characterization is to intimate that the Charleston Order lacked
ardor. While Charleston certainly established more order in their services, relative to
the charismatic spontaneity of Sandy Creek, the Charleston expression of worship was
still an expression of ardor. In particular, Oliver Hart was equally a product of revival
as his Separate Baptist brethren. Eric Coleman Smith plans to address the potential
over-amplification of this particular distinction in a future dissertation. Smith writes in
his prospectus: "The thesis of this dissertation is that, Oliver Hart was a Regular Baptist
pastor who was deeply influenced by the revival spirituality of the Great Awakening,
thus providing evidence that revival played a greater role in Regular Baptist identity
than is often suggested. The Separate Baptists of Sandy Creek were clearly birthed out of
the revival of the Great Awakening, and their contribution to the expansion of Baptist
life in the South is both undeniable and utterly remarkable. But I want to argue that the
flame of revival also touched their Regular Baptist brethren in Charleston, producing
a piety marked by both the order of their Particular Baptist lineage and the ardor of
the new evangelical awakening" (Smith, "Order and Ardor," 15). This monograph has
since been published. Eric C. Smith, *Oliver Hart & the Rise of Baptist America*, (Oxford:
Oxford University Press), 2020.

detriment to preaching. All that one needed to preach was the call of God to do so. Third, their ecclesiology was ruggedly independent. They formed the fourth Baptist association in America as the Sandy Creek Baptist Association in 1758. "But unlike the Charleston Tradition, the Sandy Creek Tradition did not spend as much time defining associational authority as they did declaring church autonomy." This is represented in part by a number of doctrinal issues related to queries that the Association put back to the inquiring church rather than seeking to answer it. Finally, their theological approach was biblicistic. "With a highly literalistic approach to Scripture, they found not two but nine Christian rites in the Bible." With roots in New England Congregationalism where non-binding creeds became substitutes for the authority of the word of God, they were "ardently opposed to confessions of faith."[9] Shurden adds the following summary, "In brief, the Sandy Creek Tradition consists of revivalistic experientialism, anticonfessionalism, exaggerated localism, fierce libertarianism, and a commitment to personal evangelism."[10]

The reasons for including Sandy Creek Baptists in this study are threefold: (1) they come most directly out of the Great Awakening which is arguably the most spiritually shaping event in American history. (2) They are among the most influential Baptist groups of the eighteenth century and changed the shape of Baptist worship in the centuries that follow. (3) They represent the Sandy Creek Tradition, which is the counterpart to the Charleston Tradition. These two worship traditions represent the totality of influence in Baptist worship. Though they appear as contrasting styles in some ways, it is their blending that accounts for most of the worship services among Baptists in the centuries that follow. Most Baptists since them have elements of worship from both worship traditions. Very few churches can authentically claim to be the practitioner of solely one tradition. Most have something from both.

A Brief History

Shubal Stearns was born in Boston in 1706, but his family moved to Tolland, Connecticut early in his life. There they joined a Congregationalist church where he remained until 1745 when he heard Whitefield preach. Stearns was converted and subsequently embraced the New Light understanding of revival and conversion.[11] William McLoughlin explains the resulting effect

9. Shurden, *Not an Easy Journey*, 205–6.
10. Shurden, *Not an Easy Journey*, 206.
11. Nettles, *Baptists*, 155. "New Light advocates, in general, favored the revival and

of so many new and zealous converts from the Great Awakening: "Religious zeal spilled over into very bitter quarrels about doctrine, church government, and ritual." Seeking to reform their churches, "many fervent New Lights were ready to conclude that it was impossible for them to reform established churches from within."[12] Their movement theme was from 2 Corinthians 6:17—"Come out from among them, and be ye separate." This is how they gained the label and stigma of "come-outers" or "Separates." Stearns did the same and separated from his Old Light, Congregational church. In 1751, Stearns became the pastor of a group of New Lights in Connecticut.

Very soon after beginning this pastorate, Stearns rejected infant baptism (as did a portion of his church) and was baptized as a believer by Wait Palmer (1728–1785). He was then ordained as a Baptist minister in March 1751. Three years later Stearns moved south, believing that the Spirit had led him to do so in order to start a great spiritual work there. It was in Opekon, Virginia that he, along with several of his church members from Connecticut, joined Daniel and Martha Marshall.[13] Here they worked among a group of Baptists associated with the Philadelphia Baptist Association. Feeling that he did not meet with the success that he had been called to, he received information from some friends in North Carolina about the need for a preacher there.[14] On November 22, 1755, "He and his party once more got under way, and, traveling about two hundred miles, came to Sandy Creek, in Guildford county North Carolina."[15] David Benedict provides the earliest description of the forming of Sandy Creek Baptist Church: "As soon as they arrived, they built them a little meetinghouse, and these 16 persons formed themselves into a church, and chose Shubael Stearns for their pastor, who had, for his assistants at that time, Daniel Marshall and Joseph Breed,

---

considered most of its phenomena as consistent with, if not directly indicative of, a work of God's Spirit. They were particularly interested in an experience of conversion— observable, communicable, and transforming" (107).

12. McLoughlin, *Soul Liberty*, 103–4.

13. Martha Marshall became famous for her exhortations. She was considered the "Priscilla" to her husband's more modest speaking gifting, as she was considered "more eloquent." Daniel Marshall was a prominent leader among the Separate Baptists and Martha a dynamic "helper in the gospel." The Sandy Creek Baptists permitted women to have a more prominent role in worship than did the Regular Baptists. They had women elders and deaconesses, in addition to allowing them a more vocal role in their services, including preaching at times. (See Semple, *Baptists in Virginia*, 374.)

14. Nettles, *Baptists*, 155. Some had to travel forty miles to hear preaching in this area.

15. Semple, *Baptists in Virginia*, 65. This is now Randolph County, North Carolina.

neither of whom were ordained." He continues regarding the manner in which the Anglican inhabitants received them:

> The doctrine of the new birth, as insisted on by these zealous advocates for evangelical religion, they could not comprehend. Having always supposed that religion consisted in nothing more than the practice of its outward duties, they could not comprehend how it should be necessary to feel conviction and conversion; and to be able to ascertain the time and place of one's conversion, was, in their estimation, wonderful indeed. These points were all strenuously contended for by the new preachers.[16]

The growth of the church was dramatic, as this group of sixteen grew to 606 members in very short order. Warren Dixon records that between 1755 and 1758, Stearns baptized over nine hundred people.[17] Benedict writes, Daniel Marshall, "though not possessed of great talents, was indefatigable in his labors. He sallied out into the adjacent neighborhoods, and planted the Redeemer's standard in many of the strongholds of Satan."[18] Several preachers were raised up in North Carolina to meet the growing need as churches (e.g., "branches") began to be formed rapidly. As church members preached to other areas and started other churches, it became clear that an association should be formed. In 1758, the Sandy Creek Association was formed, and it also grew rapidly. Of the Sandy Creek Association, Morgan Edwards writes, "In 17 years [Sandy Creek] has spread its branches westward as far as the great river Mississippi; southward as far as Georgia; eastward to the sea and Chesopeck [sic] Bay; and northward to the waters of the Pottowmack [sic]; it in 17 years, is become mother, grandmother, and great grandmother to 42 churches, from which sprang 125 ministers."[19]

16. Benedict, *General History*, 683.

17. Dixon, "Sandy Creek Separate Baptist Church."

18. Benedict, *General History*, 684. "At Abbott's Creek, about thirty miles from Sandy Creek, the gospel prospered so largely, that they petitioned the mother church for a constitution, and for the ordination of Mr. Marshall as their pastor. The church was constituted in 1756; Mr. Marshall accepted the call, and went to live among them." Marshall later continued his itinerant preaching, preaching in Virginia, South Carolina, and Georgia—establishing the Baptist church at Kiokee in 1772, which is the oldest continuing Baptist church in Georgia. His son, Abraham, eventually became the leading pastor for the pioneer Baptist movement in Georgia. He continued his ministry there for thirty-five years (Nettles, *Baptists*, 158). Abraham's son, Jabez (Daniel's grandson), became pastor after him for thirteen years.

19. Edwards, "Materials Towards the History," quoted in Nettles, *Baptists*, 157 and in Benedict, *General History*, 685. C. B. Hassell wrote in 1829: "As of now, more than a thousand churches are existing now which arose from this beginning" (Dixon, "Sandy

Stearns became known as the "Reverend Old Father" in the Sandy Creek Association. Weaver explains, "He asserted autocratic authority at times." There were occasions when ministers and churches that disagreed with the association were "disfellowshiped." Weaver also writes, "Associational gatherings focused on preaching and, according to some scholars, were evangelistic 'camp meetings' thirty-years before the nineteenth-century Second Great Awakening popularized camp meetings on the frontier."[20] In 1770, the Association split into three associations even as the Sandy Creek Church was reduced from over six hundred people to fourteen. Shubal Stearns "finished his course" at Sandy Creek on November 20, 1771.[21] The Sandy Creek Church never again regained its size or prominence, but the seeds that were planted there produced fruit both far and wide. Nettles summarizes, "Through the organizational skills of Stearns and the untiring preaching endeavors of Daniel Marshall, the Great Awakening spread deep into the South."[22]

As to the relationship between Separate and Regular Baptists, there was initially suspicion at best and outright scorn at worst. When Daniel Marshall was called to preach at Abbott's Creek soon after their arrival in North Carolina, Stearns sought help with his ordination. Believing that an ordination required a plurality of elders and Stearns being the only ordained minister among them, Stearns contacted the nearby Regular Baptist congregation at Peedee River in South Carolina. The request was sternly refused, the unnamed recipient declaring that "he had no fellowship with Stearns' party; that he believed them to be a disorderly set, suffering women to pray in public, and permitting every ignorant man to preach that chose; and that they encouraged noise and confusion in their meetings."[23] Stearns was able

---

Creek Separate Baptist Church," 1).

20. Weaver, *In Search of the New Testament Church*, 62.

21. Benedict, *General History*, 684–85.

22. Nettles, *Baptists*, 158.

23. Benedict, *General History*, 684. It is probable that the church in question here is the Welsh Neck Church, formed in 1738 out of the Welsh Tract Church in Delaware that had previously come from the Pennepek area. It was originally called the church at Peedee and the pastor during the time in question was Joshua Edwards, who ministered from 1752 to 1758. However, another minister, Robert Williams, had been ordained there in 1752 and his ministry overlapped that of Edwards. He was a highly contentious individual and a staunch Calvinist, zealous to convince others of his position. He was eventually brought under church discipline by the church regarding a matter or matters that history does not appear to record. In spite of their gentle attempts to demonstrate kindness through multiple appeals to meet with him, he would not comply. He disowned the church's authority saying that it was not a "Church of Christ," and was subsequently suspended and ultimately ejected (Townsend, *South Carolina Baptists*, 65). It is possible that Stearns' request could have been received by Edwards or

to reach out to Marshall's brother-in-law, a Mr. Leadbetter of the church on Lynch's Creek, to carry out the ordination.

A more endearing experience involves John Gano (1727–1804) who attended the second meeting of the Sandy Creek Association in 1759. Whether by assignment from the Philadelphia Association, the Charleston Association, or of his own accord, Gano visited from his pastorate at the Jersey Settlement in North Carolina. Stearns received Gano with great affection, but the tension between Separates and Regulars became quickly apparent. The other members of the Association treated him "with coldness and suspicion; and they even refused to invite him into their Association." Benedict comments benevolently of the Regular Baptist: "But Mr. Gano had too much knowledge of mankind, humility and good nature, to be offended at this treatment." He continued to observe the proceedings and was evidently prepared to return when Stearns, who was bothered by his brothers' treatment of Gano, urged them to invite Gano to preach. They did so, though they would not allow him a seat at their Assembly. Of Gano's sermon Benedict writes,

> With their invitation he cheerfully complied, and his preaching, though not with the *New Light* tones and gestures, was in demonstration of the spirit and with power. He continued with them to the close of their session, and preached frequently much to their astonishment as well as edification. Their hearts were soon opened towards him, and their cold indifferent and languid charity were, before he left them, enlarged into a warm attachment and cordial affection; and so superior did his preaching talents appear to them, that the young and illiterate preachers said, they felt as if they could never attempt to preach again.[24]

While Gano recognized certain matters of difference in doctrine and practice, his general assessment of the Sandy Creek Baptists was formulated in this statement: "Doubtless the power of God was among them; that although they were rather immethodical, they certainly had the root of the matter at heart," in that they had a genuine understanding of conversion and a theology to support it.[25]

Williams or another party.

24. Benedict, *General History*, 686; emphasis Benedict's. The "*New Light* tones" that Benedict refers to was the preaching style of Stearns and other Separates, which apparently mimicked Whitefield. Weaver describes their "holy whine" as "a shouting preaching style that evidently modulated between singing, chanting, and normal speech" (Weaver, *In Search of the New Testament Church*, 62).

25. Semple, *Baptists in Virginia*, 65–66, also quoted in Nettles, *Baptists*, 155, and commented on (162).

Theology in Practice

Gano's comment that the Sandy Creek Baptists had "the root of the matter at heart," precipitated the evaluation from Terry Wolever that Gano "did not see so much of a *doctrinal* problem with the Separates," and in this "he reflected the general sentiment of the Particular Baptists toward the Separates."[26] Nettles equally asserts, "Historical precedence makes this judgment virtually certain."[27] William H. Whitsitt (1841–1911), the Baptist historian and third president of Southern Seminary, made the following assessments of the theology of these Separate Baptists: "These Separate Baptists were all of them Calvinists by persuasion. They were not Calvinists of the stern old type that formerly had prevailed, but rather Calvinists of the school of Jonathan Edwards." The theology of Stearns and Marshall was the Calvinism of the Great Awakening. Whitsitt called them "Whitefieldian Baptists," and claimed, "Nine tenths of our denominational strength in the southern states is derived from Whitefield through the agency of Stearns and his co-laborer Daniel Marshall."[28] This form of Calvinism is considered evangelical Calvinism due to its fervent desire to see the gospel preached and men saved. Their zeal for evangelism was so great that some have considered them practicing Arminians, believing that such a combination of Calvinist theology and avid evangelism are incompatible.[29]

26. Wolever, *Life and Ministry of John Gano*, 1, 304; emphasis Wolever's.

27. Nettles, *Baptists*, 162. The Philadelphia Association had sent Benjamin Miller because members had complained about "supposed irregularities in the church, particularly under the influence of Daniel Marshall." Miller had some experience in reforming a church and he was sent to investigate the validity of the complaints. Nettles writes: "Benjamin Miller's visit to Opekon, Virginia, in 1754 provides a clear test of the doctrinal content of the preaching of Stearns and his brother-in-law Daniel Marshall. . . . Miller had served faithfully as a pastor, an active member of the Philadelphia Association, and as an itinerant preacher." After a lengthy survey of the argument, he concludes: "Unless Miller was completely without discernment (very unlikely, as he was appointed to tasks that required careful and compassionate discernment) or had shaken off the former convictions of his soul concerning the truth and the character of gospel ministry (also highly unlikely in light of his continued work and responsible leadership in the Philadelphia Association), we may be justified in concluding several things concerning the Stearns/Marshall tandem. First, their giftedness in proclamation and teaching appeared adequate in content and edifying in effect. . . . Second, their spirit, though exuberant, did not come under censure as arrogant, prideful, or improperly enthusiastic, but as warmly spiritual. . . . Third, their theology supported the strength of the exercises" (165–66).

28. William H. Whitsitt, "Baptists in America," quoted in Nettles, *Baptists*, 171.

29. R. B. C. Howell in his *The Early Baptists of Virginia* traces the Separate Baptists to the General Baptists of Virginia (and Europe before this). As such he considers them pure Arminians. Nettles adds to this: "It seems that these historians have made

Perhaps a balancing perspective is found in one of their own—John Leland (1754–1851), who wrote, "It is a matter of fact that the preaching that has been most blessed of God, and most profitable to men, is the doctrine of sovereign grace in the salvation of souls, mixed with a little of what is called Arminianism."[30] Coming from Whitefield and the Great Awakening, the clear written practice of their theology—when it was written—is that of Calvinism. At the same time, their evangelistic zeal and practices were so ardent that they appear as practicing Arminians.

Initially, the Separate Baptists were opposed to most confessions of faith. This hindered their uniting with the Regular Baptists in any formal way. They also did not record or prepare their sermons out of a fervent desire to be led of the Spirit. No extant sermon exists of Shubal Stearns so it is not possible to recover his preaching and theology. He preached extemporaneously. Their doctrinal practice in general gave at least some ability to agree to the major tenets of the Philadelphia Confession. Advocating this perspective, Semple writes regarding the union of the Separates and Regulars in Virginia in 1787: A large majority believed "as much in their confession of faith [the Philadelphia Confession] as they [the Regulars] did themselves," but "if there were some among them who leaned too much towards the Arminian system they were generally men of exemplary piety and great usefulness in the Redeemer's kingdom."[31] Morgan Edwards writes of the Separates, "The faith and order of both [Regulars and Separates] are the same, except some trivial matters not sufficient to support a distinction, but less a disunion; for both avow the *Century-Confession* and the annexed discipline."[32]

----

an assumption built upon a particular bias, that is, a convinced and consistent Calvinist cannot be evangelistic" (Nettles, *Baptists*, 170).

30. Leland, *Writings of the Late Elder*, 172, quoted in Shurden, *Not an Easy Journey*, 206.

31. Semple, *Baptists in Virginia*, 100. Nettles argues against those who claim that the theological practice of the Separate Baptists must have been Arminian due to their evangelistic zeal (see Nettles, *Baptists*, 170).

32. Edwards, *Materials Towards a History*, 43, quoted in Nettles, *Baptists*, 166. Nettles summarizes the theological distinctions among Baptists in this manner: "Distinctions urged between Stearns and the Separate Baptists on the one hand and the Philadelphia/Charleston Regular Baptists on the other are artificial. Their doctrine was the same, as was their concern for gospel preaching and Holy Spirit-induced conversion. After their union at the end of the eighteenth through the beginning of the nineteenth century, the influence of one can hardly be distinguished from that of the other. The growth of Baptists in the South comes from the strengths shared by both groups. Any dichotomy between Calvinism and evangelism in this union reveals a basic misunderstanding. The followers of Stearns helped bring into practice the evangelistic convictions of the Regulars; the confessional detail of the Regulars helped give expression

Edwards did not specify what he considered those trivial matters that were different.[33] One clear distinction, at least initially, regarded the long list of nine rites that the Sandy Creek Baptists subscribed to—baptism, the Lord's Supper, love feasts, laying on of hands, washing feet, anointing the sick, right hand of fellowship, kiss of charity, and devoting children. The extensive list was an effort to "carry out, to the letter, all suggestions of the New Testament."[34] This stands in contrast to the Regular Baptists around them who held to only two ordinances of the New Testament. While not all churches in the Sandy Creek Association practiced all nine rites, those who did still maintained association with those who did not. Most of these rites eventually fell into disuse and when they finally subscribed to principles of faith, they only listed two.

Another distinction was their emphasis of the same pneumatological practice as their founder did—seeking to hear from and act on the impressions of the Spirit. For example, early in their Association's history they did not elect a moderator, but instead waited on God to direct someone to take the lead.[35] As was mentioned above, their preachers did not generally prepare a message, but preached extemporaneously, seeking to be "Spirit-led." Another aspect of this mandate is reflected in a decision the Association made in 1758. Responding to a query from one of their churches, they decided that "dancing in the Spirit," though unusual, should be tolerated "because there was a genuine work of grace among the people."[36] Addition-

---

to the theological convictions of the Separates. The union was not an incongruous mixture of incompatibles" (172).

33. He simply writes "matters of trivial importance, such as dress, &c." as being a "bar of communion." According to Edwards these "had been for some time removed" (Edwards, "Union of Regular and Separate Baptists" in McBeth, *Sourcebook for Baptist Heritage*, 166.)

34. John Leland, *Virginia Chronicle* (Virginia, 1790), 42, quoted in Benedict, *General History*, 686. The practice of devoting children was founded upon the circumstances of bringing little children to Christ. When circumstances permitted, the mother carried the infant to the meeting and the minister either took it in his arms, or laid his hands on it, and thanked God for his mercy, and invoked a blessing on the child, at which time it received its name. This rite, which was by many satirically called a *dry-christening*, prevailed, not only in the Sandy Creek Association, but in many parts of Virginia. Most of these rites fell out of use, though still affirmed by the Association when asked about their use. The *Principles and Faith of the Sandy Creek Association* (1816) listed only the two ordinances of baptism and the Lord's Supper in article 8 (Lumpkin, *Baptist Confessions of Faith*, 358).

35. This practice changed in 1805 when they elected a moderator for the first time.

36. Purefoy, *History*, 75. The minutes from October 26, 1805, record the following answer: "We do not find in God's word, nor can we approbate it, but recommend the churches to use great tenderness with those who are exercised in that way, before they make it a bar to communion" (49).

ally, they placed a great deal of confidence in visions and divine impressions. Benedict explains that they "had strong faith in the immediate teachings of the Spirit in special instructions as to the path of duty."[37] Semple related the practice of their people seeking God to receive "tokens of his will." In following these tokens one would "inevitably be led to the accomplishment of the two great objects of a Christian's life—the glory of God and the salvation of men."[38] Many of Stearns' decisions, such as coming to Sandy Creek, were the result of impressions and/or visions perceived from the Spirit. At the same time, the Separates agreed with the Regulars that Scripture was the perfect rule and nothing contrary to it should be heeded. David McCollum observes, "They assumed immediate impressions were valid while judging them by Scriptural standards."[39]

In general, theological precision was not a priority for these Baptists, though they had deeply held convictions regarding the authority of the word of God.[40] Winning the lost to the gospel was uppermost in their priorities of belief. "These people were so much engaged in their evangelical pursuits that they had no time to spend in theological debates, nor were they very scrupulous about their mode of conducting their meetings."[41] Reflecting the latter part of this statement, Gano upon his personal visit to the Sandy Creek Baptists, reported that their practices were "rather immethodical."

The Practice of Worship

David Bebbington describes the Separate Baptist movement as having enjoyed "enormous dynamism." He continues, "Set free from the shackles of the standing order, Separate Baptists were free to itinerate in the manner of Whitefield. They carried their urgent message of the new birth around New

---

37. Benedict, *General History*, 683. William Shurden refers to the Sandy Creek Baptists as "semipentecostalists" (Shurden, *Not an Easy Journey*, 206).

38. Semple, *Baptists in Virginia*, 13.

39. McCollum, "Study of Evangelicals," 179.

40. There are examples of early doctrinal statements found in the preamble to the Sandy Creek Covenant (1757) and the Abstract of the Article of Faith and Practice of the Kiokee of the Baptist Denomination (1771–1772), established by Daniel Marshall. Both are clearly Calvinistic statements affirming particular redemption, effectual calling, imputed righteousness, and perseverance of the saints, in addition to progressive sanctification and believer's baptism. The *Principles of Faith of the Sandy Creek Association* was published in 1816 that affirms each of these again, in addition to total depravity (see Lumpkin, *Baptist Confessions of Faith*, 358).

41. Benedict, *General History*, 685.

England and then spilled over to the South."[42] He proceeds to relate the account of Elnathan Davis at a baptismal service conducted by Stearns in a North Carolina creek in 1762 or 1763:

> Davis, at first merely a curious observer, was astonished when a man who was stricken in conscience wept on his shoulder. The young man ran to report to his friends that the crowd had been seized by a "crying and trembling spirit" and decided at first not to return, but then was drawn back by "the enchantment of Shubal Stearn[s'] voice." Davis himself began to tremble, fell down in a trance, and woke up with alarm at the wrath of God against his sins. A few days later he reached an assured faith, received baptism from Stearns, and before long was serving as pastor of a Separate Baptist church in the colony. Through episodes such as this, the revival temper ensured rapid denominational expansion.[43]

The Sandy Creek model for worship was based upon a revivalistic model of mass evangelism, evidenced by bodily exercises that was observed in the Great Awakening, and predicated upon salvation as the primary purpose for gathering. There are very few written accounts of early Sandy Creek worship, but what exists are of essentially evangelistic gatherings. Even their baptismal services, a gathering for just believers in other places, often served as an opportunity for evangelistic outreach, as the account above demonstrates. The desire for unsaved people to have the opportunity to hear the gospel and respond with an experiential outpouring of the Spirit was always uppermost.

Benedict describes the similar nature of the Sandy Creek Associational meetings: "When assembled, their chief enjoyment was preaching, exhortation, singing, and conversation about their various exertions in the Redeemer's service, the success which had attended them, and the new and prosperous scenes which were opening before them." The ministers left encouraged and with their hearts inflamed for the gospel work that "no common obstacles could impede."[44] While this is often the purpose of associational meetings in other places, what was unique is that even when the Association gathered, it often drew a crowd of non-church members. Edwards writes quoting James Read, "Great crowds of people attended [the meetings of the Association], mostly through curiosity. The great power of

---

42. Bebbington, *Baptists through the Centuries*, 78.

43. Bebbington, *Baptists through the Centuries*, 78. Also, Kidd, "'Do the Holy Scriptures Countenance,'" 109.

44. Benedict, *General History*, 685.

God was among us. The preaching every day seemed to be attended with God's blessing."[45]

Preaching was the main event of Sandy Creek worship whatever the purpose of gathering, and Shubal Stearns was the exemplar. His manner of preaching defined the fundamental ethos of the Sandy Creek meetings. Benedict writes of their arrival at Sandy Creek: "Their manner of preaching was, if possible, much more novel than their doctrines [to the Anglicans they encountered in North Carolina]." He describes Stearns preaching:

> He was a man of small stature, but good natural parts and sound judgment. His voice was musical and strong, and many stories are told respecting the wonderful and enchanting influence which was exerted on his hearers by his vocal powers, and the glances of his eyes. His character was indisputably good as a man, a Christian, and a preacher.[46]

Stearns became the model of preaching to the degree that others in the movement sought to emulate him. The mode of preaching was marked by "a very warm and pathetic address, accompanied by strong gestures and a singular tone of voice" that has been described by some as "a holy whine."[47] The doctrine of the new birth appears to have been his consistent theme in preaching. Stearns' message was always the simple gospel, presented in a manner than the most uneducated among the hearers could understand. "Being often deeply affected themselves when preaching, corresponding affections were felt by their pious hearers, which was frequently expressed by tears, trembling, screams, and exclamations of grief and joy."[48] According to Isaac Backus, "Separate Baptist preachers expected to be exercised in the sense of receiving perceptible inspiration that enabled them to preach without notes."[49] George Purefoy, a nineteenth-century pastor in the Sandy Creek Association describes his forebears' conviction to God's word in preaching:

> The Baptists at this time were all strict constructionists; they then would "buy the truth and sell it not." God's word was

45. Edwards, *Materials Towards a History*, quoted in Benedict, *General History*, 685. McCullom writes, "Baptist union meetings, camp meetings, and baptisms were public events attended by many who had received little religious instruction" (McCollum, "Study of Evangelicals," 184).

46. Benedict, *General History*, 683, 686.

47. Nettles, *Baptists*, 157.

48. Benedict, *General History*, 683–684.

49. Backus, "A Fish Caught in His Own Net," 191, 235–37; quoted in McCullom, "Study of Evangelicals," 186.

strictly the main of their counsel. There was then none of that time-serving, man-pleasing, and latitudinarian construction of God's word that now prevails. Baptists then boldly and earnestly contended for the faith once delivered to the saints. Now many of them are afraid to preach the whole truth, and defend their doctrines and ordinances, for fear it will give offence to those who are teaching for doctrine the commandments of men. Baptists are the stewards of God's word, and should be found faithful in its defence and observance.[50]

Singing in congregational worship was never a question among the Sandy Creek Baptists. Nettles refers to their "fiery style of worship," which no doubt includes their singing, while Music and Richardson similarly record that they "became well known for the enthusiasm with which they sang."[51] Their hymn repertory likely began with the psalms and hymns of Watts, as did other Baptists and Congregationalists of the eighteenth century from which they came. According to Irvin Murrell, this was kept largely by oral tradition among Baptists, but mixed with the written tradition of British hymnody. "The hymns and tunes they brought with them were folk hymns and tunes that they had heard sung by their parents and grandparents. The tunes usually were those that had been associated with old love songs or ballads." The texts in use were often the most popular ones from Watts and other widely circulated hymns of the day. "There was, therefore, a joining of the written tradition of hymns with the folk song tradition from England."[52]

Northern singing school and Southern folk hymn tunes later become the steady diet of this tradition as they later "found little use for most of the British tunes."[53] The practice of lining out was beginning to be replaced with regular singing in other places. There is no evidence of traditional lining out among Sandy Creek Baptists, but the camp meeting practice of congregational response to an improvised melody from the preacher may have developed in the Sandy Creek tradition. This approach to singing would have been especially effective in the itinerant ministry so often utilized by these preachers, especially among working class attendees. In this practice, "A preacher might improvise a melody for a line from a familiar hymn by Isaac Watts or another British writer, to which the congregation could respond with a 'shouting word' (for example, 'Hallelujah') or a brief

---

50. Purefoy, *History*, 51.

51. Nettles, *Baptists*, 153–54 and Music and Richardson, *"I Will Sing the Wondrous Story,"* 79.

52. Murrell, "Ardor and Order," 39.

53. Music and Richardson, *"I Will Sing the Wondrous Story,"* 79, 304.

refrain."[54] The tunes to these songs were likely adapted secular folk tunes or other familiar folk hymn tunes. Tune books for these songs began to be published around the turn of the century, indicating an established demand for their use. The music that came from this movement is often referred to as "revival hymnody" or "spiritual songs," directed toward the seeker.[55] Many of these songs came from regional collections later published by the Richmond publishing houses as early as 1802, reflecting a demand in this area of the country for this approach.[56] By this time the Baptists had become united and this reflected a united desire for congregational song. Singing occurred before the sermon in their services, and often afterwards in the form of an altar call.

Prayer is a matter of great importance, as it related to their desire for evangelism and revival. Many references are made in the Sandy Creek Association minutes to the need for prayer: opening and closing sessions with prayer; days of fasting and prayer; fasting, prayer, and laying on of hands for the ordination of a minister or evangelist; a monthly concert of prayer; special prayer for revival; prayer meetings; and to private and family prayer.[57] Their meetings were described at times as "scenes of the most solemn and affecting nature; and in many instances there was heard at the same time, throughout the vast congregations, a mingled sound of prayer, exhortation, groans, and praise." There were also times, especially in camp meetings, when worshipers exhibited,

54. Music and Richardson, *"I Will Sing the Wondrous Story,"* 289.

55. Music and Richardson describe the emergence of a new type of published collection of songs at the beginning of the nineteenth century, intended for social and revival meetings that were a part of the series of spiritual awakenings. "Texts from Watts and the evangelical Calvinist Baptists of England served effectively for both the declaration of the gospel in worship and its offer to the unsaved in evangelism. Hymns from the Wesleys were increasingly included in Baptist collections, implying—and sometimes stating—a broader reach of the gospel. The informal songs of the revivals, which lacked the literary polish of those form British writers—and, indeed, lacked any such aspiration—were increasingly found in a range of collections" (Music and Richardson, *"I Will Sing the Wondrous Story,"* 157).

56. In 1802, John Courtney (ca. 1744–1824), the second pastor of FBC Richmond, published *The Christian Pocket Companion* for the use of "United Baptists" reflecting the joining of Regular and Separate Baptists joining in 1787. "We may surmise that the distinction between hymns and spiritual songs was not a rigid one, with the same texts sometimes functioning in formal and informal contexts" (Music and Richardson, *"I Will Sing the Wondrous Story,"* 178). Irvin Murrell has suggested that the categorization of a text as a spiritual song might reflect its popularity in the particular region (Murrell, "Examination," 104).

57. The minutes of the Sandy Creek Baptist Association prior to 1805 were never printed; they were recorded in a book annually which was destroyed by fire in 1816 (Purefoy, *History*, 31–32, 49, 51, 73, 89, 116).

Falling down under religious impressions . . . religious epilep-
sies . . . not only at the great meetings, where those scenes were
exhibited which were calculated to move the sympathetic affections; but also about their daily employments, some in the
fields, some in their houses, and some when hunting their cattle
in the woods . . . in some cases, people were thus strangely affected when alone. . . . And besides falling down, there were
many other expressions of zeal, which in more moderate people
would be considered enthusiastic and wild.[58]

A unique element of Sandy Creek Baptist worship, in contrast to
the Charleston Tradition, was the practice of exhortation, at least when
distinguished from preaching. This was possibly derived from the practice of prophesying in earlier Baptist worship, but the intent was directed
to the unsaved rather than the saved. Exhorting was a common practice
both within and outside their services and men or women could practice
it. Martha Marshall became famous for her exhortations. It was suggested
that those who did not have the gift for preaching should pursue this gift.
Exhortation seems to have been an impassioned appeal to individuals to
repent of their sins and trust Christ for salvation, similar to the use of the
term "witnessing." It was practiced house-to-house and in the context of the
gathered assembly.[59] It often was also used in conjunction with prayer (e.g.,
praying and exhorting) and sometimes in the context of prophecy, though
rarely with the latter. Certain portions of the worship service were marked
by the conglomeration of the elements of praying, praising, and exhorting,
all occurring simultaneously among the worshipers. The following account
from the First Separate Baptist Associational Meeting in Virginia in 1771
serves as a period account of Sandy Creek worship:

Went for the Association about 18 miles (Saturday morning,
May, 1771). Got to the Association about one o'clock. Brother
Hargitt was then about to preach to about 1,200 souls, from 40th
chapter Isa., 11th verse ("He shall feed His flock like a shepherd; He shall gather the lambs with His arm, and carry them
in His bosom, and shall gently lead those that are with young.")
Brother Burruss got up immediately (after) and preached from
Isa., ch. 55, 3d verse ("Incline your ear and come unto Me; hear
and your soul shall live; and I will make an everlasting covenant

58. Benedict, *General History*, 687. This description is generally about the Second
Great Awakening among the Sandy Creek Baptists.

59. Semple, *Baptists in Virginia*, 7, 227, 374, 379–80. "Mrs. Marshall, being a lady of
good sense, singular piety, and surprising elocution, has in countless instances, melted
a whole concourse in tears, by her prayers and exhortations" (374).

with you, even the sure mercies of David") with a good deal of liberty, set the Christians all afire with the love of God; Assembly praising God with a loud voice; Brother Waller exhorting till he got spent; Brethren Marshall and E. Craig both broke loose together, the Christians shouting and they speaking for the space of half an hour or more; then ceased.[60]

Finally, Sandy Creek Baptists held a firm written stance on the matter of closed communion and the requirement of baptism for access to the table. It became a matter of disagreement when fostering the partnership with Regular Baptists in the Kehukee Association. When it was discovered that some of the Regulars had been baptized before their conversion by careless Arminian preachers under whose pastorate they had formerly been, it created quite a commotion and led to division. It was not until the Regulars corrected the matter that Separates returned to the process of uniting the two in the Kehukee Association. Three examples of written confessions of the Sandy Creek Baptists reviewed for this study included this requirement. The *Sandy Creek Principles of Faith (1816)* states in article 10 "that the church has no right to admit any but regular baptized church members to communion at the Lord's table."[61]

Summary

In general, the worship services were unplanned, unprepared for, untimed, and flexible in that leaders sought to make room for the Spirit to move in them. Weaver characterizes the view of some scholars in that the Associational gatherings were essentially "evangelistic 'camp meetings' thirty-years before the nineteenth-century Second Great Awakening popularized camp meetings on the frontier."[62] They were not completely without form or content. Benedict refers to "some calculation" in the meetings to "move the sympathetic affections" in the quote above. The driving desire was to see the Great Awakening from which they came, continue in the South. This required certain elements of worship—preaching in particular—and the gospel message. There are two overriding factors regarding their worship

---

60. "Observations by an Attendee": http://baptisthistoryhomepage.com/separate. bapt.assoc.html. This is an account from the journal of Elder John Williams.

61. Lumpkin, *Baptist Confessions of Faith*, 358. The Kehukee *Articles of Faith* (1955) includes in article 12: "Persons who are sprinkled and dipped while in unbelief are not regularly baptized according to God's word, and that such ought to be baptized after they are savingly converted into the faith of Christ" (356).

62. Weaver, *In Search of the New Testament Church*, 62.

that are firmly rooted in their revivalistic beginnings: (1) the Spirit will use biblical elements such as preaching and exhortation, but is free to lead in unpredictable ways; and (2) salvation of the unsaved is the primary, and often solitary, goal. This approach was believed to be supported by and, intended to be governed by, a firm commitment to the Scriptures. However, there is no evidence of a firm commitment to the regulative principle to govern the aspects of worship. While they wrestled with certain issues at the Associational level they often referred certain matters, such as dancing in worship, to the conscience of the local church. In doing so that warned against hampering the work of grace among the people.

Purefoy reveals one of the most influential practices of the Sandy Creek Baptists that became a mainstay of Baptist worship that followed. This single addition to worship represented both an *ordo* change and thematic change in Baptist worship. His purpose is to indict the Primitive Baptist churches that were previously committed to missions but became a part of the anti-missions movement. In doing so, he cites their previous practice from their own minutes: "The ministers usually, at the close of preaching, would tell the congregation that if there were any persons who felt themselves lost and condemned under guilt and burden of their sins, if they would come near the stage and kneel down, they would pray for them. . . . The act of coming to be prayed for in this manner, had a good effect."[63]

In conjunction with this comment he writes, "The ministers (in 1802) used frequently, at the close of worship, to sing a spiritual song, suited to the occasion, and go through the congregation, and *shake hands* with the people while singing."[64] The inference and affirmation in these conjoined statements reflects the Sandy Creek practice of an altar call following the sermon. The practice of the altar call and singing at the end of the service became their most influential contribution to worship services that followed, insofar as it was done with evangelistic intent. It is perhaps this influence that undergirded the inclusion of a section of hymns in the Philadelphia collection of hymnody published in 1790 for use "after the sermon."[65]

The unavailability of a preacher was a common problem in churches of this day. Philadelphia had to give instructions for this circumstance among their churches and Sandy Creek had to do the same as they attempted to keep up with their rapid growth. In the Sandy Creek Associational minutes of October 26, 1816, they encourage those churches to "meet on the Lord's

---

63. Purefoy, *History*, 32–33.

64. Purefoy, *History*, 33.

65. Jones and Allison, *Selection of Psalms and Hymns*.

day, for prayer and religious edification."[66] This seems to imply that when a preacher is not available, evangelism is not the main goal of the gathering. In 1858, they recommended to each of its churches, "to come together for worship on each Lord's Day, whether they have preaching or not. When they have no minister present, spend one hour in singing, prayer, and exhortation."[67] The presence of exhortation here in the absence of preaching could be for evangelistic purposes, or for the aforementioned goal of religious edification.

That singing, prayer, exhortation, and preaching are the Sandy Creek elements of worship is clear. There is no reference to Scripture reading in their services, though it could be reasonably assumed that the sermon text is read or recited before the sermon. There is no prayer of confession because the whole service generally is a presentation of the gospel to the unsaved. Prayer and intercession generally occurred before the service, sometimes on Saturday, for revival and salvation. It is also does not include a Call to Worship and the hymnody is not of the theme that directs one vertically toward God in worship. The message of the services and meetings are not really directed toward the saved. It is gospel-themed for the purposes of evangelism. The direction of dialogue is more often preacher to attendee ("horizontal"). The aspect of response in worship is demonstrated primarily with the goal of seeing the unsaved respond to the gospel. Participation was unpredictable at times as attendees could participate spontaneously with prayers and exhortations. Due to these factors, and the lack of substantial records, it is challenging to codify a Sandy Creek service order from this historical period.

However, some patterns of *ordo* can be approximated from the historical accounts that do exist. The typical worship service likely began with prayer. This was a common practice among Baptists in general, but the Sandy Creek Baptists in particular had the strong desire to invoke the work of the Spirit in the service. Additionally, the minutes record their practice of opening and closing the Associational gatherings with prayer so it seems probable that this was a worship service practice as well. Given that the high point of the service was the sermon, the elements that occurred between the opening prayer and the sermon likely included some combination of singing, prayers, and exhortations. This seems to have been the unstructured part of the service where things might occur in different sequences or even at the same time. This is the point of the service where participants

66. "Minutes of the Sandy Creek Baptist Association, October, 26th, 1816," quoted in Purefoy, *History*, 74.

67. "Minutes of the Sandy Creek Baptist Association, October, 2nd, 1857," quoted in Purefoy, *History*, 177.

likely participated spontaneously, but this does not preclude that possibility of this occurring at other times. The sermon(s) was the high-water mark of the service. This was the time that the gospel was presented plainly and clearly, but with great emotion. Again, spontaneous participation and/ or bodily exercises could occur here, but the attention was on the gospel message proclaimed extemporaneously by a Spirit-led preacher. This was the most anticipated part of Sandy Creek worship. There could potentially be multiple sermons and exhortations as the Spirit led. Some type of altar call response, most likely facilitated by singing again, followed the sermon. This was not a single song or brief response to close the service as is often the case today. This demonstrated the effects of the pinnacle of the service and could include a lengthy time of prayer, exhortation, singing, praising, moaning, etc., as the Spirit affected people through exercises and ultimately, repentance and salvation. Given these descriptions, a potential service at Sandy Creek might have look like the one in figure 8.

Prayer for revival (Before the service or even on Saturday)
Opening Prayer
Singing, praying, and exhorting (potentially simultaneous)
Sermon(s) (unprepared, but reliant upon the Spirit)
Response to the gospel ("altar call")
Closing Prayer

Figure 8. Potential order of worship at Sandy Creek (late eighteenth century)

William Lumpkin concludes, "More than any other group, they impressed the revivalistic stamp upon American religious life." Their additions to Baptist worship history, for better and worse, are that "successors have inherited and perpetuated: too great a dependence on mass evangelism and excessive emotional appeal . . . and too little training of their congregations in Christian faith and worship."[68]

Excursus: Separate and Regular Baptists Unite for Revival and Missions

Though the Regular and Separates began the second half of the eighteenth century wary of one another, the substantial growth of the Separates drew

68. Lumpkin, *Baptist Foundations in the South*, 148–50. Lumpkin also includes "the undervaluing of ministerial education" in this list.

the attention of the Regulars. Weaver writes reflecting the opinion of Robert Semple in 1810, "The differences between Regular and Separate Baptists were never great and . . . jealousy played a significant role in the tensions between them."[69] Both groups were Calvinistic; both preached conversion; and both practiced believer's Baptism. Additionally, both desperately desired revival and the advance of the gospel. They had much in common and this led to efforts to unite the two types of Baptists leading up to the turn of the century. Building upon the efforts of men such as Oliver Hart and John Gano, who had reached out to Separates early, Richard Furman, William T. Brantley (1787–1845), and Basil Manly became paradigmatic of this newly united Baptist front. Each was saved under Separate Baptist preaching while themselves going on to pastor the *flagship* Regular Baptist churches of FBC Philadelphia and FBC Charleston. Basil Manly became one of the leading figures in the founding of the Southern Baptist Convention.

The issue of holding to confessions in this union was a problematic one. Separates believed confessions and creedal statements led to formality and spiritual stagnation. Their concern was that a confession would lead away from the authority of the Scriptures as they felt had occurred among the Congregationalists in New England. Regulars on the other hand felt that Separates were "not sufficiently explicit in their principles, having never published or sanctioned any confession of faith [until 1816]; and that they kept within their communion many who were professed Arminians."[70] However, the Separates finally adjusted their aversion toward confessions. "They were willing to accept the Regular's confession with the stipulation that it was not a binding statement of faith on anyone's conscience. Despite differences in style and doctrine, the two groups were drawn together by revivalism."[71] It should also be pointed out that Regulars adjusted their stance as well as they permitted association without insisting upon the authority of a statement

69. Weaver is citing early nineteenth-century Virginia Baptist historian Robert Semple in these remarks (*In Search of the New Testament Church*, 64).

70. Benedict, *General History*, 61. The Sandy Creek Principles of Faith were not published until 1816. They also felt that they could "bear with some diversity of opinion in doctrines," rather than "break with godly men of exemplary piety."

71. Weaver, *In Search of the New Testament Church*, 65. The nature of their agreement in Virginia in 1787 served as a blueprint for others that followed: "To prevent the confession of faith from usurping a tyrannical power over the conscience of any, we do not mean, that every person is bound to the strict observance of every thing therein contained; yet that it holds forth the essential truths of the gospel, and that the doctrine of salvation by Christ, and free and unmerited grace alone, ought to be believed by every Christian, and maintained by every minister of the gospel. Upon these terms we are united, and desire hereafter, that the names Regular and Separate be buried in oblivion; and that form henceforth, we shall be known by the name of the United Baptist Churches, in Virginia" (Benedict, *General History*, 61).

of confession such as the Philadelphia Confession. This proved to have a significant influence upon the course that followed.

When the Second Great Awakening broke out around the turn of the century, Baptists did not stand on the sidelines this time as they had in the Great Awakening of some sixty years earlier. The growth was evident in all types of Baptists and especially in the frontier areas such as Kentucky, where Baptist work previously had been sparsely missional. However, the revivalistic practices of the Separate Baptists modified their theology over time to what some have characterized as an Arminian direction of general atonement, to mirror their evangelistic practice. This was reflected both in preaching content and in an aggressive evangelistic style.[72] Regular Baptists had to decide how they would respond to the adjusting theology of their new partners. There was room for both under the new banner of broad cooperation at the associational level, but the dynamic nature of the relationship was more evident at the local church level in the blending of two disparate worship traditions. In the words of William Shurden,

> And now a suggestion: if you marry a semipresbyterian from Charleston to a semipentecostal from Sandy Creek, you will get a whole host of Southern Baptists spreading all over the Southland. This is what happened beginning in 1777 in North Carolina and continuing until 1801 in Kentucky, the Charlestonians and the Sandy Creekers began coming together. Together they formed the Southern Baptist Convention and the blending helped shape the Southern Baptist synthesis.[73]

This blend is reflected in a number of ways. One of these is in the content of hymnody and the hymns chosen for hymnals. David Singer analyzes the progressive moderation of Calvinism over the turn of the century in the content of hymns between 1784 and 1844:

> While the decline of Arminian General Baptists and the rapprochement between the Separate and Regular Baptists converted the denomination as a whole to an evangelistic Calvinistic theology, this strict Calvinism soon began to undergo significant changes. These changes, which were attributable in part to the influence of Enlightenment ideas, but even more so to the initial impact of the powerful Arminianizing dynamic inherent in Calvinism itself, particularly in revivalist phases, were faithfully reflected in the hymnals published between 1784 and 1807.

72. Weaver, *In Search of the New Testament Church*, 64.
73. Shurden, *Not an Easy Journey*, 206.

To any careful reader of these hymnals it would have been evident that Calvinist theology had entered a transitional phase.[74]

In particular, the doctrine of limited atonement is slowly replaced by the doctrine of universal atonement by virtue of the hymn texts chosen for the hymnals of the nineteenth century. Additionally, the theocentrism of the earlier hymnals is replaced with anthropocentrism in the later hymnals. Man becomes the leading figure in the drama of salvation rather than God. Finally, greater emphasis is put on God's role as the "glorious lover of mankind."[75] The role of Christ as the atonement for sin is consistent in both.

The new partnership of Regular and Separate Baptists in cooperative effort for revival, and later worldwide missions, laid the foundation for a united Baptist effort of the nineteenth century and beyond. It was initially a problematic one for a different reason—one that mirrored the growing division in the country. That effort eventually split over the issue of slavery in the founding of the Southern Baptist Convention in 1845. What remained to be seen is what this blended worship would look like as it migrated to the frontier areas west and north into Canada.

74. Singer, "God and Man in Baptist Hymnals," 16.
75. Singer, "God and Man in Baptist Hymnals," 16–17.

PART TWO

Worship Synthesis

6

Siloam Baptist Church, Marion, Alabama (1822–1855)

Introduction

THE NINETEENTH CENTURY DAWNED with revival in the air; a freshly forming spirit of cooperation among Baptists; a vision for the evangelization of
their rapidly expanding country; and an emerging burden and capacity for
domestic and worldwide mission. Baptist numbers were surging alongside
their Methodist revival partners. The nation's western frontier was equally
a frontier for Baptists as church-planting efforts began to push from the
Atlantic Ocean toward the Mississippi River and north into Canada. A form
of worship had been established among Baptist traditions in the eighteenth
century that emphasized preaching as the main element of worship. Unac-
companied congregational singing had been embraced in both the church
and the camp meeting. What remained to be established was the synthesis
of two seemingly incompatible worship traditions: order and ardor, edification and evangelism, Calvinism and what began to look more and more like
Arminianism.

The Charleston Tradition, associated with Calvinism, was marked by
a planned service of predictably ordered elements of worship that sought
primarily to edify the saints of God. It was equated with decorum and structure. The Sandy Creek Tradition, associated increasingly with Arminianism,
was marked by a loosely patterned service of unplanned reliance upon the
Spirit of God to save sinners. It was equated with emotion and revivalism.
Both sought to glorify God and proclaim the gospel, but their distinctions

were significant. On some points, one tradition had to take precedence over the other. Most of these choices would be made in the pastor's study, with the aim of his sermons, the view he had of worship, and the hymns he chose to sing. Additionally, whereas the eighteenth century was largely a century of importing British hymnody, the nineteenth century was an age of adding diverse American hymnody to this foundation. Many hymn writers were also the pastors, making this yet another means by which direction in worship was to be determined. Baptist worship was growing, changing, and diversifying as quickly as the denomination and the country. It was also splitting.

It would be hard to find a church during this time period that was more influential in its region and state than Siloam Baptist Church. Though the Southern Baptist Convention was not founded until 1845, much of the groundwork was laid, and early growth evidenced, in Marion, Alabama. Siloam was established in 1822 and played a central role in the formation of the Alabama Baptist Convention in nearby Greensboro in 1823. Siloam's first pastor was moderator of the Cahaba Association and the first president of the Alabama State Convention. By 1841, Judson Female Institute (now Judson College), and Howard College (now Samford University) were founded from Siloam. In 1843 the *Alabama Baptist*, the Baptist state newspaper, also began in Marion. The "Alabama Resolutions," passed at the state convention's meeting at Siloam in 1844, led to the founding of the Southern Baptist Convention a year later in Augusta, Georgia.[1] Finally, in 1845, convention leaders met at Siloam to found the Board of Domestic Missions (later the Home Mission Board and now NAMB). This was a flagship church among Alabama Baptists and Southern Baptists of the mid-nineteenth century.

The connections outside of Alabama were equally significant. Many highly educated and bright thinkers came to teach at one of the two colleges. Aspiring Baptist ministers came to Howard to be trained for pastoral ministry while influential Baptist women came to Judson—one of the first colleges in America for women.[2] Mission Board personnel shuttled in and

---

1. In the years leading up to the Civil War, some northern Baptists among the Triennial Convention (formed in 1814) opposed the appointment as missionaries, those who owned slaves (essentially southern Baptists). James Reeves of Georgia became the litmus test as he was put forth in 1844 as a potential missionary. The Baptist Home Mission Society of the convention refused to ordain him. The Alabama Resolutions affirmed the right of slaveholders to serve as missionaries and rejected the jurisdiction of the Home Mission Society. These were subsequently sent out to Baptists in every slave-holding state leading up to the historic gathering in Augusta, Georgia in 1845. The Southern Baptist Convention was formed. The northern Baptists inherited the Triennial Convention, which became the Northern Baptist Convention in 1907.

2. Howard began primarily as a literary college but in January 1844, a professor

out of Marion for their duties until it was relocated in 1882 to Atlanta; and the *Alabama Baptist* heralded the news of the Baptist work across the state from this small town. The common Sunday experience for all was that they worshiped at Siloam—where the pastor was one of the most notable in the state, and the church demonstrated an exemplary synthesis of Charleston and Sandy Creek traditions.

A Brief History

When Charles Crow (1770–1845) constituted Siloam Baptist Church in June 1822, Perry County was no more than a few log cabins in the heart of the state. The town of Marion and the church were constituted within a few weeks of each other. Alabama had just been admitted to the union a few years earlier in 1819 ushering in rapid growth from the eastern seaboard. Crow was a Separate Baptist from Bush River Baptist Church in Newberry, South Carolina, where he had been saved in the revival of 1802 during the Second Great Awakening.[3] Many of these revival converts moved to Perry County almost two decades later to establish the Ocmulgee Baptist Church near Selma in 1820 with Crow as their pastor. The Siloam Women's Society of Marion contacted Crow about starting a church there. Residents were becoming "increasingly concerned" about the "moral status of the inhabitants of [wicked] Marion. Open bar rooms, bawdy houses, street fights, were common in this frontier town."[4] Western Alabama consisted of thick forests and almost every building was some form of a log cabin. Julia Lovelace records the words of W. B. Crumpton describing Marion at the time Crow arrived: "Imagine, if you can, a thickly wooded fertile section at a crossroads,

---

of theology was hired. Its purpose was to train ministers who were badly needed for the rapidly expanding Baptist work in Alabama (Flynt, *Alabama Baptists*, 59.) John R. Sampey, fifth president of the Southern Baptist Theological Seminary, was trained at Howard College (Lovelace, *History of Siloam*, 1) and (Flynt, *Alabama Baptists*, 56). It should also be noted that higher education was not highly esteemed in Alabama at the time and establishing and supporting a college in Alabama was challenging, especially for ministry.

3. The *Alabama Baptist* called Crow's doctrine that "of the high Calvinistic order, yet not ultra" ("History of Siloam Baptist Church").

4. LeBaron, *Sketches from the Life of Charles Crow*. "From records available, it appears nine persons were present when the church was organized. A meeting house was erected on a quarter acre of land set aside for churches in Marion, and the congregation received title to it on June 4, 1824. Here Charles preached one weekend a month for the next eight years. It would be less than objective to call his ministry at Siloam Church a success. He did not reform 'wicked' Marion as he intended. The people there did not respond significantly to his ministry."

a shack of a store nearby. That would about describe the place where the fine old town of Marion now stands. A crossroads church was soon established. Perhaps it was not hard to build, as labor and logs were in abundance."[5]

Hosea Holcombe (1780–1841), one of several who migrated from South Carolina, writes, "Houses for the worship of God were scarce for several years after the writer came to [Alabama] in 1818, and many of those erected were more like Indian wigwams than anything else, only they were more open and uncomfortable."[6] When the weather permitted it was common for some Alabama pastors to meet outside under a shade tree rather than suffer the accommodations of early Baptist churches. Crow pastored Siloam for its first eight years, along with his pastorate at nearby Hopewell. "There were few pastors in Perry County at this time, and every minister served several churches."[7] Crow's name is associated with at least five churches during this time, and as a result preached at Siloam only once a month—a common practice for Baptist churches then.

Sandy Creek-styled camp meeting revivals broke out in Alabama in the 1830s. Holcombe writes, "In the course of the last year [1831–1832], revivals have been experienced in many parts of the state: the Lord has, by the outpouring of his spirit, visited the people in [many] counties . . . [including] Perry."[8] Holcombe was a member of a church that experienced this revival in central Alabama, near Marion.

> The first camp-meeting, perhaps ever known in Alabama, was held with the church, where the writer has his membership. This meeting took place about the first of October, 1831, it continued for five or six days, and twelve or fifteen families tented on the ground. Here the Lord made bare his arm, and displayed his power in the salvation of many precious souls. The groans and cries of repenting sinners, the songs and prayers, the shouts and praises of Christians, formed an awful, yet delightful harmony.

5. Lovelace, *History of Siloam*, 3. Washington B. Crumpton (1842–1926) was executive secretary of the State Mission Board of Alabama for twenty-five years and delivered the Centennial Address in recognition of the one-hundredth anniversary of the church in 1922. He lived in Marion for the last ten years that the Home Mission Board was located in Marion (1872–1882).

6. Holcombe, *Baptists in Alabama*, 43. Holcombe was president of the Alabama Baptist Convention from 1833–1838. He was asked to write a historical account of Baptists in Alabama, during which time he traveled widely throughout the state collecting information to write this volume.

7. Lovelace, *History of Siloam*, 8.

8. Holcombe, *Baptists in Alabama*, 45. Holcombe lists sixteen Alabama counties but most were in the middle of the state around Perry County. Marion is the county seat of Perry County.

At this meeting there commenced the greatest general revival, ever known at that time, in middle Alabama; it continued over twelve months; during which period there were near 500 baptized in three or four churches.[9]

Three relatively brief pastorates passed before the arrival of Siloam's most notable pastor—James H. DeVotie. William Calloway (who founded the church with Crow and continued as pastor from 1830–1833 after he left), James Veazy (served 1833–1835), and Peter Crawford (served 1835–1840) all served during this remarkable period of revival and growth for the church. Though church records from this time were lost or destroyed by fire, town records record the deed to Siloam of a two-acre tract set aside for churches in 1833. S. A. Townes, in *The History of Marion* (1844), writes, "The Baptists have one of the most elegant and tasty houses of worship in the state, erected in 1837 at a cost of $7,000.00."[10] Of this time period Holcombe writes,

Siloam—this church has been one of the most prosperous in the state, is situated in the beautiful little town of Marion, Perry County. . . . This church has prospered very much recently, and is, perhaps the largest in the state, except the African church in Huntsville. There are a number of respectable, liberal, and intelligent brethren here; and many of the females are among the precious ones of the earth. . . . [This church] built for themselves a house of worship, which cost them eight or nine thousand dollars, besides a number of other liberal subscriptions, and donations for other purposes, which were given about the same time. They likewise pay their pastor $800 to $1000 annually. In the last two years, there have been about 100 baptized.[11]

9. Holcombe, *Baptists in Alabama*, 45. This revival occurred in the winter of 1831 into 1832. "From that time camp-meetings became common among the Baptists in different parts of the state; yet some churches disapprove of the course. That there was extravagance at some of those meetings, we think few will deny yet there was much good done. It was not unusual, to have a large portion of the congregation, prostrated on the ground; and in some instances they appeared to have lost the use of their limbs. No distinct articulation could be heard; screams, cries, groans, shouts, notes of grief, and notes of joy, all heard at the same time, made much confusion, a sort of indescribable concert. At associations, and other great meetings, where there were several ministers present, many of them would exercise their gifts at the same time, in different parts of the congregations; some in exhortation, others in praying for the distressed; and others again, in argument with opposers. A number of the preachers did not approve of this kind of work: they thought it extravagant. Others fanned it as fire from heaven."

10. Townes, *History of Marion*, 26.

11. Holcombe, *Baptists in Alabama*, 146.

During these years the Alabama State Convention met at Siloam three times and met there almost every other year during DeVotie's tenure as pastor. Lovelace summarizes, "The prominence and influence of Siloam Church from the time of its organization is attested by the frequency with which the Alabama Baptist Convention met in Marion."[12]

James Harvey DeVotie (1813–1891) was born in Oneida County, New York. His mother was Presbyterian and his father was "an irreligious farmer." He was converted in 1830 and moved to Savannah, Georgia, the following year to live with his uncle who was a Baptist. He was baptized and licensed to preach at First Baptist Church in Savannah. He then attended Furman Theological Seminary for less than two years and pastored the Baptist church at Camden while a student there. At the age of twenty, he served the FBC of Montgomery for one year and then FBC of Tuscaloosa for four years before coming to Siloam in 1840.[13] Basil Manly Sr. and DeVotie crossed paths several times as they "both had South Carolina connections; both pastored congregations in Montgomery and Tuscaloosa; [and] both became prominent figures in the Alabama and Southern Baptist Conventions."[14] DeVotie's early days of ministry were marked with contentious and divisive incidents, some with Manly. He withdrew from Furman "after writing insulting letters to one of the professors." At both Montgomery and Tuscaloosa "DeVotie proved to be a fractious, opinionated man whose pastorates were both stormy and generally successful." He was dismissed from the pastorate at Montgomery and finally resigned from the Tuscaloosa post in 1839, questioning his call to the pastorate. "Despite his zeal, eloquence, and enterprise (plus two marvelous revivals during his four-year pastorate), some well-educated University of Alabama officials in the congregation criticized his lack of scholarly credentials."[15] Manly—then president of the University of Alabama—filled in as interim pastor after DeVotie left. Manly likely had helped force DeVotie's resignation after two years of criticizing the job he did there.[16]

12. Lovelace, *History of Siloam*, 10.

13. "History of Samford University: Biography." See also Cathcart, "J. H. DeVotie," 321.

14. Flynt, *Alabama Baptists*, 19.

15. Flynt, *Alabama Baptists*, 18–19.

16. Fuller, *Chaplain to the Confederacy*, 208. Fuller feels that Manly's criticism of DeVotie was unfair as "typically, once convinced of his own position, [Manly] continued to hold fast to it long after his error had become obvious." At the same time, Manly had just come from the pastorate of one of the oldest and richest churches in the south—First Baptist Charleston. He was accustomed to the Charleston order of things and the young pastor at First Baptist Tuscaloosa, zealous for the revivals of that day but not for building a new building, was not measuring up to Manly's experience

DeVotie's tenure at Siloam proved in many ways to be the pinnacle of the church's history. Not only did he oversee the major accomplishments of the church's influence in the state and national conventions referenced above, he simultaneously led the church during its greatest period of growth, including the building of the brick building in Greek Revival style that still stands today.[17] Flynt writes of this time period,

> In 1840 Marion was a flourishing village of twelve hundred inhabitants and an important hub for a substantial agricultural hinterland. As the center of the northwestern edge of the Black Belt, it served as home for numerous wealthy planters, while others gained wealth in mercantile and real estate businesses. Its citizens (many originally from the Northeast) were as highly regarded for their culture and hospitality as for their wealth. So many of the prominent families were Baptist that a writer from Richmond, Virginia, who visited Marion in 1844 called the town "the Baptist Capital of Alabama."[18]

Though lacking the completion of formal education, DeVotie possessed vision, dynamic leadership skills, and a hearty work ethic. Under his leadership, Siloam reached such prominence that it was said that she was "the strongest Baptist church west of Augusta."[19] DeVotie left several volumes of his personal journals and hundreds of handwritten sermons, demonstrating his sound theological acumen, thorough hermeneutical skill, deep religious piety, and a remarkably wide acquaintance with devotional literature, including hymnody, from which he often cited.[20]

---

and expectations.

17. Jeremy Windsor estimates that he baptized at least 1,500 in his ministry ("Preaching Up a Storm from 1839 to 1889," 13–20, quoted in Flynt, *Alabama Baptists*, 18). Membership at Siloam when he arrived in 1840 was 285. When he departed in 1854 it had increased to 676, the largest in Siloam's history. The building was built and dedicated in 1849 (see Lovelace, *History of Siloam*, 15).

18. Flynt, *Alabama Baptists*, 55–56. The citation is from January 6, 1844, edition of the *Alabama Baptist*. A great part of the financial backing of these endeavors was from Julia Ann Tarrant Barron, a wealthy widow and prosperous Marion businesswoman and planter. She was cofounder of Judson and Howard Colleges as well as the early benefactor and co-owner of the *Alabama Baptist*. She donated the land upon which Siloam Baptist Church sits. After the Civil War her fortunes declined precipitously. Her son died in 1868 and her daughter-in-law died in 1875, leaving two granddaughters for her to raise alone. She had to sell her house and died in 1890 at age eighty-four, "impoverished and largely forgotten by the Baptists who owed her such a huge debt" (58).

19. Wilson, *Some Early Alabama Churches*, 139.

20 First Baptist Church of Savannah apparently spent "an hour, or two" on Sunday evenings "agreeably spent in practicing vocal music in all its parts." It is not clear if this was a select group of singers or the entire church, but the pastor, Henry Holcombe,

Theology in Practice

Flynt describes the general theology of early Alabama Baptists' in this manner, "Although the expression of their faith was altered in time by the graft of a new frontier culture, the seed they planted was doctrinally ancient and uniform." Specifically, "The principles were straightforward, generally Calvinistic in theology and Baptist in tradition." Though reluctant to adhere to anything called a "creed," they often wrote a statement of principles, confession, articles or abstracts of faith, or constitution to define their local church expression's beliefs. These were essentially uniform and often borrowed from one another. They were unashamedly Trinitarian and stood firmly upon the authority of the word of God, which "constituted their only rule of faith and practice."[21] The gospel formed the central message of the church. They practiced two ordinances of baptism and communion, with controversy in a few places over laying on of hands and foot washing. Communion was closed except to baptized church members in good standing (e.g., not under church discipline).

Given this rather broad generalization of Baptist theology in nineteenth-century Alabama, it is no surprise that closer inspection reveals the results of the dynamic synthesis of competing theologies that came out of the eighteenth century. Holcombe writes in 1840, "We have no doubt, that in a very few years, there were emigrants from more than half the states in the Union; and among those emigrants were Baptists; whose customs, manners, and views . . . were considerably discordant."[22] While the connections to the Calvinistic tradition of Charleston were present through pastors such as Manly, Holcombe, and DeVotie,[23] as at Sandy Creek, the camp meeting revivals tended to push some pastors and churches toward a revivalistic methodology more in line with Arminianism. Holcombe explains, "Some ministers . . . have been too fond, perhaps, of working on the human passions—too anxious to make a noise, and raise a ferment; and then too

---

reported it in the journal he edited. The report is from 1802, so it is not clear if this was still the practice when DeVotie arrived in 1830, but it demonstrates that the congregational singing in his first Baptist church experience was quite involved and potentially advanced. He likely became acquainted with Baptist hymnody here. (See *Georgia Analytical Repository* 1 [1802], 185, quoted in Music and Richardson, *"I Will Sing the Wondrous Story,"* 97.)

21. Flynt, *Alabama Baptists*, 4.

22. Holcombe, *Baptists in Alabama*, 58–59.

23. DeVotie was baptized at FBC Savannah, a "Charleston Tradition" church under the teaching of Henry O. Wyer who was ordained by William T. Brantly and James Shannon. DeVotie was trained at Furman and referenced both the First and Second London Confessions in his personal journals. (See DeVotie, *Personal Journals*, 1:183.)

easily satisfied with the relation of those who profess their faith, in order to baptism. Hence many are received into our churches, who have no correct views whatever of their sins being pardoned through the blood of Christ."[24]

Flynt writes, "No biblical dispute shaped early Alabama Baptists so profoundly as Calvinism. . . . Although Baptists were Calvinists in the general sense of the term, they modified the doctrine."[25] In 1844, Basil Manly wrote the annual circular letter of the Tuscaloosa Association on article 3 of its Abstract of Principles: "We believe in the doctrine of election; and that God chose his people in Christ, before the foundation of the World."[26] In doing so, Manly laid out the Scriptural foundations of the doctrine of election, but also added an emphasis upon individual effort and responsibility. "Manly's emphasis upon human exertion and individual response reflected the powerful influence of revivalism on early Alabama Baptist thought."[27] Holcombe observes, "With regard to their doctrinal views, [pastors] have been considerably diverse; in general they have appeared to occupy what is termed the middle ground; or in other words, embraced the system of Dr. Fuller."[28] DeVotie reflected this type of modified Calvinism, but from the perspective of having experienced revival, rather than simply giving theological ascent to the possibility. One of Manly's disagreements with DeVotie

24. Holcombe, *Baptists in Alabama*, 47. Holcombe referenced a "Mr. T——," who while "Mr. H——" was preaching, was very noisy. "For it was a privilege which he allowed himself, to sing, pray, or exhort, while another was engaged in the same exercise" (46–47).

25. Holcombe, *Baptists in Alabama*, 47.

26. Basil Manly, "Circular Letter," 1844, reprinted in *Alabama Baptist*, June 30, July 3, 1930. Manly's effort was to develop a compromise between Calvinist and Arminians. Manly's clarification here enabled Arminians and "strict-Calvinists" to unite in missions work, benevolence, and revivalism. Hyper-Calvinism on the other hand, developed into the Anti-Missions movement among Baptists in Alabama (and other states), particularly Primitive Baptists.

27. Flynt, *Alabama Baptists*, 27. "If Charleston, South Carolina, provides the clearest ancestry for Calvinism, Sandy Creek, North Carolina, lays firmest claim to the revival tradition. Ardent, charismatic, emotional, independent, Biblicist, the Sandy Creek tradition merged elements of both Calvinism and Arminianism." Alabama was one of many merging points for both Charleston and Sandy Creek traditions.

28. Holcombe, *Baptists in Alabama*, 59. Holcombe lists Antinomianism, Campbellism, Arminianism, Universalism, and Hyper-Calvinism as also being represented among Alabama pastors: "We are firmly of the opinion, that there has been a considerable number of ministers in Alabama, who have in some respect departed from the old Baptist foundation, in fact, from the Scriptures, in their doctrine *views*, and sometimes in their preaching. But in the main, we believe they advance good doctrine" (emphasis Holcombe's).

was the accusation that DeVotie had "thrown himself into revivalism" while in Tuscaloosa.[29]

DeVotie's sermons were consistently organized and ordered in the same manner. A single verse or brief passage served as the text for the message. An introduction led to an exegetical outline of the body of his sermon. DeVotie derived his sermon outline from the shape of his text. Flynt describes his preaching in this manner: "James DeVotie began sermons with a text, studied every word, determined the central doctrine or truth involved, compared the text to other Scriptures to assure conformity with central biblical teachings, read commentaries and sermons about the passage to eliminate possible errors in his own understanding, selected illustrations, then wrote 'pretty full notes.'"[30]

He left numerous journals that were essentially examples of the same process of exegetical work as he developed his personal theology and spirituality. Each section was prefaced with a focal Scripture text that he worked through in the following pages. Some of these sections went on for ten or twenty pages as he worked through different angles on a single verse. He also included related verses, quotes from other books, and hymn texts that related to the text. Many times he cut these proof texts out of a spare Bible and pasted them into his journal. He did the same with illustrations from other sources and hymn texts. There are places in his journal where he breaks into doxological praise upon reflecting on a particular thought or revelation. His journals are a record of his scriptural and theological growth, but also that of his personal piety. He appears to have had a dynamic relationship with God that was as doxological as it was theological.

The Practice of Worship

DeVotie advocated personal and public worship. While unbelievers were present, public worship was primarily for the believer. In his journal he wrote, "How can any one commune [with God] but a regenerate person? Unbelievers cannot discern the Lord's body." He stated the need to only permit baptized believers into the membership of the church and to maintain a converted church membership, in attempting to follow the pattern of the apostolic church. He was insistent that church members needed to be in worship on the Lord's Day. Additionally, preparation for worship was an important part of worship. "The absence of proper preparation on the part of the hearer makes many an interesting discourse to him. . . . Who enters

29. Fuller, *Basil Manly*, 208.
30. Flynt, *Alabama Baptists*, 152.

God's house expecting to hear what God the Lord will speak for he will speak peace unto his people." At the same time he encouraged unsaved attendees to be attentive listeners as well, reflecting shades of revivalism: "A careless listener may loose [sic], what saves another man's soul by his side. . . . An inattentive soul may perish of thirst at the very fountainhead of salvation."[31]

In his instructions regarding seeking God's presence, he cautioned that worshipers needed to do so "under a full sense of our sinfulness . . . Sin must be seen, felt, and turned from. . . . He that confesseth and forsaketh shall find mercy." The topic of sin and confession is a prominent one in his journals. One wonders how this was represented in worship outside of his preaching. Clearly he wanted his people to evaluate his or her life for sin and bring that to the cross. He wrote to himself, "God will abundantly pardon. . . . Repentance and remission of sins must be preached in the name of Jesus."[32] A Christ-centered gospel is for everyone present in worship:

> His warnings of danger, his threatenings against sin, are for each of us—His promises, his doctrines, his comforting belong to each believing soul. The bread of life spread out before you is prepared for each. He says, eat my friends—in faith spiritually eat of his body, and drink of his blood. For his body is meat, indeed, and his blood is drink indeed. Let the sincere honest inquiry of each soul be, Lord is it for me, Lord is it I—The gospel deals with us; our neighbors, and brethren, are hearing for themselves. We may not apply to them, that which belongs to ourselves. Take heed what ye hear. Search the Scriptures for in them ye think ye have eternal life and they are they which testify of me.[33]

He knew where to take his sin and he wanted his people to do the same. Confession led to the cross, which positioned the confessor before Christ. He was the provision and the reward. The gospel was the means. Later in his journal he included a lengthy section regarding the principle of worship: "Give to God the Glory due. Worship Him. Men may give Glory to God. His nature and perfections demand glory and praise from all creation. Perfectness of character even elicits expressions of admiration. . . . But O' what wonderful perfection in God challange [sic] our songs of praise." He listed some of those aspects of God's perfection: wisdom, power, love,

31. DeVotie, "Personal Journal," 177, 180, 217–18. He references 1 Pet 2:5–9 regarding worship and the believer.

32. DeVotie, "Personal Journal," 1:285, 292.

33. DeVotie, "Personal Journal," 1:224–25.

creation, providence, health, authority, and again, ultimately the gospel: "He deserves Glory in the highest for his works of grace and salvation. His love for miserable sinners. The sacrifice of God's only Son. Wonder angels! Wonder devils! Praise him, praise him ye blood bought ye redeemed of earth. Sin forgiven. Sinners cleansed. Regeneration, justification, the death of the rightious [sic], the resurrection of the just. Communion with God forever—heaven—Glory, Glory, highest glory."[34]

He seemed to lose himself in rapturous praise as he delighted in the beauty and worthiness of God revealed by the gospel. The benefit of worship was in reflecting upon the joy of salvation that "excels all joy." The joy of the gospel was one of knowing God!

Worship needed to be offered in holiness, spirituality, knowledge and feeling. "The mind and heart must be full of the knowledge of God to 'Give the glory due unto his name.'" DeVotie was characterized as an emotional individual[35] and that emotion was likely on full display in worship. The passion and emotion of the private worshiper certainly overflowed in public. He concluded with a prayer for his church, written on the morning of corporate worship: "Spirit divine help us thus to worship while we stand in thy presence. Father, Son, and Holy Spirit help us to worship in the beauty of holiness today."[36]

The early Baptist view of the Sabbath was that "it ought to be observed and set apart for the worship of God, and that no work or worldly business ought to be done thereon. Works of pity and necessity only exceptions."[37] Avery Reid writes of worship around the time Siloam was founded:

> Preaching was commonly held only on one Saturday and Sunday in each month, and the people came on foot or horseback for miles around. Following a shorter sermon on Saturday, a church conference was held. In this conference there was a report on the fellowship and conduct of the members. Attempts were made to settle differences between members, and those who had evidenced misconduct were called on to acknowledge their errors and request forgiveness.

---

34. DeVotie, "Personal Journal," 1:373–78.

35. Fuller, *Basil Manly*, 208.

36. DeVotie, "Personal Journal," 1:379–81.

37. Minutes of the Enon Baptist Church of Christ, 1–2, quoted in Reid, *Baptists in Alabama*, 14. Enon Baptist Church was established in 1809 as the second Baptist church founded in Alabama. Flint River Baptist Church was founded in 1808 (11–12). This is from article 7 from the Articles of Faith of Enon Church. The articles also clearly affirm closed communion.

This is likely what DeVotie referred to as preparing for worship. The Articles of Faith for Siloam, written in the 1850s, required all male members to attend regular conferences in article 12. These meetings were to ensure that a pure and repentant church body was prepared for worship in addition to carrying out the business of the church. Membership in the church required a profession of faith in the Lord Jesus Christ, "giving credible evidence of a change of heart, adopting the views of Faith and Practice held by the church, and baptism." Transfers from other churches "holding the same Faith may be received by letters of dismission from their respected churches." An objection from a current church member could keep someone from being allowed to join the church. "Excluded members may be restored on confession of their errors and giving evidence of their repentance" according to article 10. Article 15 outlines the requirements for external conduct and the potential of church discipline as a response to "immoral unscriptural amusements or acts in social business life or characters inconsistent in the judgment of this church with the becoming Christian deportment."[38]

Reid also describes singing at the time: "The Sunday morning worship service was usually two hours or more in length with much singing and a sermon of an hour or more. Only a few hymnbooks were had, and they contained only the lyrics, which the leader would read one line at a time." This was the process known as "lining out the hymn." "Then the congregation would lustily join in singing the old familiar hymns by memory."[39] Flynt adds, "Worship services in nineteenth-century Alabama Baptist churches were simple and infrequent." The services and the hymnody were both very casual. Preachers typically carried both a Bible and hymnal to be ready to sing. "Collections of hymns by Watts, Dorsey [sic], Rippon, and [Mercer's] Cluster were favorites," though Hosea Holcombe and Basil Manly compiled collections. Singing was usually animated and loud, although confusion ensued at times resulting from lining out the verses. "Some could not remember the words and mumbled their own version."[40]

DeVotie quotes numerous hymn texts in his sermons and journals. He often concludes a sermon with a hymn text, probably read but possibly sung.

38. "Constitution of Siloam Baptist Church." "Written during the 1850s" is handwritten at the top of the typewritten copy.

39. Reid, *Baptists in Alabama*, 17–18.

40. Flynt, *Alabama Baptists*, 11–12. Should be Dossey's *Choice* and Mercer's *Cluster*. "One piece of religious folklore from northwestern Alabama recalls a hapless pastor who announced that he would line out the words to 'On Jordan's Stormy Banks I Stand.' He reached for his glasses, but did not have them. Facing the congregation, he explained, 'My eyes are dim, I cannot see; I left my specs at home.' The congregation dutifully sang his words which fit the hymn's meter" (12–13; Flynt is citing an incident from Russellville First Baptist Church).

The hymns quoted in DeVotie's writing potentially give some clues regarding what may have been sung in his church. Isaac Watts, "We're Marching to Zion," Timothy Dwight's, "I Love Thy Kingdom, Lord," Samuel Stennett's, "How Charming is the Place (The Mercy Seat)" and "Majestic Sweetness Sits Enthroned," William Hammond's, "Awake, and Sing the Song," Joseph Hart's "Come, Holy Spirit, Come," John Newton's, "Amazing Grace," Anna Barbould's "Our Country is Immanuel's Ground," Charlotte Elliott's "Just as I Am," Joseph's Grigg's "Behold a Stranger's at the Door," and Michael Bruce's "Where High the Heavenly Temple Stands" are just a handful of examples from his notes. They represent a broad range of worship songs, representing the synthesis of Charleston and Sandy Creek. The synthesis required songs for both edification and evangelism.

If Siloam was not using Rippon's collection of Watts[41] before DeVotie's arrival, they may have used one of two other popular Baptist hymnbooks in the south in the early nineteenth century. Henry S. Burrage believes H. Miller's *New Selection of Psalms, Hymns, and Spiritual Songs* (1835) and W. C. Buck's *The Baptist Hymn Book* (1842) were the most frequently used hymnbooks in the south.[42] It is likely that Siloam used *The Psalmist* (1843)[43] after DeVotie's arrival. The *Alabama Baptist* printed numerous ads, endorsements from other papers, and finally a lengthy endorsement of its own after a thorough evaluation of the hymnal: "We earnestly commend *The Psalmist* to the attention of pastor and churches."[44] Given DeVotie's role on the editorial board, the "we" seems to include him, and likely Siloam as well. Later, *Baptist Psalmody* (1850) became a popular hymnal in the south.[45] S. F. Stow,

41. Published and recommended by Philadelphia Baptists in 1820 and again with significant improvements in 1827. They may have been using William Dossey's *The Choice: in Two Parts*, recommended by the North Carolina Baptist Convention in 1834, or Jesse Mercer's *The Cluster of Spiritual Songs*, popular in Georgia where Mercer was president of the Georgia Baptist Convention. But it is more likely that they were using Hosea Holcombe's *A Collection of Sacred Hymns* (1815) or some collection of Watts and Rippon before using *The Psalmist* and/or *Baptist Psalmody*.

42. Burrage, *Baptists Hymn Writers*, 652, 654. It is not apparent that Siloam was using Buck.

43. Stow and Smith, *Psalmist*. First edition was published in 1843.

44. "Psalmist," January 8, 1847. "There are admirable Hymns on all the great Doctrines of the Bible, as depravity, the atonement, repentance, regeneration, by the Holy Spirit, justification by faith, election, perseverance of the saints. . . . There are also great numbers of Hymns of peculiar excellence adapted to Revivals, Camp Meetings, Protracted Meetings, Prayer Meetings, Conferences, and Family Worship."

45. Manly and Manly, *Baptist Psalmody*. Minutes from the Southern Baptist Convention, Tuesday, May 12, 1851: "Whereas, the Southern Baptist Publication Society has published a hymnbook entitled, 'The Baptist Psalmody,' which by its evangelical character and general excellence is eminently adapted to the purpose for which it was

one of the editors of *The Psalmist*, was an outspoken abolitionist, which caused some in the south to reject that hymnal during a time when the slavery issue was a boiling cauldron of controversy. *Baptist Psalmody* was the southern response to *The Psalmist*, which also had left out a number of the most popular hymns for Southern Baptists:

> In accordance with a request of the Tuscaloosa Association, at its late session, the undersigned propose to publish a Hymn Book adapted to the use of Baptist Churches in the South. We design it to contain unaltered, the old hymns, precious to the children of God by long use, and familiarized to them in many a season of perplexity and temptation as well as spiritual joy. We shall also add such other hymns of more recent date as seem worthy to be associated with the former, in order to make a complete Hymn Book for public and private worhip [*sic*].[46]

It was edited and published by Basil Manly Sr. and Basil Manly Jr. (1825–1892) from nearby Tuscaloosa, making it more likely that it eventually found its way to Marion.[47] Both collections contain a similar organization and categorization of hymns by topical themes as well as by special occasion or service. Both also include a substantial Scripture index, demonstrating the continuing practice of attempting to match a closing hymn to the sermon text of the day. Topical themes and the order of the hymns are arranged in order of doctrinal priority: attributes of God, acts of God, worship of God, Trinity, Christ, and the Holy Spirit make up the first 284 hymns. There are 183 hymns related to the gospel and salvation that come soon after. There are also hymns specifically included for baptism and the Lord's Supper. A few hymns listed are for revival, and a number of hymns are intended to be used as the unbeliever's response to the gospel. However, the vast majority of the 1,295 hymns are for believers to sing in worship.

---

prepared; and whereas the extensive circulation of the book will contribute materially to the Treasury of the Society: *Resolved*, That the Baptist Psalmody be recommended to be used in offering their songs of praise to the Father, Son, and the Holy Ghost" (*Proceedings of the Southern Baptist Convention*, 16). DeVotie was present at that convention serving as the president of the Board of Domestic Missions (located in Marion, AL) and as a messenger for Siloam.

46. Manly and Manly, "A New Hymn Book," text in Measels, "A Catalog of Source Readings," 152.

47. While one of the hymns cited above from DeVotie's journals was found in *The Psalmist* and not in *Baptist Psalmody* ("Our Country is Immanuel's Ground"), the rest were found either in both or only in *Baptist Psalmody* (five of eleven were only in the latter). The cutout verses were of the font size and type of *Baptist Psalmody*. The two hymnbooks are structured very similarly and the primary difference is in the content of hymns favored in the South.

There also are a number of doxologies at the end of the hymnal that could be spoken or sung and were often used at the end of sermons or addresses.[48] Certain hymns are clearly suited for opening a service while others are obviously hymns of response and closing. There are also songs of confession and gospel summary in both. These may indicate a pattern of usage and emphasis in congregational singing.

It appears from the records that remain that a choir was used at Siloam from the earliest days of DeVotie's pastorate—perhaps even before DeVotie arrived. When the new building was opened in September 1849, it included galleries on three sides for the choir. This indicates a prominent use of the choir prior to this time. There was some public debate about the choir at this time so it was not an accepted practice yet, at least not without some contention. The *Alabama Baptist* records a hypothetical argument over the use of the choir specifically at Siloam, revealing the type of disagreement at the time. In this imaginary dialogue, a church member is complaining about the singing going on above his head and not knowing whether or not he should sing along. He equates their being seated above his head in the gallery with his perception of an attitude of them being above him. The paper writes in response to Brother B.,

> The members of the choir are servants of the congregation, laboring for the edification and enjoyment—spending their own time and money to make the services of the Sanctuary most pleasant for others. . . . [Brother B. threatens to go to another church] Well brother B. if you think you are too good to worship with your brethren here, you should go off to some church where you will find better men—men more worthy of your Christian fellowship.

The quoted response is signed "Asaph." The article goes on to cite the use of choirs in Baptist churches in Charleston, Richmond and Baltimore, as well as the use of organs to assist in the music at Charleston and Baltimore. It also encourages Brother B. to sing with them: "No one has told you that you cannot sing."[49] The purpose of the choir was to help worshipers such as Brother B. sing, as congregational singing was very weak in most churches of this time.[50]

---

48. Julian, "Doxologies": s.v. "doxologies," 308.

49. "Choirs."

50. A Choir and Music committee was formed in 1879 to attempt to improve congregational singing by improving an existing choir. "The duty of this Committee shall be to have in view the worship of God in his praises, and to devise and carry out such measures as will result in a more general, prompt, and regular attendance upon the

Scripture reading may have been a part of the service in more than just reading the sermon text before the sermon. Lee Allen writes of the practice of the day of numerous Alabama churches, "The Scripture reading often taken from both the Old and New Testaments, was a vital part of the service. In an era marked by illiteracy, many knew only those portions of the Bible which were read to them." Additionally, "Lengthy pastoral prayers were expected."[51] People did not feel that they were getting their money's worth—from pew rent—if they were not in church for at least two hours.

The central event of the worship service was preaching. In many instances, if there was no preaching there was no service. Services focused on hearing and speaking the word of God. DeVotie could be fully devoted to Siloam so they met weekly for worship. As mentioned above, DeVotie's preaching was well prepared. He took for his text a single verse or short passage that he could thoroughly exegete. He does not appear to have preached through books of the Bible but must have selected a text for the day. The text was probably read formally to begin the sermon and the outline of the sermon was structured around the main points of the text.[52] Doctrine, illustrations, proof texts, and application were interspersed with each point. His outlines ranged between six and eight pages and he left some room for extemporaneous additions, though the structure and main points of the sermon were prepared in his study. Communion occurred quarterly according to later records.

------

various meetings of our church on the part of the choir, and to use all of their ability and influence to promote congregational singing, and thus improve this much neglected part of the worship of God, in our congregation" (Siloam Baptist Church, *Plan of Church Work*). Though some choirs eventually took over the singing in the service, the expressly written purpose of Siloam's choir at the time was to improve congregational singing.

51. Allen, *First 150 Years*, 13. Allen also confirms the expectation of a minimum two-hour service with the sermon being at least an hour. Additionally, he confirms the practice of the regular church conference on Saturday to include prayer, Scripture reading, and preaching, as well as the business of church membership. FBC Montgomery adopted *The Psalmist* for congregational singing in 1844 and after Basil Manly Sr. arrived as pastor, he convinced them to adopt *Baptist Psalmody* in 1861. The Civil War having just begun he described the former as having been "owned and published in a *foreign country*" (43, 76; emphasis Allen's).

52. A written account by a Mr. Huntingdon, elder of the Marion Presbyterian Church, describes the nature of the sermon as preached by one of DeVotie's successors, W. T. Winkler. His experience may give some sense of the decorum and expectations for preaching during DeVotie's tenure. He attended a service at Siloam on August 25, 1872, because his minister was out of town and Huntingdon was "pleased and gratified." The sermon was "Fight the Good Fight of Faith," based upon 1 Tim 6:12. He describes Winkler as possessing good enunciation and his "quotations and illustrations appropriate and impressive" ("Tribute to Dr. Edwin T. Winkler").

Summary

The worship at Siloam Baptist Church during DeVotie's pastorate was a remarkable example of what was occurring in Baptist churches all over Alabama and across the country at this time. The synthesis of Sandy Creek revivalism and Charleston order is reflected in a number of different ways. DeVotie was exposed to the Charleston Tradition at FBC Savannah and Furman University. He was also exposed early in his pastoral career to the revivalism of the 1830s at FBC Tuscaloosa. There Manly accused him of being given too much to it. Siloam was founded by Charles Crow in 1822—a Separate Baptist converted in the Second Great Awakening. In 1872 Edwin T. Winkler became the seventh pastor at Siloam, seventeen years after De-Votie.[53] He had been the pastor at FBC Church of Charleston before the Civil War and his tenure probably signals the finalization of Siloam's migration away from its Separate Baptist and revivalistic frontier beginnings to a refined town church in the Charleston Tradition fifty years later. DeVotie's tenure (1840–1855) falls precisely in the middle of this migration.

The church membership grew through the camp meeting revivals that exploded in the 1830s across Alabama. DeVotie arrived at Siloam as revival was settling and he was maturing. His tenure at Siloam provides a fascinating example of the providential blending of the two as was demonstrated by the significant growth and influence it represents. The church held to the order of regular church conferences and church discipline when necessary. Sermons were planned and some liturgical order was maintained. At the same time, the church was hungry for gospel growth. DeVotie's emotion and passion brought a gospel zeal that resonated through the church to the lost. The *Alabama Baptist* describes DeVotie as "one of the best preachers in the State, and perhaps, the best agent—active, energetic, and persevering."[54] The tireless piety of the man in his study was reflected in his preaching on Sunday to bring fire from light to his people. As a result, Siloam was a pioneer in mission work and education.

While no *ordo* is cited in detail, the worship service focused on a lengthy expository sermon of God's word, perhaps as long as an hour.

53. Siloam's seventh pastor, Edwin T. Winkler (1823–1883), the second pastor after DeVotie, was previously pastor at FBC Charleston where he served from 1854 until the Civil War. He was educated at Brown University, and Newton Theological Institution. During his tenure and after, the services at Siloam were reflected in stately music, eloquent sermons, and as possessing decorum in the ordinances (Lovelace, *History of Siloam*, 23–39). This connection between Charleston and Marion in 1872 strengthens the argument that Marion had become an example of the "Charleston Tradition in the West."

54. "James DeVotie."

DeVotie was skilled in his task behind the pulpit and he worked hard to show his people God through the lens of the gospel. Scripture reading certainly preceded the sermon and probably also occurred earlier in the service through related Old Testament and New Testament texts. Congregational singing was a priority and a choir was utilized to improve it. Marion was a town of culture and refinement, serving as host to Howard College where ministers were taught literature and theology, and Judson Institute where women were trained for a life of service by developing the whole person. The colleges brought to Siloam a level of talent and intelligence not often experienced in most areas of Alabama. Music was eventually improved largely due to the students from Judson who provided skilled singers for the choir and a professor skilled to play the organ and direct the choir.[55] Additionally, many educators, denominational personnel, doctors, lawyers, and store owners filled the pews each Sunday. There was a requisite for order in the service and it eventually completed the journey to becoming a church of Charleston Order.

In practicing what has been characterized as "modified Calvinism" (sometimes identified with the Calvinism of Andrew Fuller[56]), DeVotie led the church to become a leader in evangelism and missions and led its growth to its largest attendance mark in history. Under DeVotie's leadership, the believer at Siloam came to worship first to apply the gospel to himself and then take it to the world outside the church doors. It was a model of balance in the mid-nineteenth century. The hymns were for the saved; the prayers and Scripture readings were for the saved; and the sermon was for the saved. A time of response was also for the saved. However, everything was done mindful of the reality that the unsaved may also be present in the service and would be present outside the building. Therefore, the gospel was always presented in a manner to which the unsaved could respond. This represented DeVotie's pietistic and emotional zeal for God, gospel, and growth. The ethos of the service reflected the heart of the young preacher who worked hard on his sermons for his people but was also accused of being given too much to revivalism. A potential order of service at Siloam may have looked like the worship order in figure 9.[57]

55. Lovelace, *Siloam Baptist Church*, 35.

56. Holcombe, *Baptists in Alabama*, 50. Holcombe writes, "In general they have appeared to occupy what is termed the middle ground; or in other words, embraced the system of Dr. Fuller." See also Brewster, *Andrew Fuller*.

57. This order is an estimate based upon brief descriptions of worship at Siloam, but also two descriptions of other Baptist churches of the time that were recorded in the Alabama Baptist. See "Dedication of the Tremont Temple" and "Thanksgiving Day in Missouri."

Call to Worship/Opening Prayer/Opening Song

Congregational Singing/Choir

Prayer

Scripture Reading

Congregational Singing

Pastoral Prayer

Sermon (with gospel invitation)

Song of Response

Closing Prayer

Figure 9. Potential order of worship at Siloam Baptist Church, Marion, Alabama (1849)

DeVotie's writing indicates such a passionate zeal for confession of sin and Christ-centered gospel reflection that these acts had to be present in worship in some way, even if simply in his sermons. He delighted in God and wanted his people to do the same. He knew the impedance of sin to this goal, so the gospel was needed every week. As his sermons resonate with these themes, it is probable that his worship leadership reflected the same. The elements of the gospel model proposed in this study are all present in his writings. Revelation and response; mediation and response; and exhortation and response are each represented in his writing and could have all been present in the proposed order of service above. However, it is unclear if he put them together in that order in public worship. It certainly was gospel-centered, and the gospel theme was the overriding theme.

7

Jarvis Street Baptist Church,
Toronto (1882–1903)

Introduction

WHILE SILOAM EXHIBITED BROAD influence among Alabama Baptists; and Charleston has been heralded as the mother of Southern Baptists; Philadelphia continued to fuel the Baptist expansion well into and through the nineteenth century. Interestingly, the Welsh also continued to play a prevalent subplot role of influence among North American Baptists in many geographical locales. They were among the earliest groups of Baptists near Pennepek (1701). Then a group relocated to Delaware to become the Welsh Tract Church (established ca. 1703). A group from this church split off and relocated to South Carolina and eventually became part of the Charleston Association (established ca. 1738). Though the influence is much greater than that, the purposes of this study now turn to Baptists in the north. It was also a Welshman who left Philadelphia bound for Toronto in 1882 to serve the people of Jarvis Street Baptist Church during a peak time of its own influence among Canadian Baptists.

A Brief History

The Jarvis Street Church is the oldest Baptist church in Toronto.[1] It was founded in 1818 in a house on Young Street and then the congregation

1. For a brief summary of the history of the church see Tomlinson and Fountains, eds., *From Strength to Strength*. For the story of its origins see Tomlinson, *From Scotland*

139

worshiped in a schoolhouse in 1826. From 1827–1831 they worshiped in Market Lane Hall before building a small chapel of their own on the corner of March (now Lombard) and Church Streets in 1832—becoming known as the March Street Baptist Church. At the time the area now called Toronto was known as Upper York.[2] The first thirty years were a struggle, but in 1844 Robert Alexander Fyfe (1816–1878) was called as the fourth pastor of the church. Fyfe was a Scottish emigrant, trained at Newton Theological Seminary in Massachusetts, and had pastored a church in Perth, Ontario before coming to what was then also referred to as the Baptist Church at York.[3] He led them through a period of significant growth and a move to Bond Street. Following the previous practice, the church became known as the Bond Street Baptist Church in 1848 under the leadership of James Pyper (1807–1884) from Michigan. During his tenure the church quadrupled in size to approximately 270 members. From 1855–1860, Fyfe returned to Bond Street Baptist Church after pastorates in Perth, Rhode Island, and Wisconsin. During this second tenure he, along with a friend, purchased the *Christian Messenger* in 1859 and renamed it the *Canadian Baptist* the following year.[4] In 1860 he also became the first principal at Woodstock College (then Canadian Literary Institute), along with editing the newly renamed paper.

Thomas F. Caldicott (1803–1869) became pastor in 1860. He had been a member and deacon of the church under R. A. Fyfe when it was on March Street. He employed the practice of "systematic beneficent." In doing so, the pew rent system was abolished and weekly offerings became the church's means of financial support, declaring every seat free in the church building. The result was the abolishing of a system of seating by financial status.[5] His nine years in this church have been described as "the solid rock foundation upon which is built the present prosperity of the Baptist church in Toronto."[6] William Boyd Stewart (1835–1912) was hired as an assistant

---

to Canada, chap. 8.

2. See *Gospel Witness*. It became the city of Toronto in 1834.

3. R. A. Fyfe is considered part of the "older generation of Regular Baptists." For years he was viewed as representing the old Calvinistic theology while liberalism and revivalism began to affect Baptist Calvinistic theology. He was an advocate of close communion. Donald Goertz writes, "Preaching the cross in a Haldane context meant a Calvinistic revival, something firmly reinforced by R. A. Fyfe" (Goertz, "Alexander Grant," 2). See also Rosser, "Fyfe, Robert Alexander."

4. For more information regarding Fyfe's work with the *Canadian Baptist*, see Trinier, *Century of Service*, chap. 4.

5. *The Gospel Witness*.

6. Meikleham, "Caldicott, Thomas Ford."

pastor in 1869, but ultimately assumed the pastoral role upon Caldicott's death the same year. He served a brief pastorate until 1872. John Harvard Castle (1830–1890) became the pastor in 1873 and led the church to build its current historic building on Jarvis Street. In 1875 it relocated and became known by its current name—Jarvis Street Baptist Church.[7] The building at the corner of Jarvis and Gerrard Streets was designed in a Neo-Gothic style by Henry Langley (d. 1907), the leading church architect in Ontario at the time. It was designed in a style referred to as "ecclesiastical amphitheatrical," noted for the close proximity of the people to the speaker. Finally, in 1882 B. D. Thomas (1843–1917) was called to Jarvis Street, possibly by the recommendation of his predecessor Castle, who had also come from Philadelphia where Thomas was serving as pastor until the move to Toronto.[8]

Thomas was born in Narbeth, Pembrokeshire, Wales, where his father was the long-standing pastor of Bethesda Baptist Church.[9] The senior Thomas had been called there in 1823 and served the church faithfully for thirty-nine years. The junior Thomas and his family emigrated in the fall of 1868 to Pittston, Pennsylvania—Pennsylvania being a common destination for Welsh Baptists. He pastored the Baptist church there for three years before moving again to serve the Fifth Baptist Church in Philadelphia. This church had been founded in 1824 by renowned Baptist pastor, John L. Dagg (1794–1884).[10] This was one of the largest Baptist churches in the state and eleven years of faithful service there demonstrated this young pastor's

7. William McMaster (1811–1887), a wealthy businessman and member of the church, was a significant benefactor of the building project. He also was instrumental in having Woodstock College relocated to Toronto, which was eventually named after him after merging with Toronto Baptist College in 1887, the year of his death—McMaster University. In collaboration, *Dictionary of Canadian Biography*, "McMaster, William." For more information about McMaster University, see Rawlyk, "A. L. McCrimmon, H. P. Whidden, T. T. Shields, Christian Education, and McMaster University," in *Canadian Baptists and Christian Higher Education*, 31–62.

8. Haykin, "Dr. Thomas of Toronto," 5–6.

9. For a history of this church, see Williams, "History of Bethesda, Narbeth," 13–20.

10. Scharf and Westcott, *History of Philadelphia*, 1310. William Staughton (1770–1829) also served as pastor, during which time it was "noted for its fine musical talent." Tom Nettles calls John L. Dagg "one of the most respected men in Baptist life and remains one of the most profound thinkers produced by his denomination." Dagg's theology has been classified as "moderate Calvinistic Augustinianism." Nettles writes: "Such nomenclature should not leave the impression that the soteriological or theological doctrines of Calvin were rejected or hidden in any way. Properly understood, the phrase paints Dagg as an experiential Calvinist, not simply a scholastic theologian" (Nettles, "Biographical Sketch of John L. Dagg").

significant strengths and capabilities.[11] Written during his tenure at Fifth Baptist Church, *The Baptist Encyclopedia* describes him in the following way:

> He is a man of fine personal appearance, of a modest and retiring disposition, and of unaffected simplicity of manners. As a preacher he brings forth things new and old from Bible treasures, and presents them to his hearers in "thoughts that breathe and words that burn." He has contributed occasionally to religious journals, and has recently published a little volume of rare merit entitled "Popular Excuses of the Unconverted." He labors earnestly to win souls to the Saviour, and has greatly endeared himself to an appreciative and devoted people.[12]

Of his preaching at Philadelphia Michael Haykin writes, "A defining mark of his ministry during this period was evangelistic preaching, preaching that made a point of seeking the conversion of unbelievers."[13] This was his hallmark at Jarvis Street as well.

One of Thomas' earliest sermons at Jarvis Street was entitled "The Glory of the Church," written around 1886. In many ways this single sermon demonstrates the pattern begun in Philadelphia and the codification of his vision for the local church in Toronto. Standing in the center of the stately building and before his congregation of influential citizens he proclaims,

> A church (I care not what her wealth or influence or numbers) is a failure unless souls are born in her, unless she walk the earth, so to speak, under the profound impulse of a divine unction and in the enthusiasm of conscious power, unless she can cast out the demons that infest society and quicken dead souls into an immortal being by the supernatural energies of her God-given life. This is her glory and her praise, that "this and that man was born in her."[14]

---

11. Haykin, "Dr. Thomas of Toronto," 4.

12. *Baptist Encyclopedia*, s.v. "Rev. B. D. Thomas," 1147.

13. Haykin, "Dr. Thomas of Toronto," 4.

14. Thomas, "The Glory of the Church," in *Sermons Preached*, 81–82. His main point in this sermon is that every nation is known by, and indeed boasts in, those who were born there. So it is with the church when Christ returns with the armies of the redeemed: "Then shall the golden gates be opened wide and the eternal city thrill with the enthusiasm of victory. Then as those who distinguished themselves above the rest, with stripes of honor on their breasts and a heavenly radiance on their brows, pass on in the grand procession, angelic voices shall indulge in exultant shouts of recognition, 'This and that man was born in her'" (96).

It was no small matter for him to leave Philadelphia. Thomas wrote to the Toronto Baptists that leaving his church in Philadelphia—who had been so kind and who were "the most earnest and united" in not wanting him to go—made the transition "one of the most painful ordeals" he had ever experienced.[15] However, the receptivity that met him in Toronto was overwhelming. Thomas kept the newspaper report of his service of induction, which reported, the reception that Thomas received from the members of his flock and Baptists of Toronto was "enthusiastic to the extreme." There were twelve hundred present for his induction service.[16] That enthusiasm continued unabated for twenty years. Thomas expressed the genuine affection between a pastor and his flock at his seventeenth anniversary when he preached from Philippians 3:13–14. The Minute Book for October 8, 1899, records, "The Pastor today commenced the 18th year of his Pastorate preaching a very appropriate sermon in which he briefly referred to the cordial relations which had always existed during all the years between him and the people of his charge."[17] There does not seem to have been a major conflict or disagreement between Thomas and his church at any point of his tenure. The minute book perfunctorily reflects, almost without exception, simply the addition and dismission of membership numbers through the years of Thomas' pastorate. There is no evidence of a crisis or significant disagreement with the pastor or the deacons. It is a remarkably lengthy and peaceful time, though always demanding upon the pastor due to the burden of the church's size and growth.

At his tenth anniversary, though reluctant to speak of the arithmetic of church growth, he celebrated the "music" of "hundreds of souls having made a profession of Jesus Christ; and of thousands of dollars that have been given to further the interests of Christianity in this and other lands."[18] In the next decade hundreds more joined the church and thousands more were given. Thomas' passion for the unsaved to be born again at Jarvis Street was realized and the church under his leadership grew steadily.[19] During his

15. "Letter to Jarvis Street Baptist Church, August 9, 1882," quoted in Haykin, "'Dr. Thomas of Toronto,'" 6. This was Thomas' letter of acceptance after receiving the call to come to Jarvis Street.

16. Newspaper clipping in Thomas, *"My Pastorate in Toronto,"* 9, quoted in Haykin, "'Dr. Thomas of Toronto,'" 7.

17. "October 8, 1899," in *Jarvis Street Minute Book*, 166.

18. Thomas, *"My Pastorate in Toronto,"* 9.

19. The membership at the church was 612 when he arrived. This was an adjusted number after an initial stated membership of 718. In the first ten years of his ministry, 432 were added by baptism and 518 by letter or experience, making a total of 956 added in that time period. In the same period 727 were either dismissed or dropped, leaving a total enrollment at the ten-year mark of 841 (Thomas, *"Harp of Ten Strings,"* 9–10).

pastorate the average attendance on Sunday morning was nine hundred and the Sunday evening service often saw a full auditorium with twelve to fifteen hundred people attending.[20]

The demands of a church the size of Jarvis Street could take their toll on any man. Most would not be up for the task and even with lengthy vacations granted during the summer for Thomas to visit his family and homeland in Wales, the years certainly were a drain. A twenty-year pastorate is a lengthy investment of energy and Thomas must have been growing weary by the turn of the century, if not before. In 1902, the minute book records the business of finding a pastoral assistant for Thomas. The records state, "After a season of prayer and praise, the pastor introduced the matter by stating what had been done by the Trustees and the Deacons." The minutes outline a two-month process that had preceded the meeting, in which a graduate of Toronto University and current student at McMaster University—Mr. R. A. Mode—had been identified. The discussion appears to have been heavily in favor of hiring this assistant for their beloved pastor and the vote was in the affirmative.[21] October 5, 1902, marked Thomas' twentieth anniversary. It passed almost unnoticed: "In consequences of a very severe storm of thunder, lightening, and rain, the congregation numbered only 250." Thomas preached from Isaiah 53:1: "Who hath believed our report and to whom is the arm of the Lord revealed." That was his last sermon before revealing the decision that he had no doubt been considering for some time. He resigned from the pastorate the following week.

In a letter dated October 9, 1902, he explained his decision was based upon the increasing demands of a large church upon his health.[22] In his

---

The membership total in 1892 is listed as beginning at 843. 48 were added by baptism; 32 by letter; and 2 by experience, making the total membership before dismission 925. 43 were granted letters of dismission; 2 were dropped from the rolls and 14 died leaving the balance of membership at 866 ("1892 Annual Meeting," in *Jarvis Street Minute Book*, 35).

20. Robertson, *Sketches in City Churches*, 26–28, quoted in Haykin, "'Dr. Thomas of Toronto,'" 5. Up to thirteen hundred could be accommodated in the building seated in the pews and gallery. Adding seats could accommodate another seven hundred.

21. "April 2nd, 1902," in *Jarvis Street Minute Book*, 217–18. The tasks of this assistant were "pastoral work and [to] preach on Sunday evenings of [the] Church's missions and visit amongst the entire membership of the church under the direction of the pastor and to assist as far as possible in keeping an oversight of them." Mode was to begin as soon as possible. Thomas resigned the next year.

22. In his appearance before the church on October 22, 1902, to confirm his resignation, he reports, "Though he did not feel so young as he did some years ago that his health was good." It is unclear if there were actual health issues or just the concern that health issues were going to arise from the obvious demand of the job ("October 22, 1902," in *Jarvis Street Minute Book*, 238).

absence, Rev. Elmore Harris (1854–1911) read the letter to the church on his behalf. The vast majority of the letter was his expression of delight at his reflection upon the time with his flock:

> My reasons for taking this step are not to be attributed to any unpleasantness that has occurred between us. I have received nothing but kindness and consideration at your hands. You have graven yourselves upon my heart by your love and your loyalty. You have been blind to my faults and considerate of my frailties. Your magnanimity of judgment, both as respects my character and my ministry, will ever remain with me as a grateful reminiscence. You have not only been more and better to me than my deserts, but your kindness has surpassed my most sanguine dreams. I have lived and worked among you as flowers bloom amid the genialities of summer. Through all the years there has not been so much as a ripple on the waters. There has been nothing in your conduct toward me that I could justly reflect upon with discomfort. If anything has ever been done or said by any of you that was intended to be discourteous or unfriendly, I have been happily oblivious of it. You are enshrined in my affections without a single embittering recollection arising from personal considerations. That this could have been possible in a pastorate of twenty years is something for which we may together feel proud and grateful.[23]

He went on to express his only regret was that some did not receive the "moral and spiritual uplift from [his] ministry which [he] devoutly sought for them." His reason for leaving was that the "ever increasing responsibilities [had] become oppressive." He continues, "The consciousness that I have not been doing all that might and ought to be accomplished in the conservation and development of so large and scattered a membership, has been an increasing sense of discomfort and irritation." He felt that another man with different gifts and in the "maturity of his powers" was needed to move the church forward.[24] The church's response was equally gracious: "We desire to express our undiminished confidence and affection in and for

---

23. "Thomas' Letter of Resignation," in *Jarvis Street Minute Book*, 232.

24. "Thomas' Letter of Resignation," in *Jarvis Street Minute Book*, 233. This came as quite a surprise to the congregation. "The occasion being the twentieth anniversary of his settlement and a review of a lengthened ministry helpful to all, favored in no small measure by all the blessings that can come to a church, with an outlook of confident expectation for the near future was uppermost in the minds and hearts of all, except the few to whom the step had officially been made known and the disappointment was visible, grievous, and painful, and formed expression in a silence that was more significant than words or action could have been" (234).

him. It is impossible that any pastor could be more beloved by his people than Dr. Thomas is by us, and we deeply regret the conclusion to which he has arrived."[25]

One newspaper clipping stated that the church membership stood at 896.[26] The *Canadian Baptist* reported the following numbers from Thomas' pastorate: "It will be interesting to learn that 768 have been received in baptism, 984 by letter and experience; 1,431 have been dismissed by letter, etc., (including deaths) leaving the present membership at 933. The total amount raised for all purposes during his pastorate has been $294,532.07."[27] The man who had declared a church "a failure unless souls were born in her," certainly must have gratefully declared Jarvis Street Baptist Church a resounding success to the glory of God.

---

25. "October 14, 1902 Special Meeting Resolution," in *Jarvis Street Minute Book*, 234. "We recognize with great [humility is crossed out with the word 'humiliation' written in its place] that the reason that greater results have not been obtained is, humanly speaking, from our failures, not his." They proceeded to counter each of Thomas' reasons for his resignation with the confidence that he was more than capable and appealed that he might reconsider his decision. He appeared in person at the October 22 business meeting to reaffirm his decision. However, the week had brought such an outpouring of affection that he explained that he had "never felt such trying circumstances in all his life. He had never realized until during the past week how dearly he and Mrs. Thomas was beloved nor how dearly they loved this church." In spite of this, he had to "decline to reconsider his resignation" ("October 22, 1902," in *Jarvis Street Minute Book*, 238).

26. "Rev. Dr. Thomas Resigns" newspaper clipping in Thomas, *"My Pastorate in Toronto,"* quoted in Haykin, "'Dr. Thomas of Toronto,'" 7. Perhaps even more remarkable is that his mid-week prayer service averaged 400 to 500 people each week during his pastorate (Robertson, *Sketches in City Churches*, 28). Unlike many other Baptist churches, church attendance typically ran higher than the actual membership of the church. The church under Thomas' leadership kept a close eye on the membership. The *Jarvis Street Minute Book: 1892–1910* is essentially the documentation of the week in and week out monitoring of a regenerate church membership. Believers became members through either profession of faith and baptism (most often), letter from another Baptist church (less often), or by an investigation of their experience (least often). Each of these required the close evaluation of the Committee on Candidates for Baptism and Membership before being extended the hand of fellowship and access to the Lord's Table. (For an example see "Entries for 1892," in *Jarvis Street Minute Book*, 12 and "Committee on Candidates for Baptism and Membership," in *Jarvis Street Minute Book*, 92.) The committee met with candidates for baptism and membership and when they were considered authentic, they were presented to the church business meeting for acceptance. When accepted by the business meeting they were pronounced members at the next celebration of the Lord's Table by the pastor as he extended the "hand of fellowship" to join the church at the Table.

27. "Canadian Baptist Clipping," in *Jarvis Street Minute Book*, 271.

Theology in Practice

Jarvis Street was established as a Regular Baptist Church, holding to the doctrines of Calvinism. Thomas' church in Philadelphia was founded under the preaching of John Dagg's "moderate Calvinistic Augustinianism," or "experiential Calvinism." This Calvinistic foundation can be heard in one of Thomas' earliest sermons preached in Philadelphia. In a memorial service sermon he proclaims, "There is not one so low, so ignorant, so unfavorably circumstanced, if brought beneath the regenerating influences of God's saving grace, but shall one day shine in burnished beauty."[28] The balance of his remarks demonstrates how he merges man's responsibility in response to God's sovereign work. His verbs in this sequence of sentences are passive, though as past participles: "Those who *have yielded* most readily to the great Artist's chisel; those who *have expanded* most joyfully to the inflowing light and warmth of heaven's refulgence; those who *have been* most true and faithful to their sacred trusts; and those who *have been* most unselfish and sincere in their activities, shall have the greater prominence and distinction."[29]

This sermon was in Philadelphia, early in his career, under the influence of the Baptists there. Later, in Toronto, he reveals a slightly different influence and potentially a greater moderation of Calvinistic thought. At Jarvis Street, he seems to attribute election to the foreknowledge, rather than predestination of God.[30] "Mere knowledge is based on evidence. We know that spring has come by the almanac or by the outbursting forms of life and beauty that greet us in field and forest. We could not dream of associating spring and summer with the cold, bleak days of December or of January." Yet with God, in his work of salvation, his view is different. "But to the eye of God from which nothing is hidden, May nestles in the bosom of

28. Thomas, "Memorial Sermon," 6.

29. Thomas, "Memorial Sermon," 6–7; emphasis mine.

30. The doctrinal position of "election by foreknowledge" was the prevailing position among Baptists in Ontario in the nineteenth century according to William Gillespie. "The pre-1840 constitutions of Ontario's Baptists derived ultimately from the British Baptists but usually arrived in Ontario via Baptists in the United States. By the end of the 1840s, the majority (76.5%) of Ontario's Baptists had adopted a version of the 1833 constitution which the Niagara Baptist Association of New York state had developed. The Grand River Association illustrates the constitution's adoption and modification." The second article of the 1844 Grand River Association constitution includes: "the election of grace according to the foreknowledge of God." It also delineates closed communion (e.g., "the Lord's supper, a privilege peculiar to immersed believers, regularly admitted to Church fellowship"). "The only changes from the Niagara Baptist Association constitution of 1833 are stylistic ones" (Gillespie, "Recovery of Ontario's Baptist Tradition," in Priestley, *Memory and Hope*, 30).

December and June smiles and blooms and sings beneath the leaden skies and snow-clad desolations of January."[31] He summarizes this passage in a more direct manner: "When infinite love sees the perfect in the incomplete, the saint in the sinner, it is no mere illusion."[32] The result is that God then saves this individual. This distinction in soteriology also seems reflected in Thomas' remarks of the untimely death of a fellow preacher and friend, Alexander Grant (1854–1897). He speaks affirming words regarding "the doctrines of grace" that his friend possessed in his life, as if he did not embrace them in the same way. He speaks of them admirably, as if they stand out as unique among his contemporaries, rather than representative of the theological ethos of the Baptist culture.[33]

R. A. Fyfe wrote in 1851, "The peculiar affliction of the Baptists in Canada has been foreign interference and influence—at one end, too English—at the other, too American. Society in Canada is neither like that of England, nor that of America."[34] William Brackney elucidates Fyfe's reflection with his own observations: "Baptist life in [Canada] was sufficiently developed to produce its own theological mosaic. The resulting Canadian Baptist character is eclectic, revealing both British and American Baptist genes." These two sources of theological thought have synthesized in four

31. Thomas, "The Far-Sightedness of Love," in *Sermons Preached*, 44.

32. Thomas, "The Far-sightedness of Love," in *Sermons Preached*, 50.

33. Thomas, "The Strong Staff, The Beautiful Rod," in *Sermons Preached*, 70. "The doctrines of grace so buttressed him that he stood four-square to every wind that blew. His convictions went down to the granite foundations of the faith and entwined themselves around the adamantine boulders of the everlasting covenant. He despised the preaching that was sentimental and apologetic. It was a tonic to weak faith and a rebuke to all skeptical and rationalistic tendencies to come beneath his influence and ministry." Donald Goertz explains: "Dominated by a strong Calvinism, Grant's roots lay in the Haldane movement and in Fyfe. This background provided the framework with which to judge all new ideas, and its central theme was a focus on God as the source of everything, including every element in salvation. Grant preached this strongly enough to be charged with robbing humanity of all responsibility." Later he writes: "Yet Grant, like Spurgeon, was also profoundly influenced by revivalism, particularly by the pragmatism inherent within it. It is very likely that Spurgeon helped shape Grant here, for he did not find it incongruous to preach complete predestination and a rejection of free will while at the same time making a direct appeal to the sinners" (Goertz, "Alexander Grant," 6–7). It is not clear if Thomas affirmed Grant's Calvinistic position in like-minded agreement, or simply admired it with some moderation on his own part. It clearly is an aspect of Grant that stood out rather than as part of the prevailing Baptist conviction of the time. Thomas writes that upon meeting Grant for the first time—"I had wont to regard him as an egotist and a cynic. I had no desire to court intimacy with him." Yet, after spending time together, "[our] hearts were thenceforward welded into a brotherhood which death has only glorified" (Thomas, "The Strong Staff, The Beautiful Rod, in *Sermons Preached*, 72–73).

34. Brackney, *Genetic History*, 467.

unique influential factors: "the Maritime revivalistic experience, British Baptist classical theology, American Baptist schools, and a unique form of Canadian Prairie fundamentalism."[35] In 1878, four years before Thomas arrived, Calvin Goodspeed (1842–1912) wrote *The Peculiar Principles of the Baptists*.[36] In this work he puts Baptist principles into three categories: (1) those that relate to the Scriptures; (2) those that relate to the ordinances; and (3) those that relate to the church. In summarizing the Canadian Baptist theology in each category, he advocates the authority of Scripture foundationally; that there is no efficacy in the ordinances and that only believers should be baptized; and the church as a spiritual body should only consist of regenerate church members. It is in this last section that he affirms the New Hampshire Confession with the added statement—"which is generally adopted by our churches."[37] It appears that the attempt to associate so many different types of Baptists in Ontario and Quebec in particular required a more general confession for agreement. The New Hampshire Confession was the result of similar eclectic circumstances elsewhere and served the same purpose here.[38] Specifically, the language of predestination is absent,

35. Brackney, *Genetic History*, 467.

36. Goodspeed, *Peculiar Principles of Baptists*. For more information about Calvin Goodspeed see Trites, "A Forgotten Scholar: Professor Calvin Goodspeed," in Wilson, *Abiding Conviction*, and Trites, "Calvin Goodspeed: An Assessment of his Theological Contribution," 23–39.

37. Goodspeed, *Peculiar Principles*, 4–5, 8, 14, and 17. His handling of the section on Scripture advocates initially the regulative principle of Calvin before acknowledging the normative principle of Luther. "Hence, Baptists have ever insisted, in reference to ordinances as well as doctrine, on the rule first announced by Tertullian, that 'the Scriptures forbid what they do not mention.'" This seems to be Goodspeed's position (5–6).

38. Lumpkin, *Baptist Confessions*, 360. Lumpkin explains: "The theological views of Calvinistic Baptists in the New Hampshire area had been considerably modified after 1780 by the rise of the Free Will Baptists. . . . The New Hampshire convention thus sought to restate its Calvinism in very moderate tones." J. Newton Brown, in 1853, added two articles to the original sixteen, one on "Repentance and Faith" and one on "Sanctification." "In various church manuals this Confession became the most widely disseminated creedal declaration of American Baptists." It became the confession of Landmarkism beginning in 1867, the General Association of Baptist Churches in 1902, the Southern Baptist Convention in 1925 (with ten new sections added), and the General Association of Regular Baptist Churches in 1933 (360–61). Article 9, "Of God's Purpose of Grace," likely identifies the doctrinal position of B. D. Thomas: "That Election is the gracious* purpose of God, according to which he [graciously] regenerates, sanctifies, and saves sinners; that being perfectly consistent with the free agency of man, it comprehends all the means in connection with the end; that it is a most glorious display of God's sovereign goodness, being infinitely [free,] wise, holy, and unchangeable; that it utterly excludes boasting, and promotes humility, [love,] prayer, praise, trust in God, and active imitation of his free mercy; that it encourages the use of means in the highest degree; that it is** ascertained by its effect in all who [truly] believe the gospel;

and election is undefined. It seems that Thomas adjusted his Calvinism from that of the Philadelphia Baptists, which was also moderating, to that of the Ontario and Quebec Baptists.

Thomas was concerned about the Calvinist-Arminian debate in his day and its potential to keep men from hearing the gospel. "They rack their brains about divine sovereignty and human free agency with their seeming antagonisms, and permit a thousand other polemical mysteries to keep their starving souls outside the home of warmth and plenty. . . . My friend, what have you to do with religious controversy if your soul is not saved?"[39] His concern regarding men's souls and the intellectual debate of the day may have pushed Thomas farther away from his and the church's more Calvinistic beginnings. This was the trend among Baptists as a whole at the turn of the twentieth century. It likely serves as a clarifying backdrop to statements such as the following by Thomas regarding the preaching of God's Word unto salvation: "Not a little of the authoritative teaching of the inspired Word is set aside because it does not exactly chime in with human taste or notion. . . . The only rational way of dealing with the Word of God is to put it to the test of experience—do what it says." This seems to be equally an appeal to man's will as confidence in the word that does not return void. His final appeal in this particular message is, as always, to the unbeliever: "Whatever you do, do not invalidate His great message to your soul by words without knowledge."[40]

H. H. Walsh offers this description of the trend of Calvinism among Canadian Baptists: "[Alexander] Grant seems to hold a very important position in the history of Canadian Baptist theology. The older generation of Regular Baptists, led by R. A. Fyfe, had been strongly Calvinistic. In the twentieth century, thorough-going Calvinism ceased to be a major factor. Grant represents the pivotal period by being open to revivalism and mediating it into Baptist circles. Yet, unlike his successors, he was serious about his Calvinism."[41] Calvinism as a whole was being tempered at least and set aside for revivalistic Arminianism in many places. As a contemporary and friend of Grant, Thomas certainly observed his Calvinistic theology merged with revivalism. As a contemporary he could not be considered one of the successors as referenced by Walsh. Nevertheless, he does seem to be a

---

[that it] is the foundation of Christian assurance; and that to ascertain it with regard to ourselves, demands and deserves our utmost diligence." Brackets ([]) indicate the changes made by Brown. *Brown used the word "eternal" in the place of "gracious." **Brown used the words "may be" in the place of "is" (364).

39. Thomas, "The Wordy Egotist," in *Sermons Preached*, 27.

40. Thomas, "The Wordy Egotist," in *Sermons Preached*, 28–29.

41. Walsh, *Christian Church in Canada*, 282.

forerunner, or possibly frontrunner, of a generation of Canadian Baptists that was not as committed to Calvinism.

This is not to say that Thomas did not point his people to God's grandeur. Thomas urged his hearers to study the things of God and seek to understand them. "To study the mighty and magnificent achievements of the Eternal . . . is our privilege and obligation. We should also inquire diligently into God's law and government both in Nature and in grace. We cannot know too much in these exalted realms." Simultaneously, he also warned those in his day who purported to have understood God through their rationalist skepticism: "It is a superlative folly to attempt by searching to find out God, or to propound a philosophy by which He shall be understood. He is too infinitely great to come within the grasp of finite comprehension."[42] Thomas was not opposed to human learning and the pursuit of knowledge. He lived in an intellectual age and among a cultured metropolitan society. He was acquainted with a wide body of literature. He was obviously familiar with theological and devotional sources, but also those of philosophy and poetry.[43] In the end, he wanted his people to know that whatever their learning, God was infinitely higher and greater. "There is nothing that men more need to know than their limitations."[44] In contrast to all human authors, it was the word of God that was the source of truth and power:

> The question paramount to me is, Is it true? Does it do what it says it would? Does it speak to my soul's need as no other book ever did or could? Do its prescriptions for the maladies of life meet the emergencies to which they are applied? These are the questions that I want to be sure about. Has the Bible come with regenerative potency into human life? Has it changed the face of society? Has it done for men and women in every degree of moral helplessness and degradation what it said it would?

42. Thomas, "The Wordy Egotist," in *Sermons Preached*, 22–23. One of the means by which he wanted his people to know God better was through the systematic study of Scripture on Wednesday nights. Apparently this had been done with the Gospel of Luke previously and in 1897 Thomas proposed the same with the book of Acts at the Annual Meeting. There was significant discussion and it was proposed somewhat reluctantly that if such a study would not interfere with the efficiency of the Wednesday night meetings, and if it would not take more than one Wednesday per month, this could be attempted. The motion was appointed to a committee and the deacons to resolve ("June 16th, 1897," in *Jarvis Street Minute Book*, 23).

43. Among the eighteen sermons published in *Sermons Preached*, he cites or references no fewer than fourteen philosophers, poets and thinkers outside of the church. At times he quotes their writing in a manner that likely engaged those of the world as Paul did with the Greek poets in Acts.

44. Thomas, "The Wordy Egotist," in *Sermons Preached*, 24.

This is the crux of the whole argument—the final word in the
controversy.[45]

These theological principles informed and inspired worship for Thomas: God's greatness and splendor; the trustworthy nature of his word; and
the need to appeal evangelistically to man to respond to the gospel's solution
for sin.

Practice of Worship

On the tenth anniversary of Thomas' pastorate, a worship service was held
in recognition of the event:

> The services on the Lord's Day were grand and impressive,
> and as the vast congregation gave forth the inspiring strains of
> "Holy, Holy, Holy, Lord God Almighty," accompanied by the
> magnificent organ, the occasion was one which will be long re-
> membered. The Doctor took as his text Psalm 144,9. He likened
> the ten years of his pastorate to a ten-stringed instrument, and
> for forty minutes, in eloquent and graphic language, the music
> of these ten years produced a harmony which was listened to
> with eager attention.[46]

Thomas taught his people that all of life should be worship and he
utilized the analogy of music in doing so. "The meaning of ['pray without
ceasing'] is not that men should do nothing but pray, but that everything
done should be enveloped in an atmosphere of devotion."[47] The Christian's
life should be a life of rejoicing evermore, even when sad. "The great thing
is to have the life attuned to melody. The soul is a musical instrument and
'to rejoice evermore' it must be strung to concert pitch; it must be set to
the key of heaven's own harmony." He clarifies, "When the life is attuned to
melody there may be strains of sadness; there may be notes burdened with
mournfulness, but there will be no discord."[48] Thomas references music
and instruments often as symbolic of the Christian life. He certainly loved
music, was acquainted with it as more than a listener, and enjoyed its em-
ployment in worship.

45. Thomas, "The Wordy Egotist," in *Sermons Preached*, 26.

46. Thomas, *"Harp of Ten Strings,"* 18–19. This was a description of the service that
appeared in the *Canadian Baptist* that was appended to this published message in recognition of Thomas' tenth anniversary.

47. Thomas, "Habitual Temper of the Christian Life," in *Sermons Preached*, 213.

48. Thomas, "Habitual Temper of the Christian Life," in *Sermons Preached*, 210.

In advocating for the cause of the Sunday gathering, Thomas warns those who would stay at home to read the Sunday paper: "No reading, not even that of the Bible, can take the place of the sanctuary services. . . . What God has instituted is not to be treated with irreverent disregard without incalculable moral injury."[49] Borrowing a music analogy once again, he describes worship in the gathered assembly as "sit[ting] beneath the Gospel's joyful sound."[50] Elsewhere he writes, "Thousands upon thousands who believe in Him, meet week after week in temples built for worship and the burden of their adoration is, 'Worthy is the Lamb that was slain,' etc. To every assumption of supremacy, to every claim of power, to every exercise of authority, to His assertion of equality with God, the Christian consciousness replies, 'Master, thou has said the truth.'"[51]

The desire in worship is for God himself. That desire can only be met in Christ. Thomas explains, "There are times in every earnest human life when the soul cries out for a revelation of God. . . . Stupid, indeed, must be the mind and cold the heart which have never longed to draw back the veil that intervenes between them and that Great Being who is the inspiration of all life."[52] There is a great desire within each person, part of the image of God that longs deeply to "gaze into the face of the Great Artist." Thomas confesses, "I have felt His presence, I have seen His works, I have caught glimpses of His passing shadow, but Himself has never passed before mine eyes. I want to see *Him*—Him who stands behind the veil of all this visible grandeur around me—Him who inbreathes life, infuses energy and imparts beauty into all I see." He represents the longing of every true Christian in worship when he prays fervently, "O God, bow the heavens and come down. Show me, I pray thee, thy face. Assume before me some form that mine eyes

49. Thomas, "Where is Zebedee?" in *Sermons Preached*, 156.

50. Thomas, "The Strong Staff, The Beautiful Rod," in *Sermons Preached*, 67.

51. Thomas, "Response of Consciousness," in *Sermons Preached*, 106. This is the closest sermon in this collection devoted to the topic of worship. After establishing the fundamental relationship between Christ's teaching and man's deepest need; and the innate nature of Christ's deity and the command upon the world to worship him; Thomas outlines the teaching of Christ in the gospel shape proposed in this study: (1) God; (2) The Soul; (3) Sin; (4) Forgiveness; (5) Immortality; (6) Hell; and (7) Heaven. Once again, the shape can be outlined as Revelation and Response (God and soul); Mediation and Response (Sin and Forgiveness); and Exhortation and Response (Immortality, Heaven, and Hell being the weightiness and outcome of our following Christ's commands). This is the gospel: the harmonization of Christ's teaching and man's deepest need. This is the need for the gospel: the reality that Christ is Lord and the world is commanded to acknowledge this and respond.

52. Thomas, "Response of Consciousness," in *Sermons Preached*, 108. Earlier in this sermon he spoke of Isaiah's revelation of God in Isaiah 6 and the disciples revelation of the glory of Christ on the Mount of Transfiguration (103).

can gaze upon." What is God's response? The answer to this longing of the heart is Jesus Christ. "He is the expression of Divinity . . . in Him dwelt the fullness of the Godhead bodily."[53]

Thomas knew that the problem of worship was in man's heart and no one understood it better than Christ. Christ spoke to this as none other. "Christ in his exposition of the law goes down beneath the surface and looks at the germinant principles of evil. Ah, no one ever understood sin as Christ did. . . . He spoke not of the gilded life of the drawing-room and of the Church, but of the inner life of the heart. And it was a startling revelation."[54] Man, who had been created in the image of God and made a little lower than the angels has rejected his Creator and sold his birthright. He has thrown off his place of high standing before God for self-worship. Thomas writes, "The dark lines of guilt; the deep furrows of discontent; and the terrible storm clouds of unrighteous passion" have marred the image. "Corruption, frivolity, cruelty, meanness; every form and variety of degrading exhibition deface the glory of the human countenance."[55] The nature of sin creates competing interests and objects of passion in competition for the delight he is to have in God. In his pursuit of sin's pleasure, he has enslaved himself. Thomas counters man's waywardness: "His rightful place is not in slavery but in sovereignty, ruling his passions, his appetites, his circumstances, and his environment with an absolute and benignant sway. This was God's intention when He laid the stamp of His image upon him."[56]

This is not just Thomas' evaluation of the world, but he sees it most tragically in the church. He writes in the aforementioned sermon, "The Glory of the Church," "What we have most to lament is not the worldliness of the world, but the worldliness of the Church; not the wickedness without, but the heartlessness within; not the skepticism of the masses, but the skepticism of our own hearts." His appeal is that the church be "emancipated from the thrall and bondage of the world and sin—a pure church, a living church, an aggressive church, a church baptized in the spirit and power of the Master's consecration."[57] Man may deny that he has sin. He may even argue that there is such a thing as sin. "But when the light of spiritual

53. Thomas, "Response of Consciousness," in *Sermons Preached*, 108; emphasis Thomas'.

54. Thomas, "Response of Consciousness," in *Sermons Preached*, 110.

55. Thomas, "God's Purpose in Man's Creation," in *Sermons Preached*, 35. Thomas continues in contrast to his focal text in Heb 2:7–9 which quotes Ps 8:5–6: "The crown has fallen from the brow of humanity and men have become, instead of sovereigns, slaves; instead of masters, serfs; instead of princes, beggars."

56. Thomas, "God's Purpose in Man's Creation," in *Sermons Preached*, 37.

57. Thomas, "The Glory of the Church," in *Sermons Preached*, 84.

illumination flashes in upon their souls, when men see themselves as they really are, when their eyes are opened and their sensibilities aroused, they no longer say [Christ] is speaking in parables." Thomas relates the power of the presence of God in worship to shine light upon the dark places: "Oh, no, no! They then realize that they are what He represents them to be—sinners of the deepest dye."[58]

The solution for worship is the gospel. Nowhere is the centrality of Christ more evident in worship than in the gospel theme that resonates there. To go to church on Sunday; to sing the songs and to read the Scriptures; to hear the word preached; indeed to be in worship is to "sit beneath the Gospel's joyful sound."[59] Thomas references the emerging waves of thinking in his day: "Men talk about a new theology. There can be no new theology so far as Christ's death and resurrection are concerned. What these great facts were at the first they must ever continue to be. . . . The old Gospel of life through the atoning sacrifice of Christ cannot be superseded."[60] Thomas called forgiveness "the keynote of [Christ's] blessed ministry." It was the "ineffable burden of His ministry." "He assumed our nature, placing Himself voluntarily under the vengeance of a violated law—laying open His very heart to the envenomed darts of death and hell that He might present to a fallen and guilty world 'an eternal redemption.'"[61] There is a correlation between Christ and his gospel. Thomas utilizes the terminology employed in worship: "To the apostle Paul, Jesus Christ Himself was the Gospel, the converging and radiating centre of all truth and life. . . . That one transcendent personality gathered into Himself all the effulgences of illumination and all the sufficiencies of being."[62] He concludes with the gospel appeal that marked the end of every sermon: "My last word to you this morning is, 'Believe on the Lord Jesus Christ.' May God grant us all, by faith in the one sacrifice and mediation of the man Christ Jesus, to rise out of defeat into victory—out of limitation into liberty—out of weakness into power—out of serfdom into sovereignty."[63]

Finally, the benefit of worship is putting man in touch with his source of strength. This once again emphasizes Christ's centrality in worship. "Sympathy with God is the secret of abiding strength. The immortal nature cannot live on bread alone. The man of faith touches the hidden springs of

58. Thomas, "Response of Consciousness," in *Sermons Preached*, 110–11.

59. Thomas, "The Strong Staff, The Beautiful Rod," in *Sermons Preached*, 67.

60. Thomas, "Uniqueness and Sufficiency of Christ," in *Sermons Preached*, 142–43.

61. Thomas, "Response of Consciousness," in *Sermons Preached*, 111–12.

62. Thomas, "Uniqueness and Sufficiency of Christ," in *Sermons Preached*, 143.

63. Thomas, "God's Purpose in Man's Creation," in *Sermons Preached*, 41.

the God life in Jesus Christ, and is supernaturalized."[64] In another sermon
he explains the process: "You must have the Christ nature before you can
have the Christ character; you must have the Christ character before you
can have the Christ likeness; and you must have the Christ likeness before
you can be an inhabitant of the world of light."[65] This process of putting man
in touch with Christ could only occur in worship and through the gospel.
"A great deal depends upon the warmth and glow of [the church's] spiritual
experiences as to the existence and perpetuity of the highest forms of life."
A cold and formal spiritual life will not lead to spiritual fruit. "But if, on
the other hand, she dwell beneath the perennial glow of heaven's effulgent
beams, her very paths will drop fatness and all her gardens and orchards will
be abounding with celestial fruitage."[66] Elsewhere he writes similarly using
the analogy of agriculture: "If you get *into Him* there will be no difficulty
about the unfolding. The best and the sweetest that are in you will be called
forth. He is both warmth and sunlight." He is not just the source of that life;
he is the archetype of that life. "Not merely are you to grow up in Him as an
environment, but into Him as an ideal."[67]

The only way that any of this can be accomplished is to behold Christ
in worship. In "The Church in Simon's House," Thomas utilizes the various
people in Simon's house—Simon, Lazarus, Martha, Mary, and Judas—to
point out different types of people in the church. In particular, he references
Martha's serving and Mary's sitting at Jesus' feet to describe two types of
worship in the church. He is not critical of Martha's service. Her type of
administration, organization, and work is required in the church. However,
he is critical of her lack of devotion while doing what she was doing. She was
watching Mary and criticizing rather than watching Christ and delighting
in him. "The Marthas are as honorable as the Marys if they are inspired by
affection for their Lord." In his eyes, this is the issue at hand. Is Christ the
focus of worship? Of course, Mary portrays the antithesis to Martha's lack
of devotion. Thomas elaborates on her model for the church's worship and
service:

> Mary was unconscious of everything but Christ. Moses, when
> he descended from the mount, wist not that his face shone. The
> greatest danger of our religious lives is looking at our shining
> faces. What we need still more and more is to be so absorbed

64. Thomas, "Memorial Sermon," 8.

65. Thomas, "The Secret of the Divine Silence," in *Sermons Preached*, 17.

66. Thomas, "The Glory of the Church," in *Sermons Preached*, 84.

67. Thomas, "Uniqueness and Sufficiency of Christ," in *Sermons Preached*, 147–48;
emphasis Thomas'.

in the contemplation of Christ's character and so receptive of His holy influence that our whole being shall shine with celestial brilliance and we remain unconscious of the fact.[68]

Her response of liberality is also a model for the appropriate response in worship. She gave the most costly thing she had. "The greater the love the greater the liberality." He describes the reaction,

> Even so the love of Christ enters into the human heart, lays open its inmost affections and aspirations to the light, melts the ice-bound fountains of its activities and joys, and so interpenetrates it with genial inspirations that, instead of barrenness and sterility, there grow in clustering affluence the fruits of righteousness and bloom in rich profusion the flowers of paradise. . . . Mary, in her spontaneous liberality, breaking upon the person of her Lord the costly ointment, is the most suggestive type of the spirit and genius of Christianity that this book affords.[69]

Thomas describes Mary's response in worship as being like the sun and its rays. Love is the source of warmth and beneficence (e.g., the pouring out of goodness) shines out from the source like the sun's rays. This is the way the response of worship should be. Out of gospel-formed and increasing affection, the rays of this "pouring out" in worship should be of the costliest treasure of the believer's life and devotion.

As with Baptist worship elsewhere, preaching is the main element of worship. Thomas' preaching often employs the use of symbolism or allegory. The memorial sermon in Philadelphia referenced above uses the imagery of a pillar of polished brass in Solomon's temple to describe the spiritual character of a departed church member. He creates an elaborate demonstration of the potential for the strength and beauty of a man's life by imagining the columns in the temple.[70] As mentioned above, he often uses music (e.g., melody, harmony, tune, etc.) as an analogy for the presence of God in one's life. "There is no mission more exalted and sublime than that of filling the dark and solitary scenes of life, with a brightness and music which men cannot create for themselves."[71] He also quotes widely beyond theological sources. The analogy of music above is followed by a quote from an anonymous poet of the late nineteenth century as he describes the

68. Thomas, "The Church in Simon's House," in *Sermons Preached*, 195, 200. It appears that Thomas mixed the accounts of Mary sitting at Jesus' feet in Luke 10:38–42 and Mary Magdalene washing Jesus' feet in Luke 7:36–51.

69. Thomas, "The Church in Simon's House," in *Sermons Preached*, 201–2.

70. Thomas, "Memorial Sermon," 6.

71. Thomas, "Memorial Sermon," 13.

Christian's capacity to bring joy to others: "To so hold the royal gifts of the soul that they be music to some, fragrance to others, and life to all."[72] This also exemplifies his competency to use the poets of the age in his preaching.

He does not preach exegetically, but topically and systematically from a focal text. This text unified the sermon as he often returns to it at the end of each point. For example, his sermon "The Secret of the Divine Silence" is based upon part of 1 Cor 15:51: "We shall all be changed." It is a sermon based upon heaven and our inability to comprehend very much about it, because it requires us to be changed into a spiritual body to engage it. He addresses four points about heaven that we do not know due to the "divine silence" of Scripture. At the end of each point he reminds the listener that the problem is that we all need to be changed.[73] In the sermon he incorporates no less than ten direct quotations from Scripture passages related to heaven, and possibly as many allusions to other passages without directly quoting them, demonstrating his knowledge of and reliance upon God's word. This is similar to Spurgeon's use of Scripture as a motto in preaching. A focal text holds together his thoughts, which are drawn from various places of Scripture rather than preaching the verse in its context.

He ends this sermon, as he does all sermons, with a gospel call to salvation. Though his message was structured for the saved, his final application is always an invitation to the unsaved:

> There are two great changes which are absolutely essential to spiritual knowledge and attainment. The one is at the entrance into the divine life, the other is at the entrance into the eternal state. The one is regeneration, the other is glorification. Without the former we cannot enter into the kingdom of God; without the latter we cannot enter into heaven. . . . We shall "see as we are seen," and "know as we are known," and dwell in the effulgence of God's all-revealing presence when we "shall have been changed."[74]

72. Thomas, "Memorial Sermon," 13. This quote is found in numerous places including Smith, *Latter Day Saints Memorial Star*, 39:823, and Beecher and Ellinwood, *Original Plymouth Pulpit*, 5:311. He also quoted from Henry Wadsworth Longfellow's, "Excelsior" in this sermon: "He pressed upward often with lacerated limbs and bleeding feet, but waving ever 'the banner with the strange device, Excelsior'" (14).

73. The four points are: (1) in regard to the life of heaven; (2) in regard to the pursuits of heaven; (3) in regard to the society of heaven; and (4) in regard to the joys of heaven; we really know very little about because Scripture says very little (Thomas, "The Secret of the Divine Silence," in *Sermons Preached*, 9–16).

74. Thomas, "The Secret of the Divine Silence," in *Sermons Preached*, 16–18.

This evangelistic practice in preaching is unsurprising given his deep conviction regarding the church as a "birthplace of souls." His demonstrative use of the pulpit for evangelism and the making of disciples is clearly outlined in "The Glory of the Church":

> To prostitute the pulpit to any other end than this, to make it the Thermopylæ for intellectual display or rhetorical effect, to use it for mercenary or ambitious designs, or to employ it as an arena for personal exhibition, must be an impertinence for which a parallel could scarcely be produced. To have no higher aim in our ministrations than to gratify and amuse, or to seek to have the interest of our audiences culminate in admiration of ourselves, is an exhibition at which angels well might weep. . . . The one dominating, controlling, all-subduing purpose of the ministerial life should be the *salvation of souls.*[75]

This quote provides two mandatory emphases for his sermons. They should be "full of Christ" and "burdened with solicitude for souls."[76]

Thomas' description of the prayer of his friend and fellow pastor, Alexander Grant, is most compelling regarding Grant's view of prayer. Grant drowned tragically and the news of his premature death was a blow to Thomas and the church. His immediate reflections upon the memory of his friend were of his voice: "I heard him shout and laugh and sing and pray. . . . I remembered his prayers, or, I might say, his prolonged agonizings, at the throne of grace for souls, and for the glory of the one great name."[77] The orientation for the priority and necessity of prayer is like that of his sermons—the birth of souls.

He references singing and music often in his sermons. In a sermon on heaven he writes, "The thought of singing without cessation is not a pleasant anticipation, nor is it scripturally well founded, save only as symbolizing a condition of exalted blessedness."[78] In another sermon he characterizes it

---

75. Thomas, "The Glory of the Church," in *Sermons Preached,* 82–83; emphasis Thomas'.

76. Thomas, "The Glory of the Church," in *Sermons Preached,* 83. "The supreme object of the Gospel ministry is . . . to reach the hearts and influence the lives of men for God and heaven."

77. Thomas, "The Strong Staff and the Beautiful Rod," in *Sermons Preached,* 65. Alexander Grant was pastor of the FBC in Winnipeg and in 1884 was appointed to the Superintendency of Home Missions. Baptist historian Titus Fitch writes: "Few men have come to the front so rapidly as Alexander Grant, and yet few men have left such a large impress upon our denominational life" (Fitch, *Baptists in Canada,* 163). For more information see, Goertz, "Alexander Grant."

78. Thomas, "The Secret of the Divine Silence," in *Sermons' Preached,* 11.

more fully: "How [heaven's] music, even in anticipation, soothes our pain and makes even our very solitude delightful."[79] His concept of music in worship was undergirded by a very high level of music quality at Jarvis Street that was unparalleled in most churches—especially Baptists.

What is known today as the highly acclaimed "Toronto Mendelssohn Choir" was originally founded in 1894, as an extension of the already existing Jarvis Street Baptist Church choir.[80] Renowned musician and organist, William Horatio Clarke (1840–1913) had been appointed the first organist-choirmaster in 1880, two years before Thomas arrived.[81] Prior to this, Susan Moulton McMaster, the second wife of William McMaster, had donated an elaborate organ at a cost of $8,000 when the building was built in 1875. There was no shortage of controversy in music as the initial introduction of an organ at Bond Street in 1857 so outraged some members that they set up an entirely different service in another building.[82] Not only was there the issue of the extravagance of the instrument itself, but that of the donor. One former member characterized her donation as hateful and self-serving. The perception among some was that of a wealthy Jarvis Street businessman and his wife displaying their commitment to effect change that would make their church socially respectable, "at the expense of pure spiritual piety."[83] The introduction of an "unofficial songbook" was another step by the wealthy patron to advance the cause of music in the church. Geoffrey Booth explains, While the step to publish this specifically for Baptist services did temper some of the criticism, "Nevertheless, it took a while to cool things off."[84] Thomas likely arrived about the time things had cooled off, but the

79. Thomas, "Response of Consciousness," in *Sermons Preached*, 115.

80. "Toronto Mendelssohn Choir," *Historica Canada*: http://thecanadianencyclopedia.com/en/article/toronto-mendelssohn-choir-emc/.

81. "Clarke," *Historica Canada*: http://www.thecanadianencyclopedia.ca/en/article/herbert-l-clarke-emc/. His son was Herbert L. Clarke (1867–1945), the famed trumpeter and bandmaster of the turn of the century. He played in numerous groups including John Philip Sousa's band. Herbert L. Clarke built the organ in his organ factory in Indianapolis and subsequently became the first organist-choirmaster (Robertson, *Sketches in City Churches*, 26).

82. Wilson, "Baptists and Business," 308. Initially the debate was over the power of music to help or hinder devotion. Later it became an issue of worldliness and materialism. "The spirituality of those Baptists who accepted musical innovation was questioned by other counter-cultural Baptists who condemned new forms of musical expression as worldly 'atrocities.'" On the other hand, "cultural liberals, who desired social integration and respectability, remained convinced that musical innovation brought spiritual and temporal rewards that Canadian Baptists could ill-afford to miss" (307–8).

83. Wilson, "Baptists and Business," 310.

84. Booth, "'Managing the Muses," 171.

foundation for music in worship, and the potential for its controversy, was firmly established years before.

The church sanctuary was furnished with Bibles and hymnals when it was built in 1875. The hymnal used before Thomas' tenure was *The Canadian Baptist Hymn Book* (1873). R. A. Fyfe was on the committee for this hymnal "prepared for the use of the Baptist Churches of Canada" by "the Baptist Home Missionary Convention of Ontario."[85] The unofficial hymnbook referenced above was H. E. Buchan's *Our Service in Song* (1875), which was published for the Jarvis Street church.[86] It is unclear which hymnbook the church was using while singing "Holy, Holy, Holy" on Thomas' Tenth Anniversary in 1892 (referenced above). It is not present in either *The Canadian Hymn Book* or *Our Service in Song.*[87] The Deacons Meeting Minutes from November 12, 1888, record the beginning of the investigation into securing a new hymnal: "The secretary was requested to ascertain the price of one containing 150 hymns and of [a] list [of] more than [approximately] 10–12 . . . subject to the approval of the pastor as to hymns selected and also as to arrangement."[88] It appears that the deacons planned to look over numerous hymnals in order to pick one to submit to the pastor for his approval regarding the content and arrangement of its hymns. However, a December 17, 1889, entry reads, "It was on consideration decided that the new hymnal should be named our Prayer Meeting Hymnal, that it should be alphabetically arranged with an index to subjects and printed on type not smaller than long primer and that a book of music be made by placing the music set to the hymns selected in a scrap book and numbering its time with the numbers corresponding to those in the hymnal."[89]

---

85. Baptist Home Missionary Convention of Ontario, *Canadian Baptist Hymn Book*, Prefatory Note.

86. Buchan, *Our Service in Song*. Buchan was a senior deacon of the church (Robertson, *Sketches in City Churches*, 28).

87. It is hymn 241 in Baptist Home Missionary Convention of Ontario, *Canadian Baptist Hymnal*. It is not present in any of the other Canadian Baptist hymnals of the nineteenth century. It is certainly possible that Thomas brought a hymnal from Philadelphia that he persuaded the church to use. Jarvis Street hosted The Baptist Congress in 1889 and each hymn listed in the minutes is in the 1883 American Baptist Publication *The Baptist Hymn, for Use in Church and Home*, compiled by W. H. Doane and E. H. Johnson. A variety of hymnals seem to have been used as some hymn numbers are from different hymnals. However, the overwhelming majority of hymns sung are from this hymnal, some by hymn number. It seems logical that this may have been the hymnal in the church.

88. "November 12, 1888," in *Jarvis Street Baptist Church Deacon's Book*, lii. Some of the handwriting is indiscernible.

89. "December 17, 1888," in *Jarvis Street Baptist Church Deacon's Book*, liii.

It appears that rather than selecting a new hymnal from a publisher, the church published their own hymnal, at least for prayer meetings. This leaves the question about a new hymnal for use in worship services on Sunday.

A few years earlier, a hymnal committee had presented six potential hymnal options to the deacons in 1886. The church was currently using *Our Service of Song* (1875) that had been printed for it with funding from the McMasters and under the oversight of the deacons. The minutes record, "A somewhat informative and lengthy discussion as the merits and demerits of various hymn books then ensued." The hymnals presented were "The English Publication named the [left blank]; the hymnal published in Philadelphia; [Our] Service of Song; [A hymnal published] by Sheldon and Co.; The Calvary Selection, [and] the Century Co[llection]." There were three requirements for the new hymnal: (1) that it contain hymns and music; (2) irrespective of price, authorship or publication, it must contain the most appropriate hymns and the best music, and (3) that "without discarding [Our] *Service of Song*, the choice seems to be between the *Calvary Selection* and *The Hymnal*."[90] "Holy, Holy, Holy" is found in both of these hymnals so either of these could have been in use on Thomas' tenth anniversary in 1892. It seems likely that one of these two hymnals was purchased for use in worship around this time, to be used alongside *Our Service of Song*. The later entry from above may have been simply to provide a different hymnbook for prayer meetings. All of this effort to secure hymnbooks after Thomas arrived does reflect an avid interest in hymnody and congregational song by the pastor and church.

The music program at Jarvis Street continued to grow after Thomas arrived. With the financial support of advocates such as the McMasters, new musical vistas continued to be expanded and new concepts gathered

---

90. "May 11, 1886," in *Jarvis Street Baptist Church Deacon's Book*, xxxvii. Buchan, *Our Service of Song* was the hymnal printed for Jarvis Street that was funded by Susan McMaster. H. E. Buchan was one of the senior deacons of the church. It is unclear what "the English Publication" may have been but it was not being seriously considered. The hymnal published by "Sheldon and Co." could have been one of the Manly hymnals (*Baptist Psalmody* or *Baptist Chorals*). "The Century Collection" was probably *The Centennial Collection* (1876), which was selected from *The Service of Song*. The *Calvary Selection of Spiritual Songs* (1883) was published by the Presbyterian compiler, Charles Seymour Robinson (1829–1899) with Robert S. MacArthur (1841–1923), a Baptist pastor in New York City. "The hymnal published in Philadelphia" was *The Baptist Hymnal: for Use in the Church and Home* (1883). The committee and deacons were supposed to meet the next Tuesday to hear some of the hymns played. The pages after this entry have been torn out of the minute book. It seems clear that they selected *The Baptist Hymnal* published in 1883. In October of 1886, later that year, they were working on hymnbook cards for the new hymnal ("October 18, 1886," in *Jarvis Street Baptist Church Deacon's Book*, xl).

strength. Some of these bolstered the effect of the worship services, such as on his tenth anniversary, and some distracted. Booth writes of a seemingly good thing getting out of hand, especially with regard to the choir that was pursuing goals outside of congregational worship:

> More attention was being paid to its secular and professional aspects. Proof of this lay in the appointment at Jarvis in 1888 of Augustus Stephen Vogt, who replaced J. F. W. Harrison as organist-choirmaster. Vogt not only significantly improved the choir, but used many of its members to assemble what eventually became the Toronto Mendelssohn Choir. Such was Vogt's reputation that when he retired in 1906, music had, in the opinion of some, literally overwhelmed other elements of the service. His replacement, Edward Broome, followed Vogt's musical program, eventually drawing the ire of the church's pastor.[91]

The pastor at the time was Thomas Todhunter Shields (1873–1955) who in 1910 noted the proportion of music to sermon time and complained: "What was designed to be an 'opening sentence' sometimes turned out to be an anthem that required ten minutes to complete. The result was that, do as one would, the Jarvis Street preacher would begin to preach about the time other congregations were hearing the benediction."[92] A sign of the choir trying to serve two masters appeared in the form of a matter that had to be addressed during Thomas' time. There was a growing concern with the spiritual condition of the choir members. The deacons passed a resolution on March 21, 1895, to appoint a committee with whom the choirmaster could "consult on any matter connected with the choir." This likely was also an attempt of the deacons to have more input into what was going on with the choir. The minutes then include the following nuanced declaration: "For the guidance of the choirmaster and congregation, it be declared that the church deems is advisable that as far as possible the choir should be composed of persons professing to be Christians."[93] It does not require much imagination to presume that musical talent had become a greater criterion for participation in the choir than spiritual orientation.

91. Lock, *Ontario Church Choirs and Choral Societies*, 158. Outside of church, Vogt taught piano and organ at the Toronto College of Music, and after 1892, at the Toronto Conservatory of Music. On the evening of June 1, 1902, word had been received that the war in South Africa was over. Thomas took the opportunity to discuss the outcome and reflections upon the painful event. The service was concluded with the singing of the national anthem and Mr. Vogt led the choir in singing the "Hallelujah Chorus" (Excerpt of the *Toronto Daily Globe* of June 2, 1902, in *Jarvis Street Minute Book*, 226).

92. T. T. Shields, quoted in Wilson, "Baptists in Business," 311–12.

93. "March 21, 1895," in *Jarvis Street Baptist Church Deacon's Book*, cxiii.

The choir initially sang an anthem while the offering was being collected. Giving by the church was collected by passing the plate during Thomas' tenure. It took approximately twenty ushers to collect the offering and a list of twelve substitutes also appeared in the minute book.[94] There were also eight special offerings taken at different times of the year. These were typically for special needs or missions' emphases.[95] This gave plenty of opportunities for the choir to sing, but as will be shown below, this had to be changed due to the choir's musical independence in the service. Baptisms were performed at the end of Sunday school sessions, morning services, and evening services.[96] The regular need for them reflected the growth of the church at the time.

The Lord's Supper was a special time for Thomas. This was the time that new members were introduced and welcomed to the table at Jarvis Street. Nevertheless, it was a challenge to get some members to attend the ordinance. Soon after Thomas' arrival, the Deacon's Meeting minutes of June 15, 1883, record his concern that "many of our members are habitually neglecting to ordinance of the Lord's Supper." As a result, he "expressed a decided wish that [some] method be adopted by which it could be ascertained definitely who of our members attend to their duty and privilege in this respect, at least once in each month."[97] This may have led to the more careful monitoring of church membership that characterized Thomas' tenure. The only solution noted in the minutes was to make sure that the time of communion was communicated more clearly, assuming that people did not attend because they may not have known. Though with the ordinance taking place at the end of regular worship services, it may have been that they were actually leaving early. The minutes record the same discussion still going on in November 1885, noting that a proposed plan was unanimously approved for presentation to the church. Apparently, the plan was secured from someone (Thomas?) having written Spurgeon "and having [received] from him a copy of the plan used by his church." This is apparently the plan put in place at Jarvis Street. The plan is not included in the minutes.[98]

94. "Plate Collections," in *Jarvis Street Minute Book*, 200.

95. "Report of the 1899 Annual Meeting," in *Jarvis Street Minute Book*, 159. This included home missions, foreign missions, ministerial education, the Sunday School, the church edifice, etc.

96. Various entries in *Jarvis Street Minute Book*, 133, 215, etc. This is one of the most frequent entries in the minute book.

97. "June 15, 1883," in *Jarvis Street Baptist Church Deacon's Book*, x. The Lord's Supper was celebrated at least monthly, and possibly more often than that at times.

98. "November 16, 1885," in *Jarvis Street Baptist Church Deacon's Book*, xxx. On March 4, 1892, the deacons encouraged Thomas to write a circular letter to those

Summary

The blazing center of worship at Jarvis Street was Christ and his gospel. To sit in worship was to "sit under the gospel's joyful sound." A great part of that sound at Jarvis Street was the music, when it was focused appropriately. The church became renowned for its majestic organ and great choir. A reporter from the *Toronto Evening Telegram* attended an evening service in the first decade of Thomas' pastorate. An account of the visit is recorded in *Sketches in City Churches*:

> "Do you wish a seat?" asked an usher on the Sunday evening in question, as a *Telegram* reporter stepped into the gallery of this church—at the same time critically inspecting his appearance as if to procure a seat accordingly; it was not a front seat but it served the purpose of the visit. Mr. Harrison, recently of Ottawa, and a very fine organist, favoured the incoming congregation with a well-executed prelude, although, when the anthem was sung and when, after prayer, Mr. Sims Richards sang a tenor solo, the organ had too much on an orchestral effect and overpowered the singers, as is too frequently the case with accompaniments. The members of the choir sit in pews built at right angles to the pulpit rostrum and immediately below it, while the keyboard of the organ is placed still lower and in front of the choir. The people stand while the hymns are sung, and every one is politely handed a book. Although the evening was rather unpleasant fully 1,000 people were present, and when a good, substantial, familiar tune was sung the effect of it was dignified and massive. During prayer the congregation sits, the large majority leaning upon the hand or the pew in front. The congregation was made up mostly of young people that were "attentive listeners and reverent in conduct." The writer also commented on the baptismal service that evening, which was "very impressive, and evidently created a good effect; the entire method of worship was simple and plain, such as in usually observed in non-liturgical churches."[99]

The description also includes the baptismal service.[100]

---

church members who lived in the city, but had not attended recently, "in hope of leading them to attend and to see their duty in this respect" ("March 4, 1892," in *Jarvis Street Baptist Church Deacon's Book*, cliii). Apparently, they were still having trouble getting people to attend communion.

99. Robertson, *Sketches in City Churches*, 28.

100. A description of the baptismal portion of the service is also provided in Robertson, *Sketches in City Churches*, 25. The phrase Thomas used to baptize was, "On

Michel R. Belzile surveyed the worship of Canadian Baptist Churches in the Baptist Convention of Ontario and Quebec for his DMin project for McMaster University in 1998. The second half of the nineteenth century was a post-revivalistic period for worship practices among Canadian Baptist churches as churches got away from the revivalistic patterns of the camp meetings and the awakenings earlier in the century. The focus of worship in many churches began to shift back toward the believer in education and teaching rather than the unbeliever for salvation. Of the two styles Belzile analyzes from this time period, the "Formal Evangelical Pattern" fits best what Jarvis Street likely did on a Sunday morning. It was a style popular among Baptists who "sought a more formal and reverent expression of worship." The Sunday morning service at Jarvis Street may have looked like the worship order in figure 10.[101]

Organ Prelude

Choir Anthem

Scripture Reading[102]

Opening Prayer

Solo

Hymn

Prayer

Choir Anthem[103]

---

profession of your repentance towards God and your faith in the Lord Jesus Christ, I baptize you my child, in the name of the Father, the Son and the Holy Ghost, Amen." The organ played "an appropriate refrain" after each person was baptized.

101. Belzile, "Canadian Baptists at Worship," 45. Belzile provides a worship order from nearby James Street Baptist Church in Hamilton, Ontario from 1895. This is his example of the "Formal Evangelical Pattern." The other pattern is the "Post-Revivalistic Order," characterized by less formality, less evangelistic, and much more didactic (42). This order contained a "quartette" and a "lesson" but it is not clear that Jarvis Street had either in their service. The choir was so prominent that it likely did all of the non-congregational singing other than solos. Other excerpts from deacon's meeting notes and the report from the *Toronto Evening Telegram* above have been combined to formulate this proposed order of worship.

102. The Deacon's Meeting minutes discuss a concern regarding seating late arriving "strangers and others" after the Scripture reading and prayer at the beginning of the service, "so that if possible there be less confusion during the reading of Scripture and prayer" ("June 15, 1883," in *Jarvis Street Baptist Church Deacon's Book*, x).

103. The Deacon's Meeting minutes record a discussion in October 1885 regarding "the fact that there was considerable disinformation in regard to some of the anthems sung, especially after the sermon. The matter was discussed at some length when it was decided to recommend to the church that the order of service be so changed that the

Offertory[104]

Hymn

Sermon

Hymn

Baptism

Doxology[105]

Benediction

Postlude

Figure 10. Potential order of worship at Jarvis Street Baptist Church, Toronto (1885)

There are clear opportunities in this service order to advance the themes of revelation and response, and exhortation and response. The beginning of the service is highlighted by the majestic organ and choir to point worshipers to a majestic God. Their response is through hymns and prayer as they gather for worship. Preaching and its related Scripture readings remained the main aspects of exhortation. Some musical elements also contributed to this. The final worship elements of a hymn response, the Lord's Supper, baptism, and the benediction served as response to exhortation. As has been pointed out above, the pastor described the entire service as "sitting under the gospel's joyful sound." This provides the overriding theme of mediation and response, as Christ and his cross were central to worship

---

collection should taken up before instead of after the sermon and that those who have charge of the singing be requested to sing more appropriate and shorter pieces and also to shorten the interludes between the hymns. Reference was also made to the quality of [wind?] lately used and the secretary was requested to ascertain whether a better quality could not be provided" ("October 13, 1885," in *Jarvis Street Baptist Church Deacon's Book*, xxviii). This may be in reference to the bellows for the organ. A proposal was made soon after for an electronic system to provide wind for the organ. The minutes from March 15, 1886, record a follow up of the matter of shortening the interludes between the hymns and to write to the publishers of hymnbooks for the most recent copies of hymnbooks. This latter item was to prepare for a hymnbook committee to consider a new hymnal for the church ("March, 15, 1886," in *Jarvis Street Baptist Church Deacon's Book*, xxxv).

104. On September 30, 1892, the deacons decided to take the offering up after anthem rather than at the same time as had been done since 1885. "After consideration it was decided that in [the] future the plate collection on the Lord's Day be taken up after singing the anthem and in a more formal and orderly manner, the collection going up with the plates at one time" ("September 30, 1892," in *Jarvis Street Baptist Church Deacon's Book*, cxvii).

105. Jarvis Street may have sung this at the end of their worship services. They sang the Doxology at the end of every business meeting and other gatherings as reflected in the minute book.

at Jarvis Street. The specific response at Jarvis Street, and where the service may have looked most revivalistic, was at the close of every sermon. The culmination of a B. D. Thomas sermon, and thus every service, was a gospel call to salvation. No matter the text, Thomas was going to end with a call for the unsaved to respond to the gospel. It seems quite likely that a formal altar call was part of the service as the theme at the end of his message was consistently an invitation to the unsaved to respond to the gospel. This was birthed in Thomas' conviction regarding the church: "If the greatest glory of the church consists in her being the birthplace of souls, then this should be the supreme aim of the gospel ministry."[106] The words of the sermon he delivered on behalf of his tragically deceased friend seem also to be the motive of his ministry. "*The time is short!* If you mean to do anything that is to tell beneficently on human destinies, do it, do it quickly, do it now. . . . A single instant may place you beyond the possibility of aught that can follow you with grateful benedictions into the eternal future."[107] This sense of urgency went with him every time he entered the pulpit and followed him out of it.

106. Thomas, "The Glory of the Church," in *Sermons Preached*, 82.

107. Thomas, "The Strong Staff, the Beautiful Rod," in *Sermons Preached*, 76; emphasis Thomas'.

8

Walnut Street Baptist Church, Louisville, Kentucky (1881–1907)

Introduction

Walnut Street Baptist Church was founded in 1849 by the merging of First Baptist Church[1] and Second Baptist Church[2] of Louisville, Kentucky. Unlike

1. First Baptist Church was formed in 1815 in the house of Mark Lampton. The church joined the Long Run Association in September 1815 and the church was constituted upon the Philadelphia Confession of Faith, upon which fellowship in the Association was also based. The church was the forty-ninth Baptist church in the association, but the first in the town of Louisville. Louisville had been founded in 1778. Kimbrough, *Walnut Street Baptist Church*, 9. Kimbrough's history of the church, written for the one-hundredth anniversary of the church, is considered the largest and most thorough of the three historical accounts of the church (Eaton and Leonard are the other two). The first Baptist church in Jefferson County was Beargrass Baptist Church, which was one of four churches disfellowshiped by the Long Run Association during the Campbellite Controversy due to their refusal to support the Philadelphia Confession of Faith. Beargrass subsequently became a Christian church, associated with Thomas Campbell (1763–1854) and Alexander Campbell's (1788–1866) Disciples of Christ movement (Allen, "Benjamin Allen's 1832 Report"). Alexander Campbell preached at First Baptist in 1825 and the church subsequently split over the matter of the Philadelphia Confession. A similar schism later took place in the Second Baptist Church as well as other Baptist churches in the area (Leonard, *Community in Diversity*, 24). A. H. Newman claims that up until that time, the Campbellite Controversy was "by far the most important schism suffered by the Baptist body in the United States" (Newman, *History of the Baptist Churches*, 487).

2. Second Baptist Church was formed in 1838 with Rev. Reuben Morey as their first pastor. In the first sixty years of Louisville's existence, only two Baptist churches had been formed (Kimbrough, *Walnut Street Baptist Church*, 49–51).

many historic churches that have lost their records due to calamity, time, or both, Walnut Street has its record book from its first meeting and has maintained it faithfully every year since its founding. The first entry in the book is the account of its organizational meeting:

> Resolved by the First and Second Baptist Churches of the city of Louisville, Ky., now in session, That said churches do now unite together and form one church, and that the entire list of members now in fellowship in both churches be considered members of the church now formed, and from and after the adoption of this resolution the 1st and 2nd Baptist Churches of Louisville cease to exist as separate organizations.[3]

At that moment, Walnut Street Baptist Church was formed and the First and Second Baptist Churches in Louisville, Kentucky ceased to exist. At the time of its founding, Louisville was growing rapidly as the population from 1840 to 1850 more than doubled.[4] Growth of the city was quickly outpacing that of the capacity of Baptists to minister to it. Walnut Street was emblematic of the fierce effort of Baptists to catch up. B. T. Kimbrough proclaimed Walnut Street "The mother of churches" in his 1949 history of the church. He listed nineteen churches started by Walnut Street to reach the city.[5]

3. Walnut Street Baptist Church, *Minutes*, June 15, 1849–November 28, 1858, 1. Both churches had become pastorless around the same time and both extended a call to Thomas Smith Jr., a recent graduate of Princeton Seminary who had attended Georgetown College previously. Neither church was aware initially that they had each extended a call to the same man simultaneously. When it was realized, the decision was made to merge the churches, dispose of their property, and unite in an entirely new church. When the churches merged, there were 399 on the combined membership rolls (Kimbrough, *Walnut Street Baptist*, 70, 74). Eaton writes: "Both the First and Second Churches were without pastors, and the eyes of both were turned to a rarely-gifted young man, the Rev. Thomas Smith, Jr. He visited both churches, delighted both, and was unanimously called by both. . . . Elder Smith accepted both calls, and led in the union of the two churches" (Eaton et al., *History of Walnut Street*, 10). The church voted on the name "Walnut Street Baptist Church" and identified itself as cooperating with the General Association of Baptists in Kentucky and the Southern Baptist Convention in the minutes of November 30, 1849 (*Minutes*, June 15, 1849–November 28, 1858, 7–8).

4. The population in 1840 was 21,210 and in 1850 it had grown to 43,194. Kimbrough, *Walnut Street Baptist*, 69. Thomas Smith, the first pastor, comments on a meeting of Kentucky Baptists and their concern to reach Louisville: "They said that if the Baptists did not take possession of Louisville now, they never would nor could; that it must be now or never; meanwhile detailing the many great efforts being made by all denominations and particularly the Catholics and pursuits to gain the ascendancy in that city. Nothing was done on the subject" (Leonard, *Community in Diversity*, 28).

5. Kimbrough, *Walnut Street Baptist Church*, 233.

A Brief History

After having secured Thomas Smith Jr. (1827–1851) as their first pastor, the church immediately began construction on a building to hold the newly combined congregation. T. T. Eaton writes in his history of the church: "Under the leadership of their young, brilliant and consecrated pastor, they began to erect a house of worship which was the wonder and the pride of the city."[6] Tragically, Smith grew gravely ill and died unexpectedly at the age of twenty-three, having served his church for barely a year and a half. His funeral was the first meeting held in the new building—though unfinished—it was held in the basement. William W. Everts (1814–1890) moved from Mumford, New York, to pastor the church in 1853. The two years between Smith's death and Everts' arrival saw the church almost come to an end. "When [Everts] arrived at Louisville, he found nothing encouraging except the field. The building was standing half finished. The meetings in the basement were reduced to an attendance of [fifty]."[7] Everts, a prominent preacher and revivalist who had served numerous churches in New York, threw himself into the work and the church immediately began to grow. In 1854 the new building, seating eight hundred, was completed and a pew rent system was employed, setting apart a reasonable number for free pews. The first baptism was administered in the new baptistery on January 27, 1854.[8] Later that year the Portland Avenue, Chestnut Street (later Jefferson Street), and German Baptist Churches were planted from Walnut Street. The General Association of Baptists of Kentucky was also formed that year.[9]

6. Eaton et al., *History of Walnut Street*, 11. "Nothing to compare with it had been known in Kentucky, and pictures of the building were published in periodicals and in books on architecture all over the land."

7. Kimbrough, *Walnut Street Baptist Church*, 81.

8. Eaton et al., *History of Walnut Street*, 14.

9. Eaton et al., *History of Walnut Street*, 15. See also, Leonard, *Community in Diversity*, 29. Kimbrough asserts that it was the Campbellite controversy that inspired the formation of the General Association of Baptists in Kentucky. Kimbrough, *Walnut Street Baptist Church*, 148. "Campbellism" was a claim to primitivism that became very attractive to many Baptists in an increasingly pluralistic America. Bill Leonard explains: "[Alexander] Campbell was a Baptist but was highly critical of certain Baptist practices which he viewed as contrary to the teaching of the Scripture. He rejected the use of creeds or confessions of faith with the watchword, 'no creed but Christ!' He denounced mission boards, Sunday Schools and the use of the ministerial title, reverend, as unknown to the New Testament church. Through simple faith, baptism 'for the remission of sins,' weekly communion, and the repudiation of denominational labels, Campbell and his followers believed that they had restored the true church as it was in the first century. This church, he believed, was composed of Christians who needed no other distinction" (Leonard, *Community in Diversity*, 24).

The Southern Baptist Convention met in Walnut Street's magnificent new building in 1857. It was at this meeting that James P. Boyce (1827–1888) offered the proposition to raise $100,000 in South Carolina to establish a seminary at Greenville, provided that $100,000 more was raised elsewhere. This is the same seminary that, after the Civil War, was relocated to Louisville; the history of which became intertwined with that of Walnut Street. Two years later in 1859, the year the Southern Baptist Theological Seminary was established in Greenville, Everts resigned to accept the call of the First Baptist Church of Chicago, leaving the church pastorless once again. Four hundred eighty-five people had been added to the church in addition to the three new Baptist churches planted in Evert's six years. Eaton explains, "The Walnut Street Church had so little of the service of the Rev. Thomas Smith as pastor, his health so soon failing him so as to unfit him for service . . . that it was Dr. Everts' pastorate that gave shape and direction to the church."[10] The years between pastors once again proved to be greatly problematic for the church. The church leadership enacted a series of resolutions during this time in an effort to unify the church through a reaffirmation to their founding declaration of faith. The following preamble reveals the troubled state of the church:

> Whereas, we are in a distressed condition as a church of the Lord Jesus Christ which we most deeply implore; we feel it to be our imperative duty to our divine Lord and Master and to each other to attempt the restoration of peace among ourselves, that we may again be happy and useful as the children of God. And in order that this much desired object may be attained, we solemnly enter upon the following resolves.[11]

George C. Lorimer (1834–1904) began his pastorate in 1862, after six months of filling in as pulpit supply. His tenure also lasted approximately six years and the church saw much growth once again. He resigned in 1868 with the membership at 761. A. T. Spalding (1831–1921) pastored from 1868 until 1871. The Southern Baptist Convention met again at Walnut Street in 1870, during which plans were discussed to move the Southern Seminary to Louisville. M. B. Wharton (1839–1908) served the church as its fifth pastor from 1872 to 1875. He was instrumental in bringing the seminary to Louisville and helped raise $45,000 towards that end. In March 1873, James P. Boyce addressed the church on the matter and subsequently

10. Eaton et al., *History of Walnut Street*, 13.

11. Eaton et al., *History of Walnut Street*, 13. Members during this time were advised, "to cease evil speaking and surmising in regard to the grievances one with another" (Leonard, *Community in Diversity*, 33).

raised more funds for the relocation. Boyce stayed in Louisville to continue raising the subscription for the required endowment to relocate the seminary from Greenville and subsequently became the supply pastor at Walnut Street after Wharton resigned. This began the close relationship between Walnut Street and Southern Seminary that was enjoyed for many years. Joseph W. Warder (b. 1825) was installed as pastor in 1875. At this time the church membership had grown to over seven hundred, though a committee in 1876 reported that between two and three hundred were "absent from the city."[12] In 1877, the seminary moved to Louisville to the corner of Firth and Broadway, very near the Walnut Street location at Fourth and Walnut. This brought many students and faculty to Louisville and Walnut Street, including John A. Broadus (1827–1895) and soon after, Basil Manly Jr. (1825–1892), from nearby Georgetown College in 1880. Both became faithful members of the church and both took turns filling the pulpit when Warder resigned in 1880. Warder resigned and became the missionary secretary for the state convention of Kentucky.

Thomas Treadwell Eaton (1845–1907) came to Louisville in 1881 from Petersburg, Virginia and served until his death in 1907. During his tenure he also served as the editor of the *Western Recorder*, the state periodical of Kentucky Baptists. Leonard calls him "one of the most colorful and controversial pastors in Walnut Street's history."[13] His was also the longest pastorate in its history.[14] While most pastors eventually succumbed to the demands of such a large church with health issues (six of the previous seven pastors) or simply the desire to go elsewhere, Eaton led the church through one of its greatest periods of growth and expansion. Broadus had an influential role in his coming as he accepted a call without first even visiting the church. One of his first acts as pastor was to organize a protracted series of revival meetings in October 1881, establishing his commitment to revivalism and evangelism. These meetings lasted for almost a month from November 13 to

---

12. Eaton et al., *History of Walnut Street*, 29. Accurate membership records were consistently a challenge as many names were on the role that did not attend worship services.

13. Leonard, *Community in Diversity*, 41. "He was one of the chief protagonists in the controversy surrounding seminary president William H. Whitsitt. He also presided over the church's jubilee celebration, wrote its first history, and moved the congregation to its present location of Third and St. Catherine Streets" (41–42).

14. Eaton was the first to benefit from an assistant to the pastor. James H. Wright was hired in 1883 as a part-time assistant to the pastor. "The purpose of the position was to share pastoral responsibilities and to work with mission churches in the city of Louisville. This position continued in this manner until Robert Young was called as full-time Associate Pastor upon his graduation from Southern Seminary in 1956." This was during the pastorate of W. R. Pettigrew (Pratt, "Community of Ministers," 82).

December 11.[15] William H. Whitsitt (1841–1911), a church history professor and later president of the seminary, was granted membership December 18, 1881, and Mrs. Whitsitt was baptized that same evening. Jamie Broome writes, "By this time, Walnut Street was considered the church of the Seminary community."[16]

Giving, along with membership, increased dramatically during this time as the church abandoned the pew rent system and employed a weekly contribution through envelopes.[17] During the first ten years of Eaton's pastorate there were 1,061, and total contributions in giving of $427,122.62. In addition, twenty men were set apart for the ministry and three new churches started.[18] The most significant of these was the granting of 711 to form the Twenty-Second and Walnut Street Baptist Church in 1887. A new building had been built and dedicated for them by the Walnut Street church. Even with this significant dismission, the Walnut Street church still reported a church membership of 1,549 the following year in 1888.[19]

In 1889, Eaton received an offer to come to Nashville, Tennessee, but declined the call. Basil Manly offered the following resolution passed by the

15. Kimbrough, *Walnut Street Baptist Church*, 125.

16. Broome, "A Community of Faith: The Baptist Connection" in Leonard, *Community in Diversity*, 116. "Students joined the church and assumed responsibilities in mission Sunday Schools. They also filled preaching points across the city. The church offered its sanctuary to the Seminary for commencement exercises and special lecture series. Basil Manly, professor, joined the church and was allowed to use one room of the church for his library. Members prepared holiday dinners, inviting the Seminary students to attend."

17. Walnut Street started out depending upon pew rents for current expenses, and special offerings for designated needs or projects. The weekly contributions on the Lord's Day supplemented these main avenues of giving. Kimbrough writes, "Now the weekly giving through the envelope had been accepted as the scriptural plan, and was bearing fruit in the increased liberality of the members" (Kimbrough, *Walnut Street Baptist Church*, 130).

18. Kimbrough, *Walnut Street Baptist Church*, 138. The three churches were Parkland, Twenty-second and Walnut, and McFerran Memorial.

19. Eaton et al., *History of Walnut Street*, 34–35. This church eventually moved to 23rd and Broadway, taking that name as their church and existed for almost a century. In 1985, the church disbanded. At times Walnut Street's membership numbers were significantly higher than church attendance and in many places the church records show adjustments to the member list, especially after a new pastor arrived. In 1864, the church approved two membership classifications: (1) "members of whom we have knowledge"; (2) "members of whose whereabouts and religious condition we have no knowledge" (Leonard, *Community in Diversity*, 34). Though the sanctuary dedicated in 1901 could seat approximately 1,000–1,600, the church did not have two morning worship services until March 26, 1967. This is in spite of reported membership numbers of 1,244 in 1915, 2,148 in 1925, 3,363 in 1929, and 4,000 in 1945. The recorded membership in 1967 was 5,020 (Leonard, *Community in Diversity*, 53).

church celebrating the opportunity to retain Eaton and describing the great satisfaction with Eaton as pastor:

> *Resolved,* That we, the Walnut Street Baptist Church, of Louisville, Ky., have heard with profound gratification the decision of our pastor, the Rev. T. T. Eaton, to decline the call to Nashville, Tenn., and remain with us; that we trust we recognize in this the good hand of the Lord our God guiding him as well as us; and that we pledge him cordially our renewed co-operation in all the work of the church, and pray God's blessing in all the work of the church, and pray God's blessing on our united labors.[20]

On February 7, 1892, the church held a joint memorial service for Charles Haddon Spurgeon (1834–1892) and Basil Manly Jr. (1825–1892), both of whom had died on January 31 of that year. This year also saw the church recognize the centennial of the start of modern missions in October. This was a convention-wide celebration that involved the likes of Eaton, H. H. Harris from Richmond, F. M. Ellis from Baltimore, R. H. Harris from Columbus, Georgia, W. Pope Yeaman from Columbia, B. H. Carroll from Waco, Texas, and J. B. Hawthorne from Atlanta. In 1895, John A. Broadus died, prompting the largest funeral in the church's history. Eaton reflects, "That was the world event of that year. The great Christian, the great scholar, the great teacher, the great writer, the great preacher, the great man, in dying, bereaved the world and enriched heaven."[21]

In 1899, the fiftieth anniversary of the church was recognized in an event drawing 1,750 church members. When Eaton first arrived the church had 573 members, making this a threefold increase in eighteen years. At this point in his pastorate there had been a total of 1,444 baptisms and total contributions of $604,426.23. Forty-three men in all had been set apart for ministry and a total of six new churches started.[22] The Southern Baptist Convention was held in the city during this year, making its third trip to Louisville (previously in 1857 and 1870). During this time period the city of Louisville had grown substantially. Barely forty thousand lived in the city when Walnut Street was formed. By the turn of the century there were two hundred thousand citizens. The church determined, after a day of prayer and fasting, that the existing building should be sold and a new building erected. The final service in the historic Gothic building was April 1, 1900. A report was prepared for the service indicating that Walnut Street had grown

20. Eaton et al., *History of Walnut Street*, 36; emphasis Eaton's.

21. Kimbrough, *Walnut Street Baptist Church*, 144.

22. Kimbrough, *Walnut Street Baptist Church*, 157. The additional churches to those listed above were Meadow Home, Third Avenue, and Hopewell.

from her small beginning to "perhaps the largest of any Baptist church in this country, or any other, with the possible exception of the Tabernacle of London."[23] Later reflection on this time period also attributed to Walnut Street "one of the largest Sunday-schools in the South, staffed by a corps of qualified teachers."[24]

On May 1, 1901, the cornerstone was laid for a new building on Third and St. Catherine Streets. The ceremony for the event happened to coincide with Eaton's twentieth anniversary as the church's pastor. Previous pastorates had never exceeded more than six or seven years and most were substantially less. A temporary worship facility was secured in a vacant Presbyterian church at Second and College for almost a year before the church held its first service in the new building on March 9, 1902. A formal dedication service was held on November 16, 1902, in which morning, afternoon, and evening services were held. The *Western Recorder* describes the building as "the finest house of worship belonging to any church in the Convention."[25] Additional baptisms, increased giving, and new ministry and mission efforts marked almost five years of service under Eaton in the new location. Again, more men were set apart for ministry. On June 29, 1907, while en route for additional ministry efforts himself, T. T. Eaton died of a sudden heart attack at a train station in Grand Junction, Tennessee. Kimbrough writes, "He collapsed in the railroad station, asking, 'Are there any Baptists here?'"[26] Under his leadership, the church had become the most influential Baptist church in Louisville with close ties to Southern Seminary and its faculty and students, giving it an influence that reached around the world.

Theology in Practice

The Articles of Faith adopted by the church on October 12, 1849, include nine articles upon which the church was founded. The first article states that the Scriptures are "the only infallible rule of Faith and Practice." The

23. Kimbrough, *Walnut Street Baptist Church*, 158. The theme of the morning service "in the old church house" was "my joy," from John 3:29. Hymns included: "Oh Could I Speak the Matchless Worth," "All Hail the Power," and "Rock of Ages" (Leonard, *Community in Diversity*, 43).

24. Eaton et al., *History of Walnut Street*, 53. The May 10, 1900, edition of the *Western Recorder*: "Tearing down the building has revealed a condition of which no man dreamed. The building was utterly unsafe and every time the congregation gathered, it was at the peril of their lives. . . . To have continued to use the old building for church purposes would have involved a serious disaster with appalling loss of life" (55).

25. "Dedication," *Western Recorder*, November 20, 1902.

26. Kimbrough, *Walnut Street Baptist Church*, 167.

second article is a statement on the Trinitarian nature of God while articles three through six contain the various elements of the gospel. There is no statement regarding election or predestination, even though the church had been founded on the Calvinistic principles found in the Philadelphia Confession of Faith. Article 6 is a statement regarding the perseverance of the saints—"they will be kept by his power through faith unto salvation." Article 7 establishes immersion in the name of the Father, the Son and the Holy Spirit as the only true baptism and "that immersed believers only are entitled to partake of the Lord's Supper." Article 8 is related to the final resurrection of the dead and eternal judgment while article 9 regards the ministry of spreading the gospel through the Christian ministry of all its members.[27] Leonard describes Walnut Street's Articles of Faith as "much briefer than the elaborate Philadelphia Confession of faith" and that it represents a more modified Calvinism.[28]

A. H. Newman writes in his late nineteenth-century history of the Baptists, "T. T. Eaton . . . represent[ed] the Baptist conservatism of the South."[29] In an age of theological pluralism, Eaton intended to stand and fight for biblical truth as held by Baptists. Karen E. Smith writes, "He was convinced that Baptist beliefs were worth fighting over, and he stopped at nothing to make his views known."[30] Eaton was a strong proponent of Landmarkism[31] and wrote many books, articles, and pamphlets on the subject, which is why Whitsitt's beliefs on baptism drew Eaton's ire. He felt that he must contend for the convictions of the Baptist faith even if it seemed no one else would. He writes in one sermon later published as a pamphlet: "Others who hold different beliefs will not advocate our doctrines, you may be sure, hence their advocacy depends upon us, and if we fail, what we believe to be true

27. "Articles of Faith, October 12, 1849," in Walnut Street Baptist Church, *Manual of Operations and Policies*, 2.

28. Leonard, *Community in Diversity*, 31.

29. Newman, *History*, 425.

30. Smith, "Community and Conflict," 162.

31. Weaver writes: "The most explicit manifestation of gospel primitivism in Baptist life was the spread of Landmarkism throughout Southern Baptist ranks in the nineteenth century. The intense denominational competition of the frontier provided the context. Alexander Campbell claimed the restoration of the New Testament church; Methodists cited the apostolic poverty (and often celibacy) of their evangelistic itinerant ministers. Baptists did not simply suggest they were restoring the New Testament, but that they *were* the New Testament church." It's inception regarded the nature of valid baptism and "alien immersion"—immersion administered by non-Baptists (Weaver, *In Search of the New Testament Church*, 153). See Tull, *High-Church Baptists in the South*. Tull calls Eaton "one of Landmark's most forceful personalities and most trenchant minds" (122).

will perish from the earth. If those who believe error advocate it, while those who believe truth will not advocate it, then truth will perish and error will prevail."[32]

In *The Faith of Baptists*, Eaton outlines his advocacy for historic Baptist beliefs on three essential matters of faith and practice related to worship. This pamphlet was published in 1895, just over halfway through his tenure as Walnut Street's pastor. They are the thoughts of a seasoned pastor who had determined upon which truths he and his church must stand. He introduces the pamphlet in this manner, "Baptists rejoice to hold in common with many others the doctrines of grace and the great principles that make up the Evangelical faith. They lay special emphasis, however, on the importance of strict conformity to Bible teaching."[33] The purpose of this publication is to elucidate where Baptist belief is different from other denominations. He highlights three areas: (1) the church, (2) baptism, and (3) the Lord's Supper. "Baptist doctrines on these subjects follow as corollaries to their fundamental doctrines of direct and personal responsibility to God and of absolute submission to Scripture teaching."[34] Regarding the church he advocates local autonomy with a distinction between the local church and the churches that make up a denomination. Speaking of the New Testament example, "These churches, the only kind known to the New Testament, were independent bodies and were subject to no central authority. . . . All that is said to the churches and about them assumes their entire independence."[35] He is consistent with historic Baptist faith and practice in his view of the ordinances. Baptism is by immersion for those who have professed faith in Christ only, thus advocating "regenerated church membership."[36] Communion was open only to those who have made this

32. Eaton, *How to Behave*, 10. This was originally a sermon given in 1891.

33. Eaton, *Faith of Baptists*, 3. Eaton wrote a defense of the Philadelphia Confession of Faith in 1900. (See Eaton, "Defense of the Philadelphia Confession of Faith," 194–97.)

34. Eaton, *Faith of Baptists*, 4.

35. Eaton, *Faith of Baptists*, 7. In this passage he also condemns the practice of any distinction between ruling elders and teaching elders, as well as the concept of a priest. "Christ is the one and only priest who once for all made the offering for sin, of which all the offerings of the Levitical priests were but types and symbols. . . . To bring in any other sin bearer or intercessor is to declare that the work of Christ is insufficient" (12–13). He also rejects the Church of England's concept of any proposed apostolic succession of their church (14). Later he writes regarding the distinction of role while maintaining the equality of rank: "No one man can outrank any other man in a New Testament church" (16).

36. Eaton, *Faith of Baptists*, 17. "Baptists affirm that New Testament baptism is the immersion in water in the name of the Trinity of a believer on a profession of faith by one duly set apart by a church for such service" (20). Eaton also writes of baptism in his

profession and had subsequently been baptized upon this profession, and been joined to a local church.[37] In all of these arguments he asserts "no Baptist scholar has been quoted, not for any lack of them, since they are abundant, but to show that the positions taken are sustained by the scholarship of other denominations."[38] His support for each of these points is from Scripture, but also a broad array of theologians. He summarizes, "A New Testament church is then a local congregation of baptized believers—or 'saints,' as Paul calls them—banded together on their profession of faith for the maintenance of the ministry of the word and of the ordinances of the gospel, and to win the world to Christ."[39]

The matter of baptism, in this case "alien-immersion," especially in light of the controversy with the Campbellites' view of baptism for the remission of sins, was of great importance to Eaton. When H. P. Fudge, who had joined the church by letter, applied for ordination in 1897, the question of his baptism was inquired upon. Eaton explains, "In his examination he told how he had been baptized by a Disciple preacher, and was received into a Baptist church in Indiana on that baptism. The presbytery were [sic] unanimous in recommending that he be baptized before being ordained."[40] He was baptized and ordained on the same day—October 5, 1897. Eaton had written in *The Faith of the Baptists* just two years earlier,

> The Disciples teach that baptism is in order to procure the remission of sins. They have cut themselves off from our Baptist churches, which Baptists are bound to believe are according to New Testament order, and therefore the Disciples have so far forth, been guilty of schism, and have turned their backs upon New Testament order. From the Baptist standpoint, therefore, they have not an orderly church membership.[41]

Baptism by immersion according to profession of faith and scriptural truth is what makes Baptists who they are. There is no more Baptist distinctive than this.

---

article "What Is Baptism?"

37. Eaton, *Faith of Baptists*, 75–76. "Turning to the New Testament we find three prerequisites laid down for participation in the Lord's Supper: first, a credible profession of faith; second, baptism; third, an orderly church membership."

38. Eaton, *Faith of Baptists*, 42. He quotes and cites Episcopalians, Presbyterians, Methodists, and Congregationalists; as well as from the Reformers and Puritans.

39. Eaton, *Faith of Baptists*, 15. He warns: "No man should join a church to be saved. He must not join until he is saved, and ready to go forward in obedience to Christ's commands. Just the worst place in the world for an unsaved man is in a church."

40. Eaton et al., *History of Walnut Street*, 48.

41. Eaton, *Faith of Baptists*, 81.

The "Whitsitt Controversy" was in large part also over the matter of baptism. Whitsitt, a church historian and then president of Southern Seminary, published his controversial claim that Baptists did not begin to practice immersion until 1641.[42] This called into question the practice of baptism by immersion in Baptistic churches since the New Testament era, refuting the argument of Landmarkism. Eaton used his role as editor of the *Western Recorder* to support a movement requiring the removal of Whitsitt as president of the seminary. Pratt explains, "As a result of the controversy, Whitsitt was forced not only to resign the presidency of the Seminary but to move his membership from Walnut Street Baptist Church as well." Whitsitt was to write the history of the church for its jubilee celebration. The resulting schism required Eaton to write it himself and "tarnished what had been a generally positive relationship between Walnut Street and the Seminary."[43] This was a price that Eaton was willing to pay. Smith writes, "He was a man driven by his desire to hold fast to what he believed to be true Baptist doctrine." Later she summarizes Eaton's pastorate in this manner,

> While his years as pastor were difficult ones for the church, he is remembered for his strong and forceful leadership, evangelistic witness, and his seemingly tireless, if not sometimes vitriolic, pen. . . . He did not hesitate to attack what he believed to be doctrinal heresy and in doing so he often spoke in terms which were not only uncompromising, but often less than charitable.[44]

Practice of Worship

Andrew Pratt writes of Walnut Street's worship, "Worship is not only central to Walnut Street, it is vital. The ability of the church to find unity amid diversity rests to some extent on the pastor's leadership in worship. In addition, worship at Walnut Street sets the tone for all the various ministries

---

42. See Whitsitt, *Question in Baptist History.*

43. Pratt, "Community of Ministers," 68. Under fire from his pastor, Whitsitt felt he had to withdraw his membership from the church. With the close ties between the seminary and the church the controversy created division within the church.

44. Smith, "Community and Conflict," 165. "Even after Whitsitt resigned . . . Eaton continued his attack on him and on others at the seminary who in his opinion were straying from what he believed to be the true principles of the faith. In 1907, Eaton launched an attack on W. O. Carver (1868–1954), Professor at Southern Seminary, who was member of Walnut Street. Eaton claimed that Carver was trying to unite Baptists and Campbellites (now known as Disciples). . . . Carver denied the charges, claiming Eaton had left a wrong impression and misrepresented him in the *Western Recorder.*"

performed by the church."[45] The vast diversity of a burgeoning inner-city church led by an evangelistic-minded pastor is most on display in worship. This likely explains why there was such a consistent thread of challenge and difficulty woven into the church's history with regard to worship. Pastors who were itinerant evangelists and camp meeting speakers led the earliest days of First and Second Baptist Churches. The establishment of the church as Walnut Street included a transition of the church's identity to that of a more formal downtown church, especially as the city of Louisville began to grow. This transition was most evident under Eaton's leadership, which saw the city grow dramatically and the church refine its image, especially musically, as a downtown Baptist church.

The church covenant describes the pattern of behavior required of all members with regard to its worship. It includes the following:

> We will not forsake the assembling of ourselves together nor omit the great duty of prayer both for ourselves and for others . . . that we will seek divine aid to enable us to walk circumspectly and watchfully in the world, denying ungodliness and every worldly lust; that we will strive together for the support of a faithful evangelical ministry among us. That we will endeavor by example, and effort to win souls to Christ. And through life amidst evil report and good report seek to live to the glory of him who hath called us out of darkness into his marvelous light.[46]

Church discipline was initially very strict and monthly business meetings were held one Friday night a month to bring public charges of inappropriate behavior of church members before the church. However, after the merging of the congregations into the Walnut Street congregation in 1849, this process was undertaken by a committee:

> Instead of "inquiring for fellowship of the church," and making that the signal for the presentation of charges, a committee on discipline was appointed. Still charges were sometimes made in open meeting by individual members. . . . Generally, however, the discipline was left in the hands of the committee, and action was taken simply on their reports.[47]

45. Pratt, "Community of Ministers: Pastors and Staff," 61. For a treatise on the principles of worship among Landmark Baptists such as Eaton at the turn of the century, see Ford, *Baptist Waymarks.*

46. Walnut Street Baptist Church, "Church Covenant," quoted in Leonard, *Community in Diversity*, 32.

47. Eaton et al., *History of Walnut Street*, 17. The role of the committee was "to

The most common charge for discipline was the lack of attendance at worship services, though there was a general concern that discipline was not consistently upheld for this or other transgressions. The motive for discipline was not as much out of concern for purity for corporate worship as was more often the case with Baptist churches in the past. This was partially the case, but more so it was that the congregation should "purify itself before in can hope to work . . . for the purification of the world."[48] This represents the shift in primary orientation from the purity of the gathered church before God in worship, to a greater concern for the purity of the scattered church in evangelism and witness. This revivalistic shift is also reflected in the preparation for worship in a manner that was more in line with preparation for evangelistic revival, but also in the orientation of the worship services, which had become more cognizant of the unbelievers gathering on Sunday. This is not to say that there was no benefit intended for the believers who attended corporate worship. Eaton lists five reasons in a sermon based on Hebrews 10:25: (1) to become more devotional (he uses the illustration of a musician not practicing); (2) to maintain and cultivate fellowship (he uses the illustration of a stalk of wheat standing alone); (3) to enable us to resist temptation against backsliding; (4) to learn of God; and (5) for the sake of others. "Where two or three are gathered . . . [there is a] special promise to meeting."[49] The promise included the salvation of the unsaved.

Eaton presented a paper to the Baptist World Congress in 1884 in Philadelphia, Pennsylvania, on the topic of the appropriate use of the word of God in worship. He writes, "Of all places and times, the Bible should be treated reverently in the pulpit and in public worship."[50] He continues with his description of worship's priority: "The aims of public worship being to awaken sinners and build up the saints who are present, such parts of Scripture should be used as are best suited to these ends."[51] Here again, the

---

look after all the members of the church who are living in fragrant violation of their covenant obligations to the church" (21).

48. Leonard, *Community in Diversity*, 40. In 1875, the business meeting was moved to Wednesday nights and prayer meetings were held on the Wednesday nights that were not business meetings (40). However, in July 1894, it was recommended to reestablish a monthly "covenant meeting" held before communion Sunday when members "reaffirmed their covenant relationship" (43).

49. Eaton, "Hebrews 10:25," box 10, Thomas Treadwell Eaton Papers, Archives and Special Collections, James P. Boyce Centennial Library, The Southern Baptist Theological Seminary, Louisville, Kentucky.

50. Eaton, "Right Use of the Bible," 84.

51. Eaton, "Right Use of the Bible," 86. In this paper Eaton castigates a common practice of preachers in the day of "using Scripture as a motto." Eaton's preaching method is discussed below.

priority in worship seems to be first, the sinner's conversion and second, the edification of the saints. It is not exclusively for the unsaved as a revival service might be, but the prioritized emphasis has shifted toward evangelism and away from edification in late nineteenth and early twentieth-century Baptist worship. The appropriate worship of God is not referenced in this paper at all, much less advocated as the primary aim. The worship gathering seems to have become a revivalistic meeting with secondary benefits for believers. Wednesday night meetings were seen as directed toward believers through Bible lectures while the events of Sunday emphasized an evangelistic theme.

Eaton's concern for preparation for worship is reflected in an unknown excerpt simply labeled as page "3." The first two pages are missing, but it appears to be a sermon about worship and the worship attender's concern for outward appearance versus inward focus. He writes, "In how many instances do undue care and anxiety about external things, rob the mind of spirituality and withdraw us from communion with God, and hinder our growth in grace!" He warns that there are "here, even in this house of God, this holy Sabbath morning" those who did not enter "this holy place" properly, since they "bestowed more thought and attention upon their external appearance . . . than they did upon the preparation of their hearts to enter this sanctuary and worship him acceptably."[52]

Eaton addresses the topic of acceptable worship in a series of sermons on the Ten Commandments. The first four commandments relate to the subject of worship. While the first commandment deals with the subject of idolatry, "the second forbids the worship of the true one in any way save that which he hath appointed."[53] Though he assumes that Protestants have less error here than the Catholics and others who use icons and statues, he acknowledges some concern. The bulk of his concern is the propensity of man to "add to his requirements" and worship God in any mode, save that which he has commanded.[54] He explains,

> But in all these things Baptists in the past have been innocent, they have borne a testimony through all their history, against any addition or changes, in spiritual worship, which is today our noblest earthly heritage. They have scorned all pleas of expediency, refused to make religion attractive to the senses by glitter and tinsel, rejec [sic] all innocent addition to God's way, and

52. Eaton, "Worship Excerpt."
53. Eaton, "2nd Commandment," 1.
54. Eaton, "2nd Commandment," 3.

through persecution and danger and death, maintained un-
shaken their obedience to this second commandment.[55]

Eaton describes Baptist worship in contrast to that of the Catholics
or similar practices. "Our religion was never intended to be attractive to
the senses and imagination; its only appeals are to the reason and the conscience . . . you seek to increase its attractiveness, so surely with [Jereboam]
will you cause Israel to sin. It will be to the end of time to the self righteous
Jew a stumbling block, and to the learned Greek foolishness; but to those
who believe, the power of God unto salvation."[56] His concern is that by
adding human additions to worship that God has not required, the gospel
will be obscured and God will not acknowledge and bless the worship. Eaton is speaking to the regulative principle in worship in a similar way to that
of his Baptist forbears from the same second commandment. He is seeking
to protect the purity of the gospel in worship:

> This second commandment forbids all reverence for places as
> sacred, or use of relics for devotion. It forbids all dependence
> for protection on charms or lucky signs, all looking for salvation
> to baptismal regeneration, priestly absolution, good works or
> anything save the grace of God, converting the soul. Whenever
> you let any of these things occupy Christ's place in the scheme
> of salvation, you are bowing down to an image, as truly as the
> Israelites to Aaron's calf. It forbids hypocrisy and formality,—the
> latter ever a growing sin among churches which are at rest from
> persecution.[57]

In Walnut Street's new building dedication service on November 16,
1902, George B. Eager, a seminary professor, provides a similar description
of Baptist worship in his sermon, "What a Baptist Church Should Stand
For." He proclaims, "The corollaries to [living stones] are simple loyalty to
Christ and to the Word, simplicity in worship, ordinances and policy. No
gorgeous ritual in worship, baptism as the formal initiation. . . . [And] the
Lord's Supper a memorial ordinance symbolizing nourishment."[58]

Eaton was not a proponent of responsive readings in worship. In fact,
he suggests responsive singing as an equally demeaning treatment of a text,
with the difference being that it was God's word being handled carelessly

55. Eaton, "2nd Commandment," 4. He has referenced such things as required bow-
ing/kneeling in the service, sprinkling for baptism, and other added ceremonies often
associated with Catholicism.

56. Eaton, "2nd Commandment," 4–5.

57. Eaton, "2nd Commandment," 5–6.

58. "Dedication," *Western Recorder*, November 20, 1902.

in the reading rather than hymns of human composure. He also was not an advocate of the unison reading of Scripture, though he does not object to an individual reading Scripture other than the pastor. "But there should not be reading aloud in concert; all the analogies are against it."[59] When the preacher reads Scripture, he explains that some explanation may be given as a common practice of the day, but common sense should prevail: "If the comments are short, pointed, and instructive, they will be useful; but if they are commonplace and really explain nothing they had better be omitted and the words of Scripture be left in their simple grandeur to make their own impression."[60] As to the choice of the Scripture reading, in most instances the context of the main text is to be preferred. However, he feels that "if the sermon is to be expository, and the text is to be brought out at length in the discourse, it may be best to read other passages of Scripture bearing on the same subject. In general, however, the preacher should read the context."[61] Eaton's practice appears to have been to employ Scripture readings of related texts to the context of his sermon text, and not the sermon text itself.

He cautions against the criticism of a particular translation from the pulpit by highlighting the original language word and scrutinizing the

59. Eaton, "Right Use of the Bible," 88. "We are God's soldiers." The soldiers don't read the orders from the Commander-in-Chief aloud together. "We are God's children." The family does not read the letter from the loving father aloud together. "God is a king." How does one deal with the proclamation of monarchs? "Can any passage of Scripture be cited in favor of all the people reading aloud in public worship?" He then cites 1 Cor 14:31 as support for one person reading at a time. This part of Eaton's presentation is at the end. When he concludes George Dana Boardman (1828–1903) stands to contest the last portion in particular. His argument is that by placing so much emphasis on the preacher in worship that the pulpit has replaced the altar and the Baptist liturgy is as rigid as that of the Episcopalians. "The preacher conducts almost every part of the service, except occasionally of the singing; he takes the place of all the old worship. It is his voice that is heard from the beginning to the end. What he says in his sermon is accounted of more worth than the prayer, that the Scripture. Many a person will not hesitate to come into the house of God during the singing or even during the reading of the Scripture or the delivery of the prayer, who does hesitate to come in when the preacher is preaching. More respect is paid to the preacher than to the word of God." His argument is for more liturgical worship that gives the congregation its voice in worship back: "Moreover, and I say it deliberately, unless you recognize more than you have this instinct of liturgical worship, you will find that the churches that do foster it will steal away your people, and especially your young people" (89).

60. Eaton, "Right Use of the Bible," 86.

61. Eaton, "Right Use of the Bible," 86. He does condemn a trite handling of Scripture in preaching: "If the text is to be used as a motto—and with due deference to the high authority to the contrary, I see no objection to such use occasionally, provided it be done openly and honestly—then it may be best to read passages elsewhere which illustrate or enforce the truths or the duties the sermon is designed chiefly to urge."

particular English word choice.[62] He feels that preaching illustrations are best derived from other places in the Scripture rather than a common practice of the day of borrowing from science. "There is danger that science will change, and so the illustration will lose its force."[63] In general, his strong urge is to rely upon the power of the word of God in worship: "Let us *use* the Bible, for that is the weapon by which all spiritual conquests are to be won. The news of the day, the most recent science, the latest philosophy, the newest theology, these may make up very interesting and attractive discourses, but they will convert no souls and build up no characters."[64]

Once again, the use of preaching here seems first for evangelistic goals and secondarily for edification. The zeal for conversion and to see the lost saved, the regular practice of protracted revival meetings each year, and the nineteenth-century emphasis on revival have slowly broadened the dialogue in worship and directed its concluding impetus to be for the unsaved.

Eaton reports in his historical account that issues regarding the use of music in worship began before the merging of First and Second Baptist churches to form Walnut Street. Apparently the choir of the First Baptist Church was accustomed to, or desirous of, using a bass viol in worship. The use of instruments in worship was still a matter of contentious debate. A resolution was submitted on February 17, 1844: "That no instrumental music be allowed in this church, without the consent of the church." Two days later there was another entry due to a violation of the resolution. The leader of the choir is reported to have responded, "[I was] directed by the choir to bring the instrument to the church, and did so supposing the objections to its introduction had been removed." This division between the choir and the church seems to have been resolved though it is unclear how this was accomplished. The report of the committee soon after indicates that the choir was invited to "resume their place in the gallery."[65] It is unclear whether or not they continued the use of the bass viol in worship.

Controversy revolving around the use of music continued in Walnut Street's history as Everts, the second pastor of the church, had to appoint a committee to "help solve the church music problem." Everts introduced the subject and "was followed by interesting and forcible remarks." The task of the special committee was "to confer together upon the subject and mature a plan for the promotion of this important part of divine worship

62. Eaton, "Right Use of the Bible," 85. His specific example is that of the word "charity" from 1 Cor 13's use of *agapē*.

63. Eaton, "Right Use of the Bible," 86.

64. Eaton, "Right Use of the Bible," 87; emphasis Eaton's.

65. Eaton et al., *History of Walnut Street*, 8–9.

(said consideration to be based upon the real merits of the subject, free, if possible, from educational bias or prejudice" and report to the church.[66] It is clear from the financial records that money for an organ was spent in 1859 as construction costs included a line item for "organ" at a cost of $3,087.28.[67] Leonard records that the organ was present when the building opened in 1854 and it was valued at $10,000.[68] If so, this expense in 1859 might have been repair cost, enhancement, or merely the reflection of a portion of the earlier costs. It is possible that the choice of music and the use of instruments remained a source of contention as the following guideline was put into place for a non-church group that wanted to rent the building for usage in 1865: "No instrumental music [may] be used except the organ, and no singing except sacred hymns."[69] The quality and balance of singing seems to have also been an issue. In 1867, the controversy was related to the singing of certain hymns. Leonard explains:

> The deacons "investigated" the matter and concluded that "the difficulty" related more to the use of numerous hymnbooks "than any indisposition of the choir to select familiar music." Noting the difficulty of defining familiar music the deacons recommended that the church elect an organist and a "leader of music." The latter's duty involved leading music for all "public and social meetings" and in Sunday School. They also encouraged the church to increase the size of the choir, to hold singing classes, and to purchase "a hymnbook with notes, with which the members of the choir can supply themselves." Most 19th century congregations used hymnbooks in which only words were printed. "Note books" with tunes and melodies were separate. Thus the Walnut Street Church began to expand its music ministry toward greater congregational participation.[70]

The church approved the recommendation. In March 1868, a committee was appointed to "make such arrangements as they can to develop the best church music, having an eye to combining choir and congregational

66. Eaton, *History of Walnut Street*, 16.

67. Kimbrough, *Walnut Street Baptist Church*, 85. The total construction cost of the building was $81,299.98.

68. Leonard, *Community in Diversity*, 29.

69. Eaton et al., *History of Walnut Street*, 22.

70. Leonard, *Community in Diversity*, 37.

singing."[71] A singing school was established in 1873 to attempt to improve congregational singing.[72]

The Psalmist was the first hymnal used by the Walnut Street congregation and it appears to have been the primary hymnal for almost forty years. The 1849 meeting that formed the Walnut Street Church and dissolved First and Second Baptist churches also voted on this hymnal as the regular hymnal.[73] While some controversy erupted later over an inconsistency of hymnal usage and the use of unfamiliar hymns as relayed above, it was recommended again in 1869 that The Psalmist "or a selection from it by the Pastor and church be used both in our Social and Sabbath meetings."[74] Apparently other hymnals were in use at other functions or at least by the choir at times. In 1872, this was changed to The Baptist Praise Book: For Congregational Singing.[75] Finally, just after Eaton's arrival, the recommendation was made to purchase the hymnal for which he sat on the editorial board: The Baptist Hymnal, for Use in the Church and Home (1883).[76] Congregational singing was aided by a group of singers (likely a quartet as had become popular elsewhere), in addition to the choir. A cornet was also used to accompany singing for a while and this person was paid. In 1887 the cornet was dispensed with and a precenter—A. Smyth—was hired in January 1888 to lead the singing.[77] There was a paid choir for at least one year and the quartet seems to have been paid for several years.[78]

In 1893, after Eaton's arrival, and upon recommendation of the Finance Committee, the paid choir was dispensed with "to save expenses." This was followed by instructions to the pastor to "appoint a committee on music, with power to act." The committee recommended the formation of a volunteer choir, and formally thanked Mr. and Mrs. George P. Weller for

71. Eaton et al., History of Walnut Street, 23.

72. Eaton et al., History of Walnut Street, 26.

73. "November 30, 1849," in Walnut Street Baptist Church, Minutes, 8. "Recommended the use of The Psalmist in the Public Worship of the Church."

74. "January 15, 1869" in Walnut Street Baptist Church, Minutes, 266. This same report also recommended a thirty-minute rehearsal for the congregation on Wednesdays after the evening lecture and the hiring of a song leader and an organist.

75. "April 12, 1872," in Walnut Street Baptist Church, Minutes, 236. See Fuller et al., Baptist Praise Book. Two of Walnut Street's former pastors were on the editorial board of this hymnal—W. W. Everts and George C. Lorimer.

76. "July 9, 1884," in Walnut Street Baptist Church, Minutes, 260. John A. Broadus and Basil Manly Jr. were also on this editorial board.

77. "January 4, 1888," in Walnut Street Baptist Church, Minutes, 154.

78. Walker, "Walnut Street Music Reader," 139–40. Walker derives this impression from looking at financial expenditures related to the music ministry.

leading the choir. A children's singing class was started in 1894.[79] Again, in 1896, "the church was still wrestling with the music problem, the record telling us 'the music committee reported progress and asked further time.'"[80]

The quartet was dispensed with in 1901 due to a budget deficit. A volunteer choir was utilized in its place.[81] The use of the organ in congregational singing continued steadily since the first one was installed in the original building when it was built. The organist was also the music director during most of Eaton's tenure. Eaton writes of the choir's function at the new building dedication in 1902: "That choir, directed by Brother Fillison Speiden [organist], won high praise as it participated in a week's celebration initiating the new church home."[82]

Robert Walker explains in his study of music at Walnut Street: "There were several recorded instances where singing classes were given permission to use the church, and also on occasion the church sponsored classes in music." He concludes, "During the period the church was located at Fourth and Walnut Streets, interest in music and music programs seems to have continually grown." After the move to Third and Catherine during Eaton's tenure, "The musical life of the church seems to have been very active during the early years at the new location."[83] This may have been due to the strong emphasis Eaton himself placed upon singing. In some notes he recorded on singing hymns, he outlines his view that "Christianity [is] a religion of song." First, he describes his interpretation of Colossians 3:16: Psalms are "musical accompanied"; hymns are "simple praise to God"; and spiritual songs are "religious aspirations [and] emotions." He also includes five thoughts regarding singing in worship: "Church music should be (1) Good music—give God the best; (2) real praise to God, not [a] concert to man; (3) spirited, yet dignified and reverential; (4) expression of Christian emotion [and] experience; [and] (5) all should sing."[84] In a sermon based on

79. Eaton et al., *History of Walnut Street*, 43–44.

80. Eaton et al., *History of Walnut Street*, 46.

81. "June 8, 1902," in Walnut Street Baptist Church, *Minutes*, 478. The motion was to dispense with the quartette until the church moved into the new building. The church vacillated between a paid choir and a volunteer choir. Immediately after moving into the new building a "first class choir had been secured." The choir being "on hand each Sunday," the congregation was encouraged to "pass judgment themselves" (491).

82. Eaton et al., *History of Walnut Street*, 57.

83. Walker, "Walnut Street Music Reader," 140.

84. Eaton, "Some Hymns." Eaton also sketches out the background of the following hymns and hymn writers in these notes: Henry Francis Lyte's "Abide with Me," Ray Palmer's "My Faith Looks Up to Thee," William Cowper's "There is a Fountain," Augustus Toplady's "Rock of Ages," Charles Wesley's "Jesus, Lover of My Soul," and George Keith's "How Firm a Foundation." Each is listed with its hymn number as found in *The*

Colossians 3:16 he writes, "Singing must be spirited, not in such haste—as if [to] race to [the] end—not so slow as to be somber and heavy." He adds his pervasive evangelistic emphasis here as well. "Congregational singing reaches [the] unconverted. This is [a] great power in Spurgeon's ch[urch]." As above, he prioritizes the need for congregational participation in singing as well. "Each of us [is] responsible to see that church music [is] as good as possible—not [a] concert—but praise."[85]

As with Baptist churches elsewhere, preaching was the main element of worship. Eaton's earlier sermons were outlines written by hand and generally consisted of the main points and some shorthand notes. His later sermons were seemingly fully scripted by hand, and even later typed. It is likely that he added to these notes extemporaneously, but his later sermons were far more scripted than his earlier notes represent. These later sermons were essentially word for word transcripts from which he preached. It is unclear why he became more thorough in his later preaching preparation. Perhaps this is due to his age, or a mature desire to be better prepared, as he was nearing his sixties by this time. The form is generally based upon a single verse or short passage. It appears to be a form of topical exposition, drawing from the context of the passage, though not full expository preaching.[86] It was not using Scripture as a motto, as Eaton demeaned in his paper before the Baptist World Congress, but seeking to preach a topic from a verse in context and elaborating upon that topic from illustrations and examples. Eaton's preaching was described as "strong evangelistic preaching" and this set a standard for preaching that Walnut Street would maintain.[87]

Summary

The order of the funeral service held for T. T. Eaton in 1907 is given in helpful detail. It was opened with one of his favorite hymns, "How Firm a Foundation." This was followed by Scripture reading, prayer, resolutions, and eulogies. The main sermon followed and then two hymns were read ("My Faith Looks Up to Thee" and "Jesus Lover of My Soul") before the

---

Baptist Hymnal, for Use in Church and Home (1883).

85. Eaton, *Colossians 3:16*, n.p. Eaton preached this message several times in various places, but twice at Walnut Street—November 1890 and October 1899. The bulk of the sermon is filled with illustrations of how singing has been used in history and the impact of hymns on the church.

86. Timothy S. Warren defines topical exposition as: "Preaching . . . that is centered in a biblical text that is authoritative . . . and focus[ed] on relevance for particular listeners" (Warren, "Can Topical Preaching also be Expository?" 419).

87. Pratt, "Community of Ministers," 69.

benediction.[88] The same core sequence of elements of hymn, Scripture reading, prayer and sermon are found in the building dedication services of November 16, 1902. From these can be derived the likely form of a Sunday morning worship service in 1902, as shown in figure 11.[89]

The general Baptist worship pattern of Scripture reading, prayer, and sermon interspersed with hymns is very clear here. Though each service has some unique qualities (the use of a choir, solo, or male chorus; the order of some elements; the presence of an offering or baptism), they each followed a similar contour, but apparently never a precise liturgy.

Organ Prelude

Choir (at times) or Opening Hymn

Doxology (if not before the choir/opening hymn)

Invocation

Hymn

Scripture Reading

Prayer

Choir (when not at the beginning)

Hymn

Sermon

Offering

Prayer

Solo or Quartet

Hymn

Baptism (usually practiced in the evening)

Benediction

Figure 11. Potential order of worship at Walnut Street Baptist Church, Louisville, Kentucky (1902)

What is more instructive are the titles of these elements from the building dedication services, informing the contour of theme and worship

88. Eaton et al., *History of Walnut Street*, 64. The practice of reading hymns rather than singing them was also a part of the building dedication services in 1902 (59). These hymns were certainly also among Eaton's favorites as each of these appear in his notes on hymns referenced above.

89. This is based upon a synthesis of the three building dedication services held on November 16, 1902, for Walnut Street's new house of worship ("Dedication," *Western Recorder*, November 20, 1902).

dialogue. All three services begin with the Doxology either first or second, and end with a spoken benediction. Variously a hymn ("Hark, Hark my Soul"), an invocation, or the choir ("Oh Come Let Us Worship") provide the other opening service element facilitating the theme of gathering for worship. Scripture Reading and another hymn ("How Firm a Foundation" or "I Love to Tell the Story") typically follow. The Scripture reading is related to the sermon text, but not the same as the sermon text. Prayer consistently follows these opening elements. This prayer is followed by music in the form of a hymn ("Glorious Things of Thee are Spoken"), a male chorus ("Lead Kindly Light") or the choir ("The Day is Past and Over" followed by the hymn "There is a Fountain"). The sermon is then presented and a hymn of response ("Coronation," "O, Safe to the Rock," or "My Faith Looks Up to Thee") provides the final congregational response to the message. Every service is closed with a spoken benediction to send the church out.

What seems to be clear is that the initial worship elements consistently seek to point the believer to God in worship and allow the congregation to respond to his presence (e.g., revelation and response). The sermon is always towards the end of the service, in typical Baptist form, and emphasized as the main element of worship. This part of the service contains the most evident evangelistic themes. A song of response regularly follows the theme of the sermon (e.g., exhortation and response). The gospel theme is prevalent throughout various service elements (e.g., mediation and response). It is most often emphasized at the end of the sermon but is also present elsewhere in the service. In many ways, the gospel becomes the overarching theme from beginning to end. The interspersed hymns give the congregation the opportunity to respond to other worship elements such as the Scripture reading, prayer, and sermon. The gospel theme seems to be emphasized more towards the unsaved at the end of the meeting, as do the other nineteenth-century churches in this study. However, the gospel theme is still the predominant theme throughout. Response to the worship elements is very important at Walnut Street as Eaton was very opposed to the concept of worship becoming a concert for the people. He wanted their engagement and participation throughout the service. In doing so, he intended they engage and participate with the gospel throughout the service.

9

Sojourn Community Church, Louisville, Kentucky (2000–2010)

Introduction

IT HAS BEEN REFERRED to as "the reluctant megachurch."[1] The founding group's intention was never to be large, as exemplified by their house church start. Mega-churches represented the epitome of what they were trying to escape. Many of them having grown up in the church, convened with a radical desire for real, intimate, and authentic church fellowship that drove them to try something they felt had to be new. While they ultimately discovered that it was not new at all, it was at least new to them. In September 2000, sixty people gathered for the first public service of Sojourn Community Church in Louisville, Kentucky. The age range of attendees was predominantly between eighteen and twenty-five. Daniel Montgomery and Mike Cosper gathered with this small group of eager clerks, waiters, and baristas who were aspiring for something unique. The result is a church the size of what they were attempting to avoid, but a practice of which has become reflective of their maturing zeal for an authentic intersection of the gospel and this life.

---

1. Smith, "Sojourn Community Church."

A Brief History

Montgomery was a twenty-five-year-old recent graduate of the Southern Baptist Theological Seminary when he contemplated his next step. He wanted to plant a church in an older neighborhood of the city. Cosper, who was nineteen years old at the time, describes himself as a "serious Christian" and musician with dreams of rock stardom. He had been leading a "small group of wandering Christians in a Louisville apartment" when a friend connected them with Montgomery. The connection was historic as the two like-minded pastors forged a gospel-centered partnership. Cosper writes: "We were all feeling disenfranchised from our home churches and were praying about what God would have us do next."[2] "We were against 'The Man,'" Montgomery is quoted as saying. "Most of our visions of 'large' were churches that were primarily driven by attendance, building, cash." They believed they might grow to one hundred and fifty members—two hundred and fifty tops—"then subdivide, starting new churches elsewhere."[3]

Montgomery became the pastor and Cosper was asked to serve as the coordinator of Sojourn's worship ministry. The church grew fast and while they did launch new campuses around Louisville and church plants across the country, they had to keep making more room for new people or turn them away. By their tenth anniversary in 2010, the three campuses of the church comprised a total of 2,400 worshipers gathering each weekend for corporate worship.[4] The interest in the church, especially among the young adults around Louisville, was explosive. The Sojourn way of doing church was certainly new to many as rooms began to fill and services had to be added in order to accommodate the burgeoning desire for this new approach to worship. Among the unique aspects of Sojourn Church were "conservative theology, high-octane worship music, casual dress, and [an] embrace of the arts and a strong emphasis on community service—reflected in its use of Louisville's fleur-de-lis symbol in its own logo." They also practiced church discipline.[5] Louisville really had not seen such a mixture among its churches and the distinct combination quickly made Sojourn one of the largest Baptist churches in Kentucky.

---

2. Cosper, *Rhythms of Grace*, 15.

3. Smith, "Sojourn Community Church."

4. Smith, "Sojourn Community Church." A fourth campus was added in New Albany, Indiana in 2011.

5. Smith, "Sojourn Community Church."

Theology in Practice

Mike Cosper's book, *Rhythms of Grace*, is his own personal treatise of the role that the gospel should play in worship design and practice. He writes: "In the churches where I'd grown up, the gospel was often treated as peripheral—the gateway to Christianity, but not central to ordinary Christian life." He continues, "If the gospel is supposed to be central to the Christian life, then we should craft our worship services in such a way that they rehearse that story. Every week, we should gather and remember that God is holy, we are sinners, and Jesus saves us from our sins."[6] This is accomplished through Scripture reading, songs, sermon and celebrating the Lord's Supper each week. He summarizes what he characterizes as "worship as gospel remembrance":

> If you look at almost any historical worship service or worship order, you'll find that all basically engage in the same dialogue; they all rehearse the gospel story. There is plenty of variation in the details or in the degree of clarity, but the dialogue is generally the same. God is holy. We are sinners. Jesus saves us from our sins. We gather, remember our identity-shaping story, and send one another back into the wider world, allowing that story to shape us as we go. . . . It's a rhythm of life, forming our identity as a gospel-shaped people. It's a gospel rhythm of grace, spurring us on to live in the life-giving outpouring of love and mercy from the God of the universe.[7]

Worship is about the gospel and the gospel is about worship. By rehearsing the gospel story in gathered worship, the lives of the worshipers are shaped by the gospel for life worship (e.g., scattered). This is what Cosper and Sojourn sought to do each week in worship.

Practice of Worship

Sojourn's approach to worship might be considered a form of liturgical practice, though it might be better characterized as *neo*-liturgical. There is a presence of formal liturgy in that the same thematic pattern is followed each week, and a written script informs the words of both the worship leaders and the worshipers. Extemporaneous speaking other than that from the pastor during his sermon is limited. Traditional liturgical exchanges such as the "passing of the peace" to conclude the service as well as the responsorial

6. Cosper, *Rhythms of Grace*, 18.
7. Cosper, *Rhythms of Grace*, 19.

phrase at the end of the sermon text Scripture reading—"This is the word of the Lord; thanks be to God"—are present each week.

The presence of liturgical art, lighted candles, and the practice of worshipers leaving their seats to partake of a common loaf and cup for communion, all mark the services as somewhat liturgical, if not ancient.[8] The nonliturgical—though traditionally Baptist—practice of a lengthy expository sermon is the main service element. The least liturgical or traditional aspect of the worship service is what was referred to above as "high-octane music." Each week varies as a blend of eclectic yet talented musicians form a rock band with screaming electric guitar solos one week, a bluegrass band with banjo licks the next, and a classical ensemble with a cello yet another. These are just a few of the diverse musical approaches to congregational singing in this church. There is a concerted effort to match the musical style to the cultural setting of each campus or church. Inner-city Louisville *sounds* different than the suburbs and predominantly blue collar has a slightly different musical approach than predominantly white collar.

In the variety of musical styles incorporated in worship, the prototypical Sojourn worship song is a historic hymn text, often from an eighteenth-century English hymn writer, married to a musical style setting that some traditional Baptists might see as misappropriated. To a congregation with an average age of twenty-six, it is exactly what they were looking for in worship.[9] It is not only what their worshipers are looking for. MP3 recordings, YouTube videos, and chord chart downloads from this group of gifted musicians are highly sought after from other churches all over the country as Sojourn Music has become a facilitator of worship elsewhere. Cosper and others from his ministry are not only popular songwriters but also authors and speakers on the subject of worship, among other cultural discussions of the day.

Cosper[10] and his worship leaders met every Wednesday as the liturgy planning team to write the liturgy for that Sunday's service. Each campus follows the same liturgy, though there are some adjustments made relevant to each location. Having received the sermon text and theme from the

8. Each worshiper has the following words spoken to them when they reach those serving the Table elements: "The body of Christ broken for you [bread]"; and "The blood of Christ shed for you [cup]." Worshipers may also dip the broken piece of bread in a goblet of juice or wine, as their conscience permits.

9. Daniel Montgomery announced at the tenth anniversary service on September 19, 2010, that the church's average age at that time was twenty-six. When the church began in September 2000, it was twenty-four. The writer was in attendance that day.

10. Mike Cosper is no longer the Worship Director at Sojourn Community Church at the time of printing.

preaching pastors, the worship leaders begin crafting a liturgy that incorporates the theme of the day in the shape of the gospel form mentioned above: God is holy, we are sinners, and Jesus saves us from our sins. This is displayed through a call to worship, time of confession/lament, assurance of peace, instruction from God's word, and benediction. Songs, Scripture and other readings, prayer, preaching, communion, and giving compose the main elements of worship. Baptisms are incorporated into the Sunday morning services periodically. The typical order of worship at Sojourn is shown in figure 12.

Band Prelude

Call to Worship (Reading)

Song(s)

Prayer of Confession/Lament

Song(s)

Assurance of Peace (Reading)

Giving

Sermon

Communion

Song

Reading

Songs

Benediction (including the "Passing of the Peace")

Figure 12. Potential order of worship at Sojourn Community Church,
Louisville, Kentucky (2010)

The readings for the liturgy are compiled from Scripture and devotional/liturgical sources such as The Worship Sourcebook, The Valley of Vision, The Book of Common Prayer, The Devotions and Prayers of John Calvin, Voicing God's Psalms, and The Message.[11]

---

11. Brink and Witvliet, *Worship Sourcebook*; Bennett, *Valley of Vision*; *The Book of Common Prayer*; Calvin, *Devotions and Prayers*; Seerveld, *Voicing God's Psalms*; and Peterson, *Message*. Cosper also recommends three websites for liturgical resources: www.textweek.com, www.cardiphonia.com, and www.worship.calvin.edu.

Conclusion

Cosper explains the motive behind the significant effort he and the liturgy planning team make in order to prepare for Sunday. "It's through our liturgies that the rubber of *lex orandi, lex credendi* (so we pray, so we believe) hits the road. As we plan and order our services, discerning the content to include, we shape the beliefs and devotional lives of our church members."[12] The shape he wants their lives to be formed around is that of the gospel. Even his tripartite outline—God is holy; we are sinful; Jesus saves us from our sins—displays the first two emphases of the gospel shape of this study. Revelation and mediation are both reflected by his model. Though he does not include the instruction from God's word as a third aspect of gospel description, it is a part of the liturgy of the service. Revelation and response; mediation and response; and exhortation and response essentially reflect the contours of the Sojourn worship service.

12. Cosper, *Rhythms of Grace*, 118.

10

Conclusion

The Gospel as Liturgical Hermeneutic

THE PRIMARY QUESTION UNDER consideration in this book has been, "How did Baptists in North America take the gospel initially brought from England and *re-present* it in worship for successive generations of Baptist worship?" The priority of worship as a re-presentation of the gospel was informed by the work of Bryan Chapell, Christopher Ellis, and Matthew Ward in chapter 1. Utilizing the tools of a field known as Liturgical Theology, a gospel-centered thread has been identified in Baptist worship history. The representative historic churches chosen for this study demonstrate how the gospel has been re-presented in worship in a variety of settings for more than three and a half centuries. In coalescing these streams of thought, a picture of the gospel's role in worship becomes much clearer and more compelling.

According to Chapell, the gospel controls its forms.[1] This means when the gospel is kept in theological practice, it will of necessity imprint itself upon the liturgy of the worship service, even in nonliturgical traditions. When the gospel is lost in theological practice, it is also lost in the practice of worship.[2] It has not been within the scope of this study to identify the specific causes of the loss of the gospel in the worship of a particular church or movement, but in general, theological errors lie at the crumbling

---

1. Chapell, *Christ-Centered Worship*, 85.

2. Each church considered in this study has been represented in three sections: (1) a brief history, (2) theology in practice, and (3) practice of worship, to show this relationship.

foundation of gospel-less worship. When the gospel is regained in faith and belief, worship reflects this recovery, and subsequently reinforces it. The model proposed in this study to identify the gospel's form in Baptist worship is threefold: (1) revelation and response, (2) mediation and response, and (3) exhortation and response. These elements in worship's dialogue between God and man in a corporate worship service help reflect the presence and practice of the gospel. The intentional highlighting of these dialogical movements in worship reinforces the power of the gospel. This effect in corporate worship serves the people of God by instilling in them the "rhythms of grace" (according to Mike Cosper) for a lifestyle of worship.[3] It also provides the opportunity for sinners to be converted as a result of the worship service.

The earliest Baptists came from England to North America with pure and authentic worship as a priority. Matthew Ward has argued that this was their primary distinctive in England. Even if one does not fully embrace all of his conclusions regarding the English Baptists, a compelling argument can be made that it was at least *a* priority. The first Baptists in Providence and Philadelphia had the opportunity to establish worship practices unhindered by persecution or coercion. The Baptists in Boston were persecuted and had less freedom, but still managed to break away over the conviction of the worship ordinances of believer's baptism and communion for baptized believers only. With Boston under persecution and Providence unstable during its early decades, Philadelphia (e.g., Pennepek) served as the starting point for this survey. The gospel content was clear there, and as much as could be reconstructed regarding worship order also reflected a gospel *ordo*. One of the best Baptist examples of gospel-shaped worship in this survey is found among these earliest Baptists in the Philadelphia Association.

Charleston has become famous as the mother of southern Baptists and the Charleston tradition of worship. While accurately reconstructing a fully orbed depiction of the worship order at Charleston is problematic, the gospel content is clear in the preaching of Oliver Hart and the most likely hymn choices of the time period. Hart was trained in the Philadelphia Association, which makes it likely that this mid-Atlantic influence was also reflected in the *ordo* of what became known as the Charleston order. Morgan Edwards provided a depiction of worship in *The Customs of Primitive Churches* (1768) that may serve as the best aid to recovering the Charleston worship service, though it is a depiction of a Philadelphia Association church.[4] Richard Furman's pastorate is generally regarded as the high point

---

3. See also, Cosper, *Rhythms of Grace.*

4. Edwards, *Customs of Primitive Churches.*

of the Charleston worship tradition, but Oliver Hart is its founder, and he learned worship in Philadelphia. Charleston also serves as a strong example of gospel-shaped worship, at least as much as can be reconstructed.

Sandy Creek is the most difficult church service to reconstruct. Very little written material exists to examine the tradition that some have considered the counterpart to the Charleston tradition. The extreme evangelistic emphasis and semi-charismatic practices of worship are the greatest distinctions in this camp meeting tradition. The gospel theme for evangelism is clear in this practice, even if a worship order or sermon cannot be recovered. What remains unclear is what type of worship order existed. Broadly, the services seemed to contain three main sections: (1) preliminaries of singing, praying and exhortations; (2) sermon(s); and (3) evangelistic response to the gospel. It is not a stretch to believe that some form of the threefold model presented in this study was present. The opening portion of worship certainly intended to reveal the greatness of God, if in the manner of 1 Corinthians 14:24–25.[5] The subject of the atonement of Christ was the main message and a call for a response to the gospel was the main reason for gathering. However, the radical spontaneity of the services, and the lack of historical accounts and written records, makes such a conclusion indefinite, if not irresponsible.

Three churches have been presented in this study as examples of Charleston and Sandy Creek worship tradition synthesis of the nineteenth century. None of these fits either tradition exclusively, and all three reflect aspects of both. The synthesis of these traditions is quick and thorough. Siloam, Jarvis Street, and Walnut Street Baptist Churches are each marked by certain worship decorum as downtown churches in the Charleston tradition, but also a zeal for evangelism and revival that seems more rooted in the Sandy Creek tradition. DeVotie, pastor at Siloam, was accused by Basil Manly of having "thrown himself into revivalism."[6] B. D. Thomas considered the Jarvis Street church "a failure unless souls are born in her."[7] T. T. Eaton's preaching at Walnut Street was considered "strongly evangelistic" and set a standard for his successors.[8] All were intentional about the gospel and congregational participation in worship. Each of these churches represent a facet of the nineteenth-century worship practice of gospel content and form that is exemplary among Baptists. Though the late

5. "But if all prophesy, and an unbeliever or outsider enters, he is convicted by all, he is called to account by all, the secrets of his heart are disclosed, and so, falling on his face, he will worship God and declare that God is really among you" (1 Cor 14:24–25).

6. Holcombe, *Baptists in Alabama*, 59.

7. Thomas, "The Glory of the Church," in *Sermons Preached*, 81–82.

8. Pratt, "Community of Ministers," 69.

nineteenth and twentieth centuries gave way to a wide variety of practices, these three churches represent some of the best examples of gospel-shaped worship. They exemplify a Baptist trend in worship that seems prevalent at mid-century, but less so as the end of the century neared. This practice of gospel-shaped worship for the believer, with zeal for the conversion of the unbeliever, is typical of the best examples of Baptist worship that ushered in the twentieth century.

The worship practice at Sojourn Community Church is seemingly unique retrospectively, but representative of a current trend. This *neo-liturgical* approach to worship in a free church tradition is becoming widespread in the twenty-first century. Many churches are *returning* to a liturgy that their tradition never possessed. Yet this reclaiming of a sense of *ordo* from the past is often accompanied by elements of worship that are very contemporary in another sense. The merging of Prayer Book readings, lengthy expository sermons, and weekly communion, with electronic instruments and contemporary musical styles is refreshingly relevant to a young generation; as is evidenced by the remarkably young average age of their congregations. Yet Cosper makes it very clear that the motive behind their worship planning is to allow the gospel to resonate in their content and form.

Baptist Worship and the Gospel

What Bryan Chapell refers to as "letting the gospel shape our practice," has been characterized in a variety of different ways, but all point to worship's function as a *re-presentation* of the gospel in worship.[9] Constance Cherry writes, "The Christ Event now drives worship, for the object of our worship is Jesus Christ, the content of our worship is the story of Jesus Christ, the word proclaimed in Christian worship is the gospel of our Lord and Savior, Jesus Christ."[10] Bruce Leafblad writes,

> An evangelical church celebrates and enacts the Evangel—the gospel of Jesus Christ—in its worship. Worship centers in Christ. The good news of redemption in Christ brings rejoicing, thanksgiving, and celebration in the "psalms, hymns, and spiritual songs" of worship. Sermons declare the manifold blessings and glories of salvation. The Lord's Table reenacts and proclaims the heart of the good news.[11]

9. Chapell, *Christ-Centered Worship*, 85.
10. Cherry, *Worship Architect*, 8.
11. Leafblad, "Evangelical Worship," 93.

Matthew Ward refers to this practice among Baptists as "us[ing] the gospel as the liturgical hermeneutic."[12] This has been reflected in the story of Baptist worship because it has been the intention of Baptists to advance the gospel and allow it to shape their practice.

Christopher Ellis' study of Baptists in England concluded that the confession "Jesus is Lord" is the "presiding conviction" in Baptist worship. In addition, he identified the priorities of Baptist worship as being—attention to Scripture, devotion and openness to the Spirit, concern for the community, and an eschatological orientation in worship. Finally, he considers the central actions of worship as those of praying, preaching, singing, and the ordinances.[13] Some very similar statements can be made resulting from this study regarding the nature of Baptist worship in North America, as those who came from these English beginnings.

The central act of worship among Baptists in North America is preaching. Other consistent elements of worship include praying, singing, Scripture reading, and later giving (which does not become a consistent element of the worship *ordo* until the mid to late nineteenth century). Baptists celebrate the Lord's Supper intermittently (e.g., once a month or less frequently) and baptism as needed. Choral participation has been quite common among Baptist churches since the mid-nineteenth century and, to a lesser degree, the use of a quartet or soloists during the same time period. Franklin Segler and Randall Bradley have characterized Baptist worship in the following manner: "The general pattern of Baptist worship in England has remained about the same to the present, consisting of Scripture reading, prayers and sermons, interspersed with hymns by the congregation and the choir."[14] This is an apt description of Baptist worship in North America as well. The more that the Baptist worship service evolved in the time period in view in this study, it did so by adding more elements of worship interspersed with more congregational and choral singing. The late nineteenth- and early twentieth-century orders of worship could have five or more singing elements in the service with the other elements of Scripture reading and prayer filling in between them. This highlights a priority in Baptist worship in America—that of congregational participation, but more importantly—response.

The interspersion of singing among these elements might have been done just to keep the congregation engaged periodically in its basic form. However, it seems more likely that this was done to give the congregation

12. Ward, *Pure Worship*, 143.
13. Ellis, *Gathering*, 74, 99, 229–32.
14. Segler and Bradley, *Christian Worship*, 40.

the opportunity to respond to the preceding element. This facilitates the dialogue of worship as God's voice in the dialogue is heard through the call to worship or Scripture reading, to which the people respond in song. Another manner in which this is done is to have the choir or a prayer represent an aspect of the worship dialogue, to which the congregation could then also respond through singing. The most obvious aspect of this potential is the very common practice of having the congregation respond to the sermon through song. At times, and in some places, this took on the feel of an altar call, especially entering the twentieth century. However, whether it consisted of the words of an unsaved person responding to the gospel, or the saved person responding to the teaching of the word of God, most pastors and worship leaders worked hard to have the right words to put in the people's mouths at that strategic moment. These were the words that the worshiper carried into the rest of the week to inform a lifestyle of worship.

Revelation, mediation, and exhortation are representative of God's part of the dialogue in Baptist worship. Opening worship elements such as the call to worship, opening hymns and anthems, and opening prayers almost always represent this aspect of entering into corporate worship. The gathering nature of opening a worship service reflects the nature of a holy God who has revealed himself to his people and called them to worship through Jesus Christ. Baptist worship is clearly contoured to aim toward the preaching of God's word as the main point of exhortation. While other elements of Scripture reading, congregational and choral singing, and written liturgies often include instruction from God's word, it is the sermon that worshipers expect to be the message from God, through the preacher, to speak to their lives. As has been mentioned above, the gospel content of mediation can take many forms and be placed in various places in the service. Elements throughout the service can reflect this part of the gospel shape, but many times the middle section of a service draws people to these aspects of the gospel. This seems especially true of the eighteenth-century examples at Philadelphia and Charleston. The end of the service also often points people to this aspect of the gospel, especially if there is a gospel presentation to unbelievers, or the Lord's Supper is celebrated. This latter point seems to be true of all of the examples in this study.

The emphasis of a proposed model for Baptist worship is not that Baptist worship services should rigidly follow this order. Baptist worship will not rigidly follow any order. The point of the model is to show that these aspects of the gospel shape the service. God reveals himself and worshipers respond through worship's dialogue. Jesus is identified as the Savior by whom worship is made possible and worshipers (and unbelievers) respond through the words of worship. The Spirit instructs in the ways of following

Christ through the word of God and worshipers (and unbelievers) respond verbally in song, prayer, and life. There is a coalescing and comingling of these themes throughout the service, but where the gospel is embraced, its identifying markers are clearly identifiable in worship. The variety of examples represents the myriad of potential approaches to gospel-shaped worship. This is reflective of a multifaceted, yet consistent, gospel shape.

Another aspect of this study has been the demonstration of worship liturgy among a free church tradition. The concept of liturgy is somewhat foreign to many Baptist worship practitioners. The last thing Baptists want to be is conformed to formal liturgy. Yet, for all of this, Baptists are famous for their ruts of tradition. It is the nature of the church, and of people in general, to carve out patterns of routine and practice that seem to work best. This is not simply a drive for efficiency, though that has impacted worship in both positive and negative ways. In tradition's more beneficent examples, it has been the result of worship leaders seeking to lead people through a contour of worship that highlights what is most important and eliminates what is not. The desire to keep Christ and his gospel central and the word of God foundational has persistently driven Baptist worship. These are the patterns that have historically shaped the Baptist worship service and therefore the Baptist worshiper.

Three questions were introduced in chapter 1 as necessary criteria for evaluating gospel-centered worship in this study of North American Baptists: (1) Is Christ central to worship? (2) Is gospel content present in worship? (3) Is the gospel faithfully "re-presented" in worship? The evidence presented above is conclusive in the affirmative to each of these criteria. As a result, a gospel-shaped approach to Baptist worship has formed gospel-shaped people who have been being conformed to the image of Christ—the one that they have held in view.

Characteristics of Baptist Worship in North America

Baptist worship in North America can be broadly characterized by five worship characteristics. First, the preaching of God's word is the main worship element and is often perceived as the main reason for gathering for worship. The sermon often takes up to half, and in some cases even more, of the total service time. The aim of the first portion of the service is to point toward the sermon as the climax of worship. This has led to the unfortunate habit of some referring to Baptist worship as having two services: the song service and the preaching service. It is a much more appropriate perspective to see all worship elements as part of the same worship service, as the examples in this study reflect. Proper response to the sermon was one of the earliest concerns of Baptists in North America. This emphasizes the importance of the word of God and the pulpit in Baptist worship within the context of the service as a whole.

Second, singing is an important part of worship to Baptists and it is often interspersed throughout the service as the primary means by which the congregation responds in worship's dialogue. God's portion of the dialogue is represented by the various means of employing his word (e.g., Scripture reading, songs, readings, etc.) and worshipers are given the opportunity to respond through song to what God *says* in worship. Even unbelievers have hymns written for them to verbalize their response of faith to the gospel. The human response to God and his gospel is an important part of Baptist worship and singing is used throughout the service as the vehicle to facilitate that response. This is how the correct words are put in the worshipers' mouths and this is as much a part of the conforming process as the *ordo*.[15]

Third, while worship is primarily for believers, the presence of unbelievers has always been a consideration in worship planning and practice in North America. Initially it prevented some congregations from singing out of a fear of "conjoined" worship. However, this concern quickly gave way to the reality that unbelievers were always going to be present in Baptist worship and the worship commands of Scripture included singing. The appeal to unbelievers to respond to the gospel is a prevalent theme in Baptist worship history beginning in the nineteenth century. A deliberate altar call is an emerging element of worship as Baptist worship enters the twentieth century. It seems likely the ethos for this stems from the influence of the great awakenings, Sandy Creek, and camp meetings. Jarvis Street almost certainly employed one during Thomas' pastorate and Walnut Street probably did as well. However, gospel presentation in a manner that unbelievers could hear and respond to has been a consistent aspect of Baptist worship since the earliest days in Philadelphia. This is reflected in their holding separate services for communion that were for only for church members (e.g., believers). Even those churches that did not include a formal altar call presented the gospel in a manner that the unbeliever could hear and understand, and by responding, he or she could potentially be converted.

---

15. For the importance of these words in worship see Rienstra and Rienstra, *Worship Words*. Rienstra and Rienstra write: "The words we hear, sing, and speak in worship help form: our images of God; our understanding of what the church is and does; our understanding of human brokenness and healing; our sense of purpose as individuals and as a church; our religious affections: awe, humility, delight, contrition, hope; our vision of wholeness for ourselves and all creation; and our practices of engaging with God, with each other, and with the world" (28).

A fourth observation has to do with giving in Baptist worship. This is marked by a change in practice from a pew rent system that was a common practice in the eighteenth century, to beneficent giving which became predominant in the nineteenth century (see Jarvis Street Baptist Church above). In some churches this was done with collection boxes at the rear of the meeting place. However, it became increasingly more common to have a worship element in the service order for the purpose of collecting the tithes and offerings as a congregation. This was often associated with a musical component known as the offering or offertory. This movement away from the pew rent system is a gospel change among Baptist churches. The pew rent system led to seating by socioeconomic status. Those who could afford it sat in the best seats, which was often also nearest to the source of heat in the winter. Those who could not sat farther away or did not have designated pews. Visitors could only sit in those pews designated as "free" pews for such a purpose. This created a class system in the church, which was supposed to be devoid of such segregating elements (see Gal 3:28). The system of beneficent giving not only obscured some of the pretense and favoritism associated with the pew rent system (see Jas 2:1–13), it also emphasized the gospel truth that all were equally needy for Christ and his word. It declared every seat in the sanctuary "free."

Finally, the fifth observation is the main characteristic of Baptist worship and of this study. The theme of the gospel has been prevalent in Baptist worship since the first Baptists arrived on this continent. The gospel they brought from England was the gospel they intended to pass on to subsequent generations through their worship. When Baptists pressed on to frontier areas, they immediately employed worship elements that could convey the gospel as clearly as possible. It has been the *main thing* in Baptist worship since the churches in Providence, Boston, and Philadelphia held their first worship services. In the words of B. D. Thomas, pastor at Jarvis Street Baptist Church, to come to worship is to "sit under the gospel's joyful sound." This is the main theme of Baptist worship in North America. If North American Baptists have a "presiding conviction" to parallel that of Christopher Ellis' study of Baptists in England, it is that attending corporate worship is "sitting under the gospel's joyful sound."

In other words, it has been the Baptist conviction in worship that it is by the gospel that sinners are called out of darkness to be joined to the body of Christ. It is therefore by the gospel that the church can gather for worship. This makes the worship gathering both a celebration and expression of the gospel. It is in the ordinances and elements of worship that the gospel is rehearsed, and its effects of grace applied and employed. It is this paradigm of worship that the Baptists brought to North America and one of the primary reasons that they came. It is the conviction that they, and subsequent generations, have maintained. Baptist worship is intentionally, and unintentionally (by the Spirit's power), a *re-presentation* of the gospel.

Appendix 1

The Word of God and the Regulative Principle among Baptists

Introduction

THE REFORMATION WAS FUNDAMENTALLY about reclaiming the authority of the Word of God, including its authority in worship. In the English Reformers' view, the "imaginations and devices of men" (e.g., tradition and mysticism in the liturgical forms of worship) had obscured the gospel and therefore blurred the worshipers' view of the gospel and the glory of God. This historical conviction has often been represented by the Westminster Divine's (1643–1649) written conviction in the *Westminster Confession of Faith* (1647): "The acceptable way of worshipping the true God is instituted by Himself, and so limited by His own revealed will."[1] As will be demonstrated below, this was no less a concern for the Baptists and in some ways, their concern was greater. Only the word of God could fix the liturgical confusion represented by the Roman Catholic and Anglican practices of the seventeenth century. In their quest to recover the worship of the primitive church (e.g., New Testament church), the Puritans looked to Calvin.

In John Calvin's opening discussion of the Word of God in the *Institutio*, Calvin compares the Bible to spectacles: "Just as old or bleary-eyed men and those with weak vision, if you thrust before them a most beautiful volume, even if they recognize it to be some sort of writing, yet can scarcely construe two words, but with the aid of spectacles will begin to read distinctly; so Scripture, gathering up the otherwise confused knowledge of

1. "Westminster Confession of Faith," in Schaff, *Evangelical Protestant Creeds*, 646.

God in our minds, having dispersed our dullness, clearly show us the true God."[2] Commenting on this section Matthew Boulton writes, "Thus Calvin casts Christian Scripture as a clarifying instrument that 'clearly shows us the true God.'"[3] It is from the school of Scripture (e.g., special revelation) that believers learn to see God in the school of creation (e.g., general revelation). Boulton explains, "To characterize the 'special gift' of Scripture, Calvin uses terms strikingly reminiscent of his portrait of creation. He calls Scripture, 'The very school of God's children,' for example, and 'a mirror in which [God's] living likeness glows' (1.6.4; 1.14.1). That is, describing the Bible, Calvin recapitulates key terms he uses to describe the universe: 'school,' 'mirror,' 'living likeness' of God, and so on. In this way, Calvin portrays Scripture as a school within a school, a likeness within a likeness, a reflection within a reflection."[4]

Due to Scripture's function as "spectacles" to see God in everything, its role in the liturgy of worship is critical to worship's function in the liturgy of life. In his *Commentaries on Genesis*, Calvin asserts that Scripture for worshipers functions as a "herald who excites [their] attention, in order that [they] may perceive [themselves] to be placed in this scene" both "for the purpose of beholding the glory of God" and "to enjoy all the riches which are here exhibited."[5] Boulton highlights Calvin's intention here:

> It is as if a sanctuary functions as a kind of studio and stage in the midst of creation, a place where what should be audible anywhere ("all the voices of God") is amplified, and what should be happening everywhere (humanity's praise of God) is manifest, by the Spirit's gift. Again, Calvin's case conjures up the image of a microcosm within a macrocosm, this time a temple within a temple: God's voice perpetually fills the temple of creation but

2. Calvin, *Institutes of the Christian Religion*, 1.14.1.

3. Boulton, *Life in God*, 96. Boulton continues with a section regarding Calvin's view of the necessity of the Spirit in coordination with the Word in this effort. "Merely reading the Bible will not do. The Spirit must be present with and in the reader, 'sealing' Scripture with an 'inward testimony' so that 'it seriously affects us' (1.7.5)." And later, "Thus in Calvin's view, the Holy Spirit is both the 'Author' of Scripture and the necessary companion in our interpretation of it, illuminating our minds and persuading our hearts 'both to read and to hearken' to biblical texts 'as if there the living words of God were heard' (1.9.2; 1.7.1)" (98). Finally, "Indeed, for Calvin, Scripture and Spirit are so intimately joined 'by a kind of mutual bond' that they are, from the human point of view, inseparably linked: 'the Word is the instrument by which the Lord dispenses the illumination of his Spirit to believers' (1.9.3). Accordingly, if the Bible is God's 'special gift' to the church for dispersing human dullness and oblivion, the paideutic program Calvin has in mind here is as pneumatological as it is biblical (1.6.1)" (99).

4. Boulton, *Life in God*, 100.

5. Calvin, *Commentaries on Genesis*, 62.

goes unrecognized and therefore unheeded by human beings; but in the microcosmic temples of the church, God's Word is amplified and clarified. That is, in the smaller sanctuaries God's voice may be discerned more clearly in the "school" and "mirror" of Scripture, the sermons of well-trained preachers, the psalm singing of the whole congregation, and so on. But the smaller sanctuary should by no means eclipse the cosmic one; rather, it should point toward it, disclose it, and train disciples so that their whole lives may be lived out as liturgies writ large.[6]

This is *why* Scripture's use in worship is so important to Calvin.[7] The question remains as to *how* this importance should be demonstrated in worship. There are two aspects to this question. One regards Scripture as worship's content, which shall be saved for later. The other is Scripture as worship's regulator.

Calvin and the Puritan Regulative Principle

Baptists inherited this emphasis on the regulative principle from the Puritans who in turn inherited from Calvin. In *The Necessity of Reforming the Church* Calvin wrote,

> Moreover, the rule which distinguishes between pure and vitiated worship is of universal application, in order that we may not adopt any device which seems fit to ourselves, but look to the injunctions of him who alone is entitled to prescribe. Therefore, if we would have him to approve our worship, this rule, which he

6. Boulton, *Life in God*, 101–2. "The Bible must always serve as the privileged text at the center of Christian *paideia* (1.6.1). But that formative program itself is geared toward making disciples who can contemplate not only God's word in Scripture but also God's work and life in the world. For Calvin, the Bible is not merely the church's spectacle, a special sacred site set off from ordinary things; it is also and crucially the church's 'spectacles,' a clarifying instrument for seeing ordinary things more clearly, and thereby living into the world more deeply, wisely, and realistically" (110).

7. Calvin prescribed a rigorous regimen of Scripture for the saints in Geneva. Boulton summarizes, "Twice-weekly corporate worship attendance was mandatory in Geneva, preaching services occurred daily, and more intensive lectures on Scripture were often held in the afternoons. Reformed sermons were lengthy expositions of biblical texts, but Calvin's prayers, too, including the daily prayer cycle and Day of Prayer service on Wednesdays, were drenched in scriptural language and images. Likewise, morning and evening domestic worship properly included passages of Scripture read aloud, and psalm singing dominated Reformed devotion both at home and at church—to say nothing of the songs laborers may have sung or hummed 'in the houses and in the fields,' as Calvin hoped. Thus in the *Institutio*, Calvin can write in passing, 'And in our daily reading of Scripture . . . (3.2.4)" (Boulton, *Life in God*, 110–11).

everywhere enforces with the utmost strictness, must be carefully observed. For there is a twofold reason why the Lord, in condemning and prohibiting all fictitious worship, requires us to give obedience only to his own voice. First, it tends greatly to establish his authority that we do not follow our own pleasure, but depend entirely on his sovereignty; and, secondly, such is our folly, that when we are left at liberty, all we are able to do is to go astray. And then when once we have turned aside from the right path, there is no end to our wanderings, until we get buried under a multitude of superstitions. Justly, therefore, does the Lord, in order to assert his full right of dominion, strictly enjoin what he wishes us to do, and at once reject all human devices which are at variance with his command. Justly, too, does he, in express terms, define our limits, that we may not, by fabricating perverse modes of worship, provoke his anger against us.[8]

This manner of regulating worship by only permitting what Scripture allows for worship (e.g., the regulative principle) is by many set against Martin Luther's (1483–1546) view that while the Bible contained the "articles of belief necessary for salvation," in matters of worship and church government "the Bible is not to be treated as a new Leviticus."[9] This led to the view ascribed to Luther by which only that which was forbidden by Scripture should be excluded from worship (e.g., the normative principle). The Anglican Church essentially agreed with Luther in the matter while the Puritans embraced Calvin. Horton Davies writes, "The Puritan said that if the Bible is binding on one issue, it is binding on all issues."[10] While many Puritans attempted to reform worship and church government from within the Church of England, others eventually separated from the established church in an attempt to establish "a more biblical way of worship in their secret conventicles," (e.g., Separatists).[11] The basis of both groups was ref-

---

8. Calvin, "Necessity of Reforming the Church," 128. Elsewhere Calvin states quite clearly the priority of worship's regulation by seemingly giving it equal priority with the source of salvation—"If it be inquired, then, by what things the Christian religion has a standing existence among us, and maintains its truth, it will be found that the following two not only occupy the principal place, but comprehend under them all the other parts, and consequently the whole substance of Christianity: that is, a knowledge, *first*, of the mode in which God is duly worshipped; and *secondly*, of the source form which salvation is obtained" (126; emphasis Calvin's). See also his *Reply to Cardinal Sadoleto's Letter* (in vol. 1), and *The Adultero-German Interim Declaration of Religion with Calvin's Refutation (The True Method of Giving Peace to Christendom and of Reforming the Church)* (in vol. 3).

9. Davies, *Worship of the English Puritans*, 3.

10. Davies, *Worship of the English Puritans*, 3.

11. Davies, *Worship of the English Puritans*, 10.

ormation according to the Word of God and according to Davies, "Both parties asserted positively that only such ordinances as were warrantable by the Word of God should be tolerated in public worship."[12]

A subsequent generation of Puritans eventually codified their forefathers' view through the Westminster Assembly of Divines (1643–1649) in their adoption of the *Directory of Public Worship* (1645), *Larger Catechism* (1647), and the *Westminster Confession of Faith* (1647). Thus, according to Davies, "The Puritan tradition . . . originated from the practice of the Church at Geneva under John Calvin."[13] In their *Confession of Faith*, the Westminster Divines expressed their version of Calvin's regulative principle in the section entitled "Of Religious Worship, and the Sabbath Day" (21:1):

> The light of nature showeth that there is a God, who hath lordship and sovereignty over all, is good, and doth good unto all, and is therefore to be feared, loved, praised, called upon, trusted in, and served, with all the heart, and with all the soul, and with all the might. But the acceptable way of worshipping the true God is instituted by Himself, and so limited by His own revealed will, that He may not be worshipped according to the imaginations and devices of men, or the suggestions of Satan, under any visible representation, or any other way not prescribed in the holy Scripture.[14]

More than forty years later, the London Baptist Confession of 1689, chap. 22, section 1, repeats this text from the Westminster Confession in almost verbatim fashion:

> The light of nature shews that there is a God, who hath lordship and sovereignty over all; is just, good and doth good unto all; and is therefore to be feared, loved, praised, called upon, trusted in, and served, with all the heart and all the soul, and with all

12. Davies, *Worship of the English Puritans*, 77.

13. Davies, *Worship of the English Puritans*, 111. Davies highlights the prominent role of John Knox (1514–1572) a Scottish clergyman and "Calvin's most fervent disciple" in his adaptation of the work of Calvin to the Reformation through Puritan worship, specifically through Knox's Liturgy (e.g., *The Book of Common Order* [1564]) (26, see also 30, 36, 111, and 116–18). For an additional perspective see R. J. Gore Jr., who argues, "The Puritan regulative principle of worship was an exaggeration of, and departure from, the worship practice of John Calvin" and "has been fraught with difficulties from the very beginning. . . . The Puritan regulative principle exceeded the bounds established in Scripture and imposed strictures on its adherents that were unduly narrow" (Gore, *Covenantal Worship*, 163). See also Gore, "Pursuit of Plainness."

14. "Westminster Confession of Faith," in Schaff, *Evangelical Protestant Creeds*, 646. London Baptists had expressed a similar conviction prior to this in their 1644 Confession (Lumpkin, *Baptist Confessions of Faith*, 144).

the might. But the acceptable way of worshipping the true God, is instituted by himself, and so limited by his own revealed will, that he may not be worshipped according to the imagination and devices of men, nor the suggestions of Satan, under any visible representations, or any other way not prescribed in the Holy Scriptures.[15]

The Philadelphia Confession of Faith (1742) is an almost entire adoption of the Second London Confession (1689) with the addition of two articles: chap. 23 on Singing Praises and chap. 31 on The Laying on of Hands. Chap. 22 and the recitation of the Regulative Principle from the London Confession are included word for word in the Philadelphia Confession. The addition of chap. 23 is an important statement regarding worship:

> We believe that (Acts 16:25, Eph. 5:19, Col. 3:16) singing the praises of God, is a holy ordinance of Christ, and not a part of natural religion, or a moral duty only; but that it is brought under divine institution, it being enjoined on the churches of Christ to sing psalms, hymns, and spiritual songs; and that the whole church in their public assemblies, as well as private Christians, ought to (Heb. 2:12, Jam. 5:13) sing God's praises according to the best light they have received. Moreover, it was practiced in the great representative church, by (Matt. 26:30, Matt. 14:26) our Lord Jesus Christ with His disciples, after He had instituted and celebrated the sacred ordinance of His Holy Supper, as commemorative token of redeeming love.[16]

Early Baptists in America clearly inherited and embraced some interpretation of Calvin's regulative principle, as passed to them through the Puritanical Reform of England's Baptists and their Second London Confession

15. Lumpkin, *Baptist Confessions of Faith*, 280. The first London Confession (1644) contained a briefer statement in chap. 7: "The Rule of this Knowledge, Faith, and Obedience, concerning the worship and service of God, and all other Christian duties, is not man's inventions, opinions, devices, lawes, constitutions, or traditions unwritten whatsoever, but onely the word of God contained in the Canonicall Scriptures" (Lumpkin, *Baptist Confessions of Faith*, 158). One of the signatories of the Second London Confession (1689) was Benjamin Keach (1640–1704); who was pastor at Horseleydown, Southwark, and whose son, Elias Keach (1666–1701) had pastored a Baptist Church near Philadelphia. Upon Elias' return to London to pastor the Tallow Chandler's Hall Church in London in 1692, he subsequently concurred with his father to write a series of articles that were essentially the Second London Confession with two additional articles regarding hymn singing and the laying on of hands. William Lumpkin writes, "The Keach Confession, which had only one edition in England, found its way to America, through Elias Keach's influence, and became the body of the Philadelphia Confession, the dominant early Calvinistic Baptist Confession in the New World" (240).

16. George and George, *Baptist Confessions*, 82.

of 1689. How this was interpreted and applied specifically in the churches included in this study through subsequent centuries has been discussed as part of this work on each church. However, some general understanding of the historic interpretation of this principle is possible here. This is the understanding that Baptists would have carried with them into worship in the New World.

A Baptist Perspective on the Regulative Principle

Steven R. Harmon writes, "In general, Baptists identify Scripture as the supreme earthly source of authority. Many early Baptist confessions lacked articles on the Scriptures, but they evidenced a radical Biblicism in their copious prooftexting of confessional statements with parenthetical and marginal biblical references."[17] The fundamental understanding of the regulative principle is that "the acceptable way of worshipping the true God, is instituted by himself, and so limited by his own revealed will." Unlike the normative principle, which prescribes freedom to use anything in worship that is not forbidden in Scripture (often associated historically with the Lutheran and Anglican church), the regulative principle requires positive support from Scripture for the use of any element of worship.[18] It prohibits the use of elements "according to the imagination and devices of men, nor the suggestions of Satan, under any visible representations, or any other way not prescribed in the Holy Scriptures." William Cunningham (1804–1865) explains regarding the Reformers' view: "There are sufficiently plain indications in Scripture itself, that it was Christ's mind and will that nothing should be introduced into the government and worship of the Church, unless a positive warrant for it could be found in Scripture."[19] Baptists likewise

17. Harmon, *Towards Baptist Catholicity*, 28.

18. R. J. Gore Jr. contends that there are at least five different approaches in the Western church today. The "pragmatic" approach, which argues "in practice if not in theory, whatever works is allowed" (which he associates with the "free church" worship of the United States in particular); The Roman Catholic "ecclesial" approach, which maintains "that whatever the church deems to be correct is allowed"; the normative principle associated with the Lutheran and Anglican churches; the Reformed or Covenantal approach, which says, "Whatever is consistent with covenant faithfulness is appropriate" (which he advocates); and the regulative principle (Gore, *Covenantal Worship*, 9–10).

19. Cunningham, *Reformation of the Church*, 38. Jeremiah Burroughs (1599–1646), an English Independent Anglican (e.g., Puritan) and Westminster Divine, wrote the treatise *Gospel Worship* as a definitive Puritan application of the Regulative Principle. His subtitle is "The Right Manner of Sanctifying the Name of God in General and Particularly these 3 Great Ordinances: (1) Hearing the Word, (2) Receiving the Lord's

generally required a biblical precedent for everything done in worship, though they have not been as stringent with the application of the regulative principle in some places and in some cases have added the principle of accommodation.[20]

Ernest C. Reisinger and D. Matthew Allen, both Baptists, explain, "Under the regulative principle, true worship is only that which is commanded. False worship is anything other than what is commanded."[21] With that seemingly unequivocal statement, Reisinger and Allen proceed to suggest four qualifications to the regulative principle to avoid some of the more extreme applications of this principle:

1. The regulative principle applies only to church ordinances, church government, and acts of worship and not to the remainder of the Christian life.

Supper, (3) Prayer." However, he does not ever question the practice of infant baptism. (See Burroughs, *Gospel Worship*.) Baptists leaned heavily upon the regulative principle to argue for baptism by immersion as "the plain testimony of Scripture" (See Weaver, "Plain Testimony of Scripture").

20. Tom Ascol defines this principle as "The willing restriction of the exercise of legitimate Christian liberties for the purpose of redeeming people and circumstances which are governed by the ignorance and misunderstanding which results from man's fallen nature" (Ascol, *Accommodation and Compromise*, loc. 151). Ernest Reisinger and Matthew Allen explain, "The doctrine of accommodation is an extremely important doctrine for Southern Baptists and others seeking to minister in the twenty-first century." It seeks to answer the question, "Is it ever permissible and morally legitimate for the Christian minister to forego insisting on change in certain areas until he can make an appeal for change on the basis of biblical instruction and teaching which he has provided?" It is largely an argument out of the principle of Christian Liberty and the teaching of Paul in Rom 14–15 and 1 Cor 8 (Reisinger and Allen, *Worship*, 131–32). R. J. Gore Jr. asserts that in order to understand Calvin's approach to the regulative principle one must understand his interpretive method and the role of *adiaphora*, or "things neither commanded nor forbidden." In doing so he "warns against binding the conscience, forcing it to believe or to observe that which is 'indifferent'" (Gore, *Covenantal Worship*, 34). See also, chap. 5 "Worship, Genevan Style" for a clarification of worship as Calvin practiced (71–89). With regard to the Puritan "strict" application of the regulative principle, Gore explains that challenges need to be considered in "(1) understanding the nature of Puritan biblical interpretation, and (2) integrating the practices of Jesus concerning the worship of God into our understanding of the regulation of worship" (91–92). Essentially, Gore asserts that the Puritans, "when interpreting a text that had bearing on the regulative principle of worship, failed to take into account the larger context of the Scriptures" (97). Additionally, "The evidence concerning the worship practices of our Lord has significantly undermined the traditional Puritan formulation of the regulative principle of worship" (110).

21. Reisinger and Allen, *Worship*, 25–26. Extreme Presbyterian applications of the regulative principle would never have accepted hymn singing or the use of musical instruments as an accompaniment to psalm singing. Most of the Baptist disputes over the regulative principle were attempts to expand the use of music in worship (71–72).

2. Under the regulative principle, an explicit command from Scripture is not required to legitimize a worship practice.

3. The regulative principle applies to "things" or "elements" of worship but not to "circumstances" of worship.

4. The regulative principle does not apply to the "mode" of worship.[22]

There are a variety of approaches to the strictness of application of the regulative principle. Even the Second London Confession left some aspects of worship up to the local church. Chapter 1, section 6 reads, "There are some circumstances concerning the worship of God and government of the Church, common to human actions and societies, which are to be ordered by the light of nature and Christian prudence, according to the general rules of the word, which are always to be observed."[23] Benjamin Keach was a signer of the Second London Confession, a proponent of the regulative principle, and yet a fierce advocate for hymn singing in worship for which the London Confession did not provide. He worked for six years slowly to introduce the practice of hymn singing. By 1691 his church had voted to have a hymn sung following the service each Sunday. This would have been the first Baptist church to do so.[24]

Considering the third and fourth qualifications above, some have attempted to clarify the differences between elements, circumstances, and modes (e.g., forms) of worship.[25] Elements are the essential features of worship and are the means by which the church worships. Chap. 22 of

22. Reisinger and Allen, *Worship*, 29–32. They cite one such extreme example that they reject: "All worship by unwarranted means, and all dishonest use of authorized means, would seem to be included in false worship, and may be designated devil worship, for all beast worship is devil worship" (32).

23. Lumpkin, *Baptist Confessions*, 250–51.

24. Reisinger and Allen, *Worship*, 72. Keach wrote *The Breach Repaired in God's Worship; or Singing of Psalms, Hymns, and Spiritual Songs, proved to be an Holy Ordinance of Jesus Christ* (1691) to defend the practice of hymn singing. He cited Eph 5:19; Col 3:16, and Jas 5:13 in defense of hymn singing and the regulative principle. The Philadelphia Confession (1742) added a section regarding hymn singing largely due to Keach's direct influence (73).

25. John Frame, an advocate of the regulative principle, disagrees with this distinction, as its application is not easy. He writes, "Is a song in worship an element, as John Murray taught, or is it a 'form' or 'circumstance,' a *way* of praying and teaching? Is instrumental music an element (as the covenanter tradition holds) or a circumstance (helping the congregation to sing in a decent and orderly way)? Is a marriage essentially a taking of vows and therefore a proper element of worship, or is it part of a broad group of activities that should be excluded from worship because it is not prescribed? All these questions have been disputed among those who have accepted the distinction between elements and circumstances" (Frame, "Fresh Look at the Regulative Principle").

the 1689 Confession identifies the approved elements of worship as prayer, the reading of Scripture, preaching the word, singing, and practicing the ordinances of baptism and the Lord's Supper.[26] Some also include taking an offering based upon Paul's request in 1 Corinthians 16:2 that the church at Corinth collect a gift on the first day of the week, though the confessions did not provide specifically for that element in their prescriptions for worship.

By contrast, circumstances for worship have to do with the conditions most conducive to worship. These aspects of worship such as the time to meet, whether or not to use pews or chairs, what kind of building should be used for worship, etc., do not fall under the restrictions of the regulative principle because the Bible does not expressly mandate the circumstances of worship. In light of this, the Second London Confession explains that the circumstances of worship should be "ordered by the light of nature and Christian prudence, according to the general rules of the word."[27]

The modes or forms of worship have to do with the content and structure by which an element is expressed. Reisinger and Allen explain, "Although Scripture prescribes the elements of worship, it does not always detail how those elements are to be carried out."[28] How long a sermon should be or how many there should be is not determined by Scripture. Whether or not a prayer should be fixed, such as the Lord's Prayer, or free, such as a spontaneous prayer, is also not prescribed by Scripture. Obviously, there should be congruence between mode and the element expressed. In general, the regulative principle requires a positive warrant from Scripture for a particular element or expression of worship to be included in corporate worship; there is some freedom regarding the forms or modes of worship; and simple common sense regarding its circumstances should prevail. The ultimate concern is that Scripture be the guide in all matters related to worship

26. Lumpkin, *Baptist Confessions*, 281. Chapter 22, para. 3—"Prayer, with thanksgiving, being one part of natural worship, is by God required of all men. But that it may be accepted, it is to be made in the name of the Son, by the help of the Spirit, according to his will; with understanding, reverence, humility, fervency, faith, love, and perseverance; and when with others, in a known tongue." Chapter 22, para. 4—"Prayer is to be made for things lawful, and for all sorts of men living, or that shall live hereafter; but not for the dead, nor for those of whom it may be known that they have sinned the sin unto death." Chapter 22, para. 5—"The reading of the Scriptures, preaching, and hearing the Word of God, teaching and admonishing one another in psalms, hymns, and spiritual songs, singing with grace in our hearts to the Lord; as also the administration of baptism, and the Lord's supper, are all parts of religious worship of God, to be performed in obedience to him, with understanding, faith, reverence, and godly fear; moreover, solemn humiliation, with fastings, and thanksgivings, upon special occasions, ought to be used in an holy and religious manner."

27. Lumpkin, *Baptist Confessions*, 250–51. See chap. 1, para. 6.

28. Reisinger and Allen, *Worship*, 31.

and life, under the influence of the Holy Spirit. Chapter 1, paragraph 6 of the Philadelphia Confession reads (as did the same section of the Second London Confession),

> The whole counsel of God concerning all things necessary for his own glory, man's salvation, faith and life, is either expressly set down or necessarily contained in the Holy Scripture: unto which nothing at any time is to be added, whether by new revelation of the Spirit, or traditions of men. Nevertheless, we acknowledge the inward illumination of the Spirit of God to be necessary for the saving understanding of such things as are revealed in the Word, and that there are some circumstances concerning the worship of God, and government of the church, common to human actions and societies, which are to be ordered by the light of nature and Christian prudence, according to the general rules of the Word, which are always to be observed.[29]

The Reformers and Sola Scriptura

John Frame writes of the reformers, "The Protestant Reformers, particularly Calvin and his followers, emphasize *sola Scriptura* as the chief rule of worship. What we do in worship must be warranted by Scripture."[30] Horton Davies explains, "The basic doctrines held in common by the Reformers [Calvin and Luther] were three: the Bible as God's Revelation, Justification by Faith, and Christ as the sole Mediator between God and men. The last two doctrines, of course, were derived from the first all-inclusive doctrine of the Scriptures."[31] Davies later writes, "First and foremost, the Puritans were the champions of the authority of the 'pure Word of God' as the criterion not only for church doctrine, but also for church worship and church government."[32] Their goal was to return the church to the purity and sim-

29. George and George, *Baptist Confessions, Covenants, and Catechisms*, 58.

30. Frame, *Contemporary Worship Music*, 16.

31. Davies, *Worship of the English Puritans*, 15.

32. Davies, *Worship of the English Puritans*, 49. While Calvin admitted a principle of accommodation to inessential matters, the early Puritans did not. This was most likely in their haste to purify the church from its Anglican and Catholic impurities. William Bradshaw (1571–1618) writes in 1605, "IMPRIMIS they should hould and maintaine that the word of God contained in the writings of the Prophets and Apostles, is of absolute perfection, given by Christ the Head of the Churche, to bee unto the same, the sole Canon and rule of all matters of Religion, and the worship and service of God whatsoever. And that whatsoever done in the same service and worship cannot bee justified by the said word, is unlawfull" (Bradshaw, *English Puritanism*, 5, quoted in

plicity of the apostolic church. They believed that the worship of the church was to be characterized by six ordinances: (1) Prayer; (2) Praise; (3) the proclamation of the Word; (4) the administration of the Sacraments of Baptism and the Lord's Supper; (5) catechizing; and (6) the exercise of Discipline. Their source for these elements was Acts 2:41–42 and "other places in the New Testament."[33]

Unlike the Puritans who remained in the state church in hopes of reforming it, "The Separatists, on the other had, desired 'Reformation without tarrying for any.'"[34] While generally both Puritans and Separatists were agreed liturgically and pled for a three-fold reformation—gospel-doctrine, gospel-government, and gospel-discipline—there were some distinctive emphases that the Separatists were able to implement immediately while the Puritans could only theorize. There are three groups of Separatists that have varying degrees of influence upon the Baptists of North America— Barrowists, Anabaptists, and Particular Baptists. The Barrowists were the first of these persecuted groups to organize, many of whose leaders died for their faith.[35] Their services were held in secret locations that moved each week and would meet as early as five o'clock and stay until sundown so as not to travel by daylight. Their worship elements consisted largely of "expound[ing] out of the Bible so long as they are assembled" and a form of prayer that was "not liturgical, but extempore in character. They would not even repeat the Lord's Prayer, which they regarded as the perfect model of prayer." Barrowists believed that "all liturgical forms, the Lord's Prayer included, were a hindrance to the operation of the Spirit of God."[36] They still held to baptizing children by washing their faces, just not in the churches of the establishment. They used 1 Corinthians 11 to practice the Lord's Supper in a manner that was rather simple, but true to the New Testament. The Barrowists also practiced excommunication. Davies emphasizes, "All Barrowists' sermons were expository, and it appears they were delivered in a homely, if not a rough, manner. The exercise of 'Prophecie' was recognized

Davies, *Worship of the English Puritans*, 50).

33. Davies, *Worship of the English Puritans*, 51.

34. Davies, *Worship of the English Puritans*, 77.

35. Davies, *Worship of the English Puritans*, 80. Followers of the basic teachings of Henry Barrow(e) (ca. 1550–1593) and John Greenwood (ca. 1554–1593). These were two of the earliest leaders of the Separatist movement.

36. Davies, *Worship of the English Puritans*, 80–81. This type of praying demonstrated their view of what it was to worship "in spirit and in truth" (John 4:24). Anabaptists would go even farther in this effort to have the Holy Spirit's witness to that truth through extemporaneous praying and prophesying/preaching in corporate worship. John Smyth advocated this type of worship as truly "spirituall worship." See also, McKibbens, "Our Baptist Heritage in Worship."

by Puritans and Separatists alike as 'a valuable means of inculcating doc-trine. Various speakers would preach and expound the same passage of Scripture *seriatim*, allowing members of the congregation to state their dif-ficulties, which the Church officers would attempt to resolve.'"[37]

A second early group of dissenters are the Anabaptists—generally as-sociated with John Smyth (died ca. 1612) and Thomas Helwys (1575–1616). There are two important differences between the Barrowists and the Ana-baptists.[38] While their worship services of the latter shared many common characteristics, the Anabaptists' mode of administering baptism was for believers, not children.[39] The Anabaptists also were adamantly opposed to set forms in their worship. Davies writes, "They were logical enough in their attempt at attaining a pneumatic worship to put away the Bible early in their service, as a form of words. John Smyth describes this view toward worship in *The Differences of the Churches of the Separation*:

> Wee hould that the worship of the new testament properly so called is spirituall proceeding originally from the hart: & that reading out of a booke (though a lawfull ecclesiastical action) is no part of spiritnall worship, but rather the invention of the man of synne it being substituted for a part of spirituall worship. Wee hould that seeing prophesiing is a parte of spirituall worship; therefore in time of prophesjng it is vnlawfull to have the booke as a helpe before the eye wee hould that seeing singinging [*sic*] a psalme is a parte of spirituall worship therefore it is vnlawfull to have the booke before the eye in time of singing a psalme.[40]

37. Davies, *Worship of the English Puritans*, 85–86.

38. Davies distinguishes between Anabaptists and Baptists in his text. The earliest congregations that were opposed to infant Baptism and only baptized professing adult believers are Anabaptists. Then there are the Baptists who were divided into General Baptists and Particular Baptists. However, in the index, he groups them all under the subject index of "Baptists" and under the subject heading of "Anabaptists" he lists "*v.* Baptists." Davies, *Worship of the English Puritans*, 297. According to Davies, the Ana-baptists appear to have had no organization in England before 1612. "The first Baptist (e.g., Anabaptist) congregation to be settled in England was that over which Thomas Helwys (ca. 1550–c. 1616) presided with Thomas [John] Murton (1585–1626?). This withdrew from John Smyth's (ca. 1554–1612) congregation in Amsterdam and returned to England about 1612 (Davies, *Worship of the English Puritans*, 88–89).

39. Davies, *Worship of the English Puritans*, 89. Davies later explains, "Whilst Helwys did not insist that the mode of administration should be either sprinkling or dipping, immersion appears to have been insisted upon by the London Baptists in 1633. This church, under the leadership of [Henry] Jessey [(1603–1663)] and [Richard] Blunt, used immersion as the only legitimate method of administration" (91).

40 Smyth, "Differences of the Churches," 81.

Davies summarizes, "The rejection of forms of worship was so complete that one stage further would have led to Quakerism. This 'spiritual worship' while it does not altogether do away with the use of books, regards the part of the service in which they are used as a mere preparation of the pure worship, which proceeds without them."[41] The English Baptists led by Helwys and Morton advocated the same practice:

> They as partes or meanes of worship read Chapters, Textes to preache on & Psalmes out of translacion, we alreddy as in praying, so in prophesiinge & singinge Psalmes laye aside the translacion, & we suppose yt will prove the truth, that All books even the originalles themselves must be layed aside in the tyme of spirituall worshipp, yet still retayninge the reading & interpretinge of the Scriptures in the Churche for the preparinge to worship, Iudginge of doctrine, decidinge of Controversies as the grounde of or faithe & of or whole profession.[42]

While singing in unison was not a feature of early Anabaptist worship,[43] another group of baptizers or "dippers" arose, many of whom would embrace congregational singing as part of their worship.

The third group of Separatists in view here is the Particular Baptists. They are the most influential of the three for this study and must be considered in more detail. The First London Confession of 1644 was the confessional agreement of seven like-minded baptizing churches in London—believed to be the first of the Particular Baptists. As other Separatists, they left the established church in an effort to form true gospel churches. It appears that the 1644 confession was an effort to unify in cooperation as well as distinguish themselves from (continental) Anabaptists, Anarchists, or Arminians.[44] These churches came out of the Jacob-Lathrop-

41. Davies, *Worship of the English Puritans*, 90.

42. Thomas Helwys, "Letter of Sept. 20, 1608," quoted in Burrage, *Early English Dissenters*, 166.

43. Specific individuals gifted in "bringing the Psalm" (1 Cor 14:26) were allowed to do so. "To singe Psalmes in the Gospel is a speciall gift given to some particular member in the church, whereby he doth blesse, praise, or magnifie the Lord through the mighty operation of the spirit. Ep. 5, 18.19 which is to be performed I say, by one alone, at one time to the edification one of another and therefore it is an ordinance flowing from a cheerfulle heart" (Draper, *Gospel-Glory Proclaimed Before the Sonnes of Men* (1649), quoted in Davies, *Worship of the English Puritans*, 91).

44. See Ward, *Pure Worship*. Ward believes that by penning the 1644 Confession they "vehemently denied being (continental) Anabaptists, Anarchists, or Arminians" (47). William Lumpkin writes similarly: "In order to distinguish themselves from both the General Baptists and the Anabaptists, the Calvinistic Baptists of London determined to prepare and publish a statement of their views" (referring to the 1644 Confession)

Jessey Church, named for the first three pastors of this congregation of the 1630s.[45] This church went through a series of secessions in 1633–1638 as separate-leaning members began leaving this non-separatist church. One group joined with John Spilsbury (1593–1668) as pastor and is generally considered the first Particular Baptist Church (1638) by their adoption of the practice of immersion. Several others formed in the ensuing years until seven churches sent representatives to meet in 1644. The confession was drafted under the guidance of Spilsbury with the help of Samuel Richardson (fl. 1646) and William Kiffin (1616–1701). Another secession from the JLJ church in 1644 called Hanserd Knollys (1599–1691) as pastor and that church joined the group in 1646. Kiffin and Knollys are instrumental in discipling Benjamin Keach (1640–1704), who had been a General Baptist. Keach became a prominent figure in the next associational gathering of Particular Baptists in London and the Second London Confession of 1689, as well as the dialogue and development of Baptist worship.

Many of the early Particular Baptists refused to sing corporately in worship, though some allowed solo singing. The concern was regarding "conjoined" or "promiscuous" singing (the joining of unbelievers with believers) in worship. At the 1689 assembly led by Kiffin, Knollys, and Keach, Keach sought to raise the matter of congregational singing. Recognizing the volatility of the matter, the body declined to debate it and left the matter to be determined by each congregation. The debate was subsequently made by the exchange of pamphlets over the matter between Isaac Marlow (1649–1719) and Keach.[46] Eventually Benjamin Keach persuaded his Baptist congregation at Horsley-down to bring the matter to a vote in 1691. They had been singing one song together after the Lord's Supper and on certain thanksgiving days since the mid-1670s, affording those who opposed it to depart early. The vote passed by a wide margin and congregational singing became a regular part of the church at Horsleydown, though the debate among Baptists continued for years to

---

(Lumpkin, *Baptist Confessions*, 145).

45. Henry Jacob (1563–1624), John Lathrop (1584–1653), and Henry Jessey (1603–1663).

46. Music and Richardson, *"I Will Sing the Wondrous Story,"* 10–11. Isaac Marlow's *A Brief Discourse Concerning Singing in the Publick Worship of God in the Gospel-Church* (1690) began the debate with Keach's *The Breach Repair'd in God's Worship: or Singing of Psalms, Hymns, and Spiritual Songs Proved to Be an Holy Ordinance of Jesus Christ* (1691) as the reply. By the end of 1692, fifteen publications had been exchanged in the debate.

come.[47] David Music and Paul Richardson call Keach "the seminal figure in congregational singing among Baptists."[48]

However, long expository sermons were the predominant elements of Baptist worship from the beginning. Davies notes, "The sermons, we may surmise from the importance of the exercise of 'prophesying' in their worship, were long expositions of Scripture. These were of three quarters of an hour to an hour's duration."[49] Marlow referred to the Baptist worship gathering as a "lecture-meeting," demonstrating both his anti-singing position and this emphasis on preaching.[50] Davies adds, "The peculiar contributions made by the Baptists to the worship of the English Separatists were three. They practiced believer's baptism by immersion. . . . In the second place, they went further than the other Separatists in their opposition to forms in worship. . . . The third influence . . . was to become a regular feature of Puritan worship. This was the method of running exposition of interpolated comment during the public reading of the Scriptures."[51] The priority of *sola Scriptura* is clear here. Not only should Scripture regulate worship in order to make it pure, but it should also inform the content of worship. While the mode of prayer and prophecy were to be free from set forms, and all books, including the Bible, were to be set aside during the time of pure worship, Baptists were confident that the Holy Spirit would confirm the truth of the word that was previously established from the reading of Scripture. This was their understanding of worship in spirit and truth and Jesus described it in John 4:24. The form and progress of worship would be shaped by the rule of the Holy Spirit through scripture-regulated elements of worship filled with scripture-informed content.

---

47. Ward, *Pure Worship*, 189.

48. Music and Richardson, *"I Will Sing the Wondrous Story,"* 12. Keach was the first to establish the practice of singing hymns, as distinguished from psalms, in the regular worship of any English Church (Baptist or otherwise). His son, Elias Keach would carry this same influence to some of the first Baptist churches in the New World—in Philadelphia—as demonstrated by the addition of chap. 23 to the Philadelphia Confession (1742) regarding singing in worship as a holy ordinance.

49. Davies, *Worship of the English Puritans*, 91.

50. Ward, *Pure Worship*, 186.

51. Davies, *Worship of the English Puritans*, 95. Davies emphasizes that it was this second contribution of "radical opposition to any set forms in worship" that is "probably more than any other factor, which accounts for the Puritan departure from the liturgical customs of the Continental Reformed Churches" (97).

Appendix 2

Historic Worship Service Examples

1609: General Baptists in Amsterdam (from England), Recorded Order of Worship[52]

Prayer

Prophesying (Read one or two chapters and "give the sense thereof")

Confer upon the same

(All books are laid aside)

Solemn Prayer by the Speaker

Read Scripture and Prophesy out of the same text (45 minutes to an hour)

A second speaker does the same, then third, fourth, fifth, etc. as time allows

First speaker concludes with prayer

Exhortation to contribute to the poor

Collection

Prayer

Note: This service was reported to have lasted about four hours (eight o'clock until twelve o'clock) in the morning and then a second service in the afternoon lasted about three or four hours (two o'clock until five or six

---

52. Letter from Hughe and Ann Bromheade who were evidently part of the John Smyth exodus from England to Amsterdam. See Burrage, *Early English Dissenters*, 2:172–77. See also McBeth, *Sourcebook for Baptist Heritage*, 22.

o'clock). The government of the church is handled after the second service. This is believed to be the oldest record of Baptist worship.

17th Century: Congregationalists (Puritans) in England, Potential Order of Worship (Davies)[1]

Scriptural Call to Worship

Prayer of Confession

Metrical Psalm of Praise

Old Testament Scripture Reading (w/ brief explanation)

Metrical Psalm or New Testament Lection

Prayer of Intercession (led by minister and followed by congregational "amen")[2]

Sermon

Metrical Psalm

Blessing

17th and 18th Century: Baptist Worship at Providence, Reenactment in 1963 ("Forefathers' Service")[3]

Organ Call to the Meeting House (Handel, "Concerto in B flat")

Entrance of Ministers and Deacons

Prayer

Psalm 100 (OLD HUNDREDTH)

Reading of Scriptures with Comments (Job 7:1–8; Heb 3:7–15)

Psalm 65 (ST. ANNE)

The Announcement of the Text

Sermon—"The Weaver's Shuttle"

---

1. Davies, *Worship of the English Puritans*, 246–47.

2. In a Presbyterian church "this item would be postponed until after the sermon, and it would conclude with all saying the Lord's Prayer aloud" (Davies, *Worship of the English Puritans*, 246).

3. "The First Baptist Church in America, 325th Anniversary Year, May 5, 1963," Worship Bulletin (Providence: First Baptist Church, 1963), 4 o'clock service. The program notes under the worship service order: "The service today follows the order used in the Meeting Houses in the 17th and 18th centuries."

Prayer

The Gathering of the Offering

Choral Anthem—"Before Jehovah's Awful Throne"

Psalm 23 (DUNDEE)

The Blessing

The Dismissal

Organ Postlude (Bach, "Fantasie in G minor")

1768: Baptist Worship in Philadelphia, Potential Order of Worship (Morgan Edwards)[4]

Opening Prayer

Opening Hymn*

Scripture Reading*

Prayer*

Hymn before the sermon

Sermon closed with prayer

Lord's Supper (when celebrated)

Collection for the saints

Closing Hymn

Benediction

*Order of these elements varied.

Late 18th Century: Baptist Worship in the Charleston Tradition (Furman Pastorate), Potential Order of Worship[5]

A short prayer, suitably prefaced

Reading of Scripture

A longer prayer

4. Based upon Edwards, *Customs of Primitive Churches*, and other source material referenced in this study.

5. Edwards, *Customs of Primitive Churches*, 100. Don Hustad suggested worship at Charleston probably looked like this order from Morgan Edwards (Hustad, "Baptist Worship Forms," 32).

Singing (congregational)

Sermon

A third prayer

Singing

The Lord's Supper (on appointed Sundays)

Collecting for the necessities of saints

Benediction

Late 18th Century: Baptist Worship in the Sandy Creek Tradition (Shubal Stearns Pastorate), Potential Order of Worship[6]

Opening Prayer

Singing, praying, and exhorting (potentially simultaneous)

Sermon(s) (unprepared, but reliant upon the Spirit)

Response to the gospel ("altar call")

Closing Prayer

Late 18th Century: Puritans (Congregationalists) in New England, Potential Order of Worship (Davies)[7]

Opening Prayer of Intercession and Thanksgiving

Reading and exposition of a chapter of the Bible

Psalm singing

Sermon

Psalm singing

Prayer

Blessing

6. This order is based upon the research gathered for this study. Sandy Creek Baptists did not record or plan their services or their sermons. Their services were marked by spontaneity; therefore this is a very loose approximation from the scant service descriptions available.

7. Davies, *Worship of the American Puritans*, 8.

1801: Puritans in Hubbardston, Massachusetts, Recorded Order of Worship[8]

<u>A.M. Service</u>
Short Prayer
Reading the Scriptures
Singing
Long Prayer
Sermon
Prayer and Blessing

<u>P.M. Service</u>
Short Prayer
Reading the Scriptures
Singing
Long Prayer
Singing
Sermon
Prayer
Singing
Blessing

1801: The Baptist Meeting-House at Charlestown, MA Recorded Order of Worship ("Building Dedication," May 12, 1801)[9]

I. *By the Rev Jedidiah Morse, D.D.*
Read the 24th Psalm—*The earth is the Lord's, etc.*
Address, explanatory of the occasion
Prayer

8. Believed to be the oldest extant order of worship in North America—handwritten in the front pages of *The Psalms of David, together with Hymns and Spiritual Songs* (Boston, 1801)—pulpit hymnal of the church, reproduced in Rivera, *Jonathan Edwards on Worship*, 9.

9. *Sacred Performances at the Dedication*, 3. Samuel Stillman (1737–1807) was the pastor of First Baptist Church of Boston from 1765 until his death.

Read 2 Chronicles 6:12, 14, 18–42

Dedicatory Poem—Sung

II. *By the Rev. Mr. Grafton of Newton*

Dedication Prayer

III. Read and Sung Dedicatory Hymn

IV. *By the Rev. Samuel Stillman, D.D.*

A Sermon on Brotherly Love and Christian Fellowship from 133rd Psalm, 1st verse—*Behold, how good, and how pleasant, etc.*

V. *By the Rev. Thomas Baldwin, A.M.*

The Recognition of the Church—An Address

—The Fellowship of Sister Churches given.

Concluding Prayer, and singing 132d Psalm—*Arise, O King of grace, arise, etc.*

VI. Sung an Anthem from the 48th Psalm

VII. Benediction by the Rev. Dr. Stillman

1849: Siloam Baptist Church (Marion, Alabama), Potential Order of Worship[10]

Call to Worship/Opening Prayer/Opening Song

Congregational Singing/Choir

Prayer

Scripture Reading

Congregational Singing

Pastoral Prayer

Sermon (with gospel invitation)

Song of Response

Closing Prayer

---

10. This order is an estimate based upon brief descriptions of worship at Siloam, but also two descriptions of other Baptist churches of the time that were recorded in the *Alabama Baptist*. See "Dedication of the Tremont Temple" and "Thanksgiving Day in Missouri" in *Alabama Baptist Advocate*, June 6, 1844.

December 1860: Old Cane Springs Baptist Church (Madison County, Kentucky), Recorded Order of Worship from a historical account of Augustine "Gustin" Hart[11]

Hymns (lined out)

Scripture Reading

Prayer

Hymn

Sermon (Psalm 8)

Hymn ("Amazing Grace")

1885: Jarvis Street Baptist Church (Toronto, Ontario), Potential Order of Worship[12]

Organ Prelude

Choir Anthem

Scripture Reading

Opening Prayer

Solo

Hymn

Prayer

Choir Anthem

Offertory

Hymn

---

11. Chenault and Dorris, *Old Cane Springs*, 50–56. James Noland, who lined out the hymns, invited worshipers to extend the hand of Christian fellowship to the preacher, Rev. William Rupard, during the final hymn. This opportunity was likely afforded because he had to go on to the next locale for preaching and there would not be time for everyone to greet him after the service.

12. This order is based on various entries in the minutes of Jarvis Street Baptist Church, a newspaper account of one of their services in 1885, and the work of Michel Belzile (see Belzile, "Canadian Baptists at Worship," 45).

1895: James Street Baptist Church (Hamilton, Ontario), Recorded Order of Worship from church bulletin dated April 14, 1895 ("Easter")[13]

Prelude

Anthem—"Break Forth Into Joy"

Doxology and Invocation

Hymn 182 (words printed in bulletin)

Lesson—Matthew XXVIII, 1–8

Solo—"I Know That My Redeemer Liveth"

Lesson—Acts XVIII, 1–8

Anthem—"God Hath Appointed a Day"

Prayer

Offertory

Anthem—"The Lord is King"

Hymn 198 (words printed in bulletin)

Sermon

Quartett—"Christ, Chime Ye Bells"

Hymn 189 (words printed in bulletin)

Benediction

Postlude

1902: Walnut Street Baptist Church (Louisville, Kentucky), Recorded Order ("New Building Dedication Service")[14]

Organ Prelude

Choir (at times) or Opening Hymn

Doxology (if not before the choir/opening hymn)

13. Belzile, "Canadian Baptists at Worship," 45. Belzile considers this the Formal Evangelical Pattern of worship. "It had risen out of a dissatisfaction among some Baptists with the Post-Revivalist style which they perceived to be too informal, irreverent, and passive. This dissatisfaction was by no means unique to Canadian Baptists, but rather characterized Baptists in both Britain and the United States."

14. This is order based upon a synthesis of the three building dedication services held on November 16, 1902, for Walnut Street's new house of worship ("Dedication," *Western Recorder*, November 20, 1902).

Invocation

Hymn

Scripture Reading

Prayer

Choir (when not at the beginning)

Hymn

Sermon

Offering

Prayer

Solo or Quartet

Hymn

Baptism (usually practiced in the evening)

Benediction

1912: First Baptist Church (Shreveport, Louisiana), Recorded Order of Worship from Church Bulletin dated April 19, 1912[15]

The Organ

Voluntary—Holy! Holy! Holy!

Invocation

Anthem

The Scriptures

Prayer

Hymn

The Lord' Treasury

Sermon

Hymn

Benediction

Doxology

The Organ—Postlude

15. Carter, "Southern Baptist Heritage of Worship?," 44.

1913: First Baptist Church (Ottawa, Ontario), Recorded Order of Worship from Church Bulletin dated November 30, 1913[16]

Organ

Doxology

Invocation: "My God I Thank Thee"

Hymn

Scripture Reading

Prayer

Offertory Anthem

Children's Talk

Sermon

Hymn No. 416

Benediction

1949: Walnut Street Baptist Church (Louisville, Kentucky), Recorded Order of Worship from Church Bulletin dated October 9, 1949[17]

Sunday School Convocation

Hymn—"Jesus Saves"

Prayer

Peaks of Progress

Hymn 74—"Holy, Holy, Holy"

Announcements

Centennial Hymn[18]

Scripture

16. Belzile, "Canadian Baptists at Worship," 42. Belzile considers this a post-revivalistic pattern of worship. "Actually a moderate form of Revivalist worship, the Post-Revivalist style claimed for itself a less evangelistic and more didactic role, concerning itself with nurturing, equipping, and instructing its worshippers in the fine details of Scripture and doctrine."

17. Walnut Street Baptist Church, "Centennial Celebration, October 9, 1949," ii. This is a special service celebrating the one hundredth anniversary of the founding of Walnut Street Baptist Church from the merging of First and Second Baptist Churches.

18. This was written for this occasion by Mrs. W. O. Carver and Dr. Claude Almand.

Prayer (Emeritus Pastor Dr. Finley F Gibson)

Hymn 67—"For All the Saints"

Offertory Anthem—"Psalm 100"

Sermon—"Why Baptists?" (Dr. Ellis A. Fuller)

Hymn 361—"Have Thine Own Way, Lord"

Benediction

1949: First Baptist Church (West Palm Beach, Florida), Recorded Order of Worship from Church Bulletin dated March 27, 1949[19]

Call to Worship

Doxology, Invocation and Response

Hymn 10—"Safely Through Another Week"

Solo—"The Lord is My Light" (Allitsen)

Scripture Reading

Prayer

Offertory—Litany

Hymn 24—"How Tedious and Tasteless the Hours"

Sermon—"The Secret of His Life"

Hymn of Invitation 417—"Holy Spirit, Breathe on Me"

(Sung by Choir while Christians Pray)

Reception of New Members

Benediction 480—"God Be With You"

Postlude—"Marche Militaire" (Clark)

1950: First Baptist Church (Shreveport, Louisiana), Recorded Order of Worship from Church Bulletin dated June 4, 1950[20]

The Organ—(Raff, "Andantino")

19. First Baptist Church, "March 27, 1949," iv.

20. Carter, "Southern Baptist Heritage of Worship," 44–45. This service included a special recognition for Nursery and Cradle Roll Department Workers.

Call to Worship and Hymn No. 4 ("Come, Thou Almighty King")

Pastoral Prayer, ending in Lord's Prayer

Recognition of Nursery and Cradle Roll Department Workers

Call for Nursery and Cradle Roll Members

Prayer of Dedication

The Scriptures

Solo—The Twenty-Third Psalm (Malotte)

Welcome to Visitors, Announcements, Doxology, Prayer, Tithes and Offerings

"Offertory in G"

Anthem (Wagner, "O Sing to Thee")

Sermon—"The Motherhood of God"

Invitation Hymn No. 209 ("My Faith Looks Up to Thee")

Benediction—Choral and Pastoral

1950s: Unidentified Rural Church (Baptist), Recorded Order of Worship (from the Pastor's recollection)[21]

Hymn

Prayer

Welcome to Visitors and Announcements

Hymn

Hymn

Offertory

Special Music, either a solo or another hymn

Sermon

Invitation Hymn

Benediction

21. Carter, "Southern Baptist Heritage of Worship," 45. Carter explains that this was the worship order for every Sunday of the church he pastored for many years and while rural churches did not have worship bulletins, a similar order was followed in most rural Baptist churches of that time.

1955: Canadian Baptist Minister's Handbook, Suggested Order of Worship ("Formal Evangelical Pattern")[22]

An Organ Prelude

The Doxology or Sanctus

The Lord's Prayer

A Responsive Reading

A Hymn

The Scripture Lesson

An Anthem

The Pastoral Prayer

The Presentation and Dedication of Tithes and Offerings

An Anthem

The Announcements

A Hymn

The Sermon

A Hymn

The Benediction

An Organ Postlude

1963: Pennepek Baptist Church (Lower Dublin Baptist Church, Pennsylvania), Recorded Order of Worship ("275th Anniversary Service")[23]

Organ Prelude

Hymn ("O God, Our Help in Ages Past")

Call to Worship

Gloria Patri/Invocation/The Lord's Prayer

Responsive Reading, New Testament

Presentation and Dedication of Flags

---

22. *Canadian Baptist Ministers' Handbook*, 70. Belzile cites this example as representative of the Formal Evangelical Pattern found in Baptist worship in Canada (Belzile, "Canadian Baptists at Worship," 47).

23. *Pennepack Baptist Church 275th Anniversary Program*, n.p.

Morning Prayer and Choral Response

Hymn ("Lead on, O King Eternal")

Announcements and Offertory Prayer

Offertory ("'Tis the Blessed Hour of Prayer")

The Doxology

Scripture Reading: Philippians 3:7–17

Anthem ("Battle Hymn of the Republic")

Sermon ("Look to the Galleries")

Hymn ("We Would Be Building")

Benediction

Meditation

Organ Postlude ("America the Beautiful")

1963: First Baptist Church (Providence, Rhode Island), Recorded Order of Worship ("325th Anniversary Service")[24]

Organ Prelude (Franck, "Prelude, Fugue & Variation")

Choral Call to Worship

Sentences

Invocation and Lord's Prayer

Hymn ("We Gather Together")

Responsive Lesson

Gloria Patri

Anthem (Gibbons, "Almighty and Everlasting God")

Scripture Lesson—Hebrews 11

Sermon ("Roger Williams—Though Silent, Still He Speaks")

Hymn ("Now Thank We All Our God")

Call to Prayer

Prayer and Choral Response

Registration of Attendance

24. "The First Baptist Church in America, 325th Anniversary Year, May 5, 1963," 11 o'clock service. This service was a part of the 325th Anniversary celebration. Musical selections were intended to be from the founding period, but the *ordo* is reflective of the mid-twentieth-century practice of the church.

Sentences

Gathering of the Offering

Anthem (Handel, "How Excellent Thy Name, O Lord")

Doxology

Prayer of Consecration

Hymn ("I Greet Thee, Who My Sure Redeemer Art")

The Lord's Supper

Prayer and Blessing

Hymn ("O Sacred Head, Now Wounded")

Organ Postlude (Marcello, "The Heavens Declare")

1977: Walnut Street Baptist Church (Louisville, Kentucky), Recorded Order of Worship from Bulletin dated January 9, 1977[25]

Call to Worship—"All Praise to Thee" (Vaughan Williams)

Doxology and Invocation

Hymn 419—"Glorious Things of Thee are Spoken"

Church Announcements

Hymn 344—"Blessed Assurance"

Morning Prayer

Choir Hymn—"The Banner of the Cross" (McGranahan)

Message in Music (solo)

Hymn 192—"Nail-Scarred Hand"

Recognition of Visitors

Anthem—"Sanctus"

Choral Meditation—"Break Thou the Bread of Life"

The Reading of the Scripture (Pastor)

Hymn 255—There's a Sweet, Sweet Spirit in this Place

Offertory Prayer

God's Tithes and Our Offerings

Hymn 71—"His Name is Wonderful"

Message in Music (solo)

25. Walnut Street Baptist Church, "Church Chimes, January 9, 1977," ii.

Sermon

Invitation Hymn 190—"Softly and Tenderly"

Benediction

Choral Response—"I Have Decided to Follow Jesus"

1979: I. Judson Levy, *Come, Let Us Worship*, Suggested Order of Worship, Liturgical Pattern[26]

Music

Call to Worship

Prayer of Invocation and/or Adoration

Hymn

Prayer of Confession

Words of Assurance

Scripture: Old Testament

Response Reading (Psalm)

Gloria Patri

Scripture: New Testament

Affirmation of Faith (optional)

Hymn

Prayer

Sermon

Prayer

Offertory and Offering

Announcements

Prayers of Thanksgiving and Intercession

Hymn

Blessing (Benediction)

Music & Quiet Meditation

26. Levy, *Come, Let Us Worship*, 106–7. Belzile cites this example as representative of the Liturgical Pattern among Canadian Baptists (Belzile, "Canadian Baptists at Worship," 54).

1995: First Baptist Church (West Palm Beach, Florida), Recorded Order of Worship from Church Bulletin dated April 9, 1995[27]

Call to Prayer

Prelude

Baptism

Praises to the Triumphant King—"He is Jehovah" (Choir and Orchestra)

"Blessed Be Your Name"

"All Hail the Power of Jesus' Name"

Hymn 234—"Crown Him with many Crowns"

Welcome of Visitors

Welcome Hymn—"In One Accord"

Offertory Prayer

"The Trial of Jesus" [drama] (First Act)

Offertory Praise—"The Way of Sorrows" (Choir and Orchestra)

Sermon

Invitation Hymn 342—"Just As I Am"

Benediction

2001: Walnut Street Baptist Church (Louisville, Kentucky), Recorded Order of Worship from Church Bulletin dated September 9, 2001 ("Celebrate a New Beginning")[28]

Processional Hymn—"O for a Thousand Tongues to Sing"

Invocation

Choral Call to Worship—"Then Will the Very Rocks Cry Out" (Hayes)

Recognition of Special Guests

Songs of Praise—Shout to the Lord, Lord I Lift Your Name on High, Sanctuary

Children's Sermon

27. First Baptist Church, "First Day, April 9, 1995," iv.

28. Walnut Street Baptist Church, "Celebrate a New Beginning, September 9, 2001," 6. This was a special service celebrating the dedication and completion of renovations to the sanctuary one hundred years after the building had been opened.

Scripture Reading (Isaiah 60:1–5) and Pastoral Prayer

Choral Anthem—"God so Loved the World" (Stainer)

New Testament Reading (Matthew 16:13–19)

Prayer of Dedication

Old Testament Reading (Psalm 150)

Congregational Hymn—"Joyful, Joyful, We Adore Thee"

Message—"Reflections in Stained Glass"

Invitation Hymn—"Amazing Grace"

Offertory—"Jesu, Joy of Man's Desiring" (Bach) / "My Beloved Father" (Puccini)

Closing Comments

Prayer of Dedication and Benediction

Choral Benediction—"Hallelujah!" from *Messiah* (Handel)

Postlude

2010: Sojourn Community Church (Louisville, Kentucky), Recorded Order of Worship[29]

Band Prelude

Call to Worship (Reading)

Song(s)

Prayer of Confession/Lament

Song(s)

Assurance of Peace (Reading)

Giving

Sermon

Communion

Song

Reading

Songs

Benediction (including the "Passing of the Peace")

29. This order is based upon the assimilation of five different Sunday liturgies provided by Sojourn Community Church for this project. The "passing of the peace" occurs at the beginning of the liturgy in other examples.

2020: First Baptist Church (Jacksonville, Florida)[30]

Prelude

Choral Call to Worship

Opening Prayer

Call to Worship Scripture Reading

Congregational Singing (generally three songs)

Scripture Reading

Offertory Prayer

Choral Offertory

Pastoral Scripture Reading and Prayer

Sermon

Call to Response

Congregational Singing

Announcements/Benediction/Postlude

30. This order is based on the order used at the time of printing at First Baptist Church where the author is Pastor of Worship.

Bibliography

Allen, Benjamin. "Benjamin Allen's 1832 Report." http://beargrass.org/about-beargrass/history/benjamin-allens-1832-report/.

Allen, Lee N. *The First 150 Years: Montgomery's First Baptist Church, 1829–1979.* Montgomery, AL: First Baptist Church, 1979.

Allmen, J. J. von. *Worship: Its Theology and Practice.* London: Lutterworth, 1965.

Aniol, Scott. "The Mission of Worship: A Critique of and Response to the Philosophy of Culture, Contextualization, and Worship of the North American Missional Church Movement." PhD diss., Southwestern Baptist Theological Seminary, 2013.

———. *Worship in Song: A Biblical Approach to Music and Worship.* Winona Lake, IN: BMH, 2009.

Ascol, Tom. *Accommodation and Compromise.* N.d.: Poimen, 2020. Kindle.

Augustine. *The Confessions.* Translated by Maria Boulding. Hyde Park, NY: New City, 1997.

Backus, Isaac. *The Atonement of Christ Explained and Vindicated, Against Late Attempts to Exclude It Out of the World.* Boston: Samuel Hall, 1787.

———. *The Diary of Isaac Backus.* Providence, RI: Brown University Press, 1979.

———. *A Discourse, Concerning the Materials, the Manner of Building and the Power of Organizing of the Church of Christ.* Boston: John Boyles, 1773.

———. "A Fish Caught in His Own Net." In *Isaac Backus on Church, State, and Calvinism; Pamphlets, 1754–1789,* edited by William G. McLoughlin, 167–288. Cambridge, MA: Harvard University Press, 1968.

———. *A History of New England: With Particular Reference to the Baptists.* Religion in America. New York: Arno, 1969.

———. *Isaac Backus on Church, State, and Calvinism: Pamphlets, 1754–1789.* John Harvard Library. Cambridge, MA: Belknap of Harvard University Press, 1968.

———. *Your Baptist Heritage, 1620–1804.* Rev. ed. Little Rock, AR: Challenge, 1976.

Baker, Robert A., et al. *History of the First Baptist Church of Charleston, South Carolina 1682–2007.* 325th anniversary ed. Charleston Association Series. Springfield, MO: Particular Baptist, 2007.

The Baptist Encyclopedia: A Dictionary of the Doctrines, Ordinances, Usages, Confessions of Faith, Sufferings, Labors, and Successes of the General History of the Baptist Denomination in All Lands. Philadelphia: Louis H. Everts, 1883.

Baptist History Celebration Steering Committee. *Baptist History Celebration, 2007: A Symposium on Our History, Theology, and Hymnody: Convened as a Tercentenary Anniversary Tribute to the Founding of the Philadelphia Baptist Association in 1707, Held at the First Baptist Church of Charleston, South Carolina on August 1–3, 2007.* Edited by Michael A. G. Haykin et al. Springfield, MO: Particular Baptist, 2008.

Baptist Home Missionary Convention of Ontario. *The Canadian Baptist Hymn Book.* Toronto: Copp & Clark, 1873.

Barrows, C. E. *Historical Sketch of the First Baptist Church, Newport, R.I.* Newport, RI: Sanders, Mercury, 1876. https://archive.org/details/historyoffirstbaoobarr.

Bartholomew, Craig G., and Michael W. Goheen. *The Drama of Scripture: Finding Our Place in the Biblical Story.* Grand Rapids: Baker Academic, 2004.

Basden, Paul. "The Theology and Practice of Worship." *Theological Educator* 57 (Spring 1998) 82–90.

———. *The Worship Maze: Finding a Style to Fit Your Church.* Downers Grove: InterVarsity, 1999.

Beale, G. K. *We Become What We Worship: A Biblical Theology of Idolatry.* Downers Grove: IVP Academic, 2008.

Bebbington, David W. *Baptists through the Centuries: A History of a Global People.* Waco, TX: Baylor University Press, 2010.

Beecher, Henry Ward, and T. J. Ellinwood. *The Original Plymouth Pulpit: Sermons of Henry Ward Beecher in Plymouth Church, Brooklyn; From Stenographic Reports by T. J. Ellinwood.* Boston: Plymouth, 1897.

Belcher, Joseph, ed. *The Complete Works of the Rev. Andrew Fuller.* 3 vols. Harrisonburg, VA: Sprinkle, 1988.

Belzile, Michel R. "Canadian Baptists at Worship: A Survey of Congregational Worship within the Baptist Convention of Ontario and Quebec." DMin project, McMaster University, 1998.

Benedict, David. *A General History of the Baptist Denomination in America and Other Parts of the World.* New York: Lewis Colby, 1848.

Bennett, Arthur. *The Valley of Vision.* Carlisle, PA: Banner of Truth Trust, 1975.

Benson, Bruce Ellis. *Liturgy as a Way of Life.* The Church and Postmodern Culture. Grand Rapids: Baker Academic, 2013.

Benson, Louis F. *The English Hymn: Its Development and Its Use in Worship.* Richmond, VA: John Knox, 1963.

Best, Harold M. *Unceasing Worship: Biblical Perspectives on Worship and the Arts.* Downers Grove: InterVarsity, 2003.

Blomberg, Craig L. *Matthew.* New American Commentary 22. Nashville: Broadman & Holman, 1992.

The Book of Common Prayer. New York: Church, 2011.

Booth, Geoffrey James. "'Managing the Muses': Musical Performance and Modernity in Public Schools of Late-Nineteenth Century Toronto." PhD diss., University of Toronto, 2012.

Boswell, Matt. *Doxology and Theology: How the Gospel Forms the Worship Leader.* Nashville: Broadman & Holman, 2013.

Boulton, Matthew Myer. *Life in God: John Calvin, Practical Formation, and the Future of Protestant Theology*. Grand Rapids: Eerdmans, 2011.

Brackney, William H. *Baptists in North America: An Historical Perspective*. Religious Life in America. Malden, MA: Blackwell, 2006.

———. *A Genetic History of Baptist Thought*. Macon, GA: Mercer University Press, 2004.

Bradshaw, Paul, and John Melloh, eds. *Foundations in Ritual Studies: A Reader for Students of Christian Worship*. Grand Rapids: Baker Academic, 2007.

Bradshaw, William. *English Puritanism*. Reprint. Shropshire: Quinta, 2011.

Brewer, Paul D. "Embracing God's Word in Worship." *Baptist History and Heritage* 27 (1992) 13–22.

Brewster, Paul. *Andrew Fuller: Model Pastor-Theologian*. Nashville: B & H Academic, 2010.

Bridges, Jerry. *The Discipline of Grace: God's Role and Our Role in the Pursuit of Holiness*. Colorado Springs: NavPress, 2006.

———. *The Transforming Power of the Gospel*. Colorado Springs: NavPress, 2012.

Brink, Emily, and John D. Witvliet, eds. *The Worship Sourcebook*. Kalamazoo, MI: Faith Alive Christian Resources, 2003.

Brown, R. LaMon. "Theology, Spirituality, and the Church." *Theological Educator* 57 (1998) 113–21.

Buchan, H. E., ed. *Our Service of Song: A Collection of Psalms and Hymns for Divine Worship*. Toronto: Globe, 1875.

Buck, W. C. *The Baptist Hymn Book*. Louisville: Buck, 1842.

Bunyan, John. *A Confession of My Faith, and a Reason of My Practice*. London, 1672.

Burrage, Champlin. *The Early English Dissenters in the Light of Recent Research (1550–1641)*. 2 vols. Cambridge: Cambridge University Press, 1912.

Burrage, Henry S. *Baptist Hymn Writers and Their Hymns*. Portland, ME: Brown Thurston, 1888.

Burroughs, Jeremiah. *Gospel Worship*. Edited by Don Kistler. Reprint. Morgan, PA: Soli Deo Gloria, 2003.

Byars, Ronald P. *What Language Shall I Borrow? The Bible and Christian Worship*. Grand Rapids: Eerdmans, 2008.

"Calvin Institute of Worship." http://worship.calvin.edu/about/mission.html.

Calvin, John. *Commentaries on Genesis*. Grand Rapids: Baker, 1981.

———. *Commentary on the Epistles of Paul the Apostle to the Corinthians*. Grand Rapids: Baker, 2003.

———. *The Devotions and Prayers of John Calvin*. Edited by Charles E. Edwards. Whitefish, MT: Literary Licensing, 2011.

———. *Institutes of the Christian Religion*. Edited by John T. McNeill. Translated by F. L. Battles. Philadelphia: Westminster, 1961.

———. "The Necessity of Reforming the Church." In *Tracts and Treatises on the Reformation of the Church*, 1:184–216. Translated by Henry Beveridge. Grand Rapids: Eerdmans, 1958.

———. *Tracts and Treatises on the Reformation of the Church*. Translated by Henry Beveridge. Grand Rapids: Eerdmans, 1958.

Campbell, Iain D. "Jonathan Edwards' Religious Affections." *Scottish Bulletin of Evangelical Theology* 21 (2003) 141–62.

———. "Jonathan Edwards' Religious Affections as a Paradigm for Evangelical Spirituality." *Haddington House Journal* (2008) 141–62.

Canadian Baptist Ministers' Handbook. Toronto: Baptist Federation of Canada, 1955.

Carson, D. A. *The Cross and Christian Ministry: Leadership Lessons from 1 Corinthians.* Grand Rapids: Baker, 2004.

———. *Worship by the Book.* Grand Rapids: Zondervan, 2002.

Carter, James E. "Southern Baptist Heritage of Worship." *Baptist History and Heritage* 31 (July 1996) 38–47.

———. "What Is the Southern Baptist Heritage of Worship." *Baptist History and Heritage* 31 (1996) 38–47.

Castleman, Robbie. *Story-Shaped Worship: Following Patterns from the Bible and History.* Downers Grove: IVP Academic, 2013.

Cathcart, William, ed. "J. H. DeVotie." In *The Baptist Encyclopedia: A Dictionary of the Doctrines, Ordinances, Usages, Confessions of Faith, Sufferings, Labors, and Successes of the General History of the Baptist Denomination in All Lands,* 331–32. Philadelphia: Louis H. Everts, 1883.

Challies, Tim. "The Gospel-Centered Everything." Challies.com. March 7, 2013. http:// challies.com/articles/the-gospel-centered-everything.

Chandler, Matt, and Jared C. Wilson. *The Explicit Gospel.* Wheaton, IL: Crossway, 2012.

Chan, Simon. *Liturgical Theology: The Church as Worshiping Community.* Downers Grove: IVP Academic, 2006.

Chapell, Bryan. *Christ-Centered Preaching: Redeeming the Expository Sermon.* Grand Rapids: Baker Academic, 2005.

———. *Christ-Centered Sermons: Models of Redemptive Preaching.* Grand Rapids: Baker Academic, 2013.

———. *Christ-Centered Worship: Letting the Gospel Shape Our Practice.* Grand Rapids: Baker Academic, 2009.

———. *Holiness by Grace: Delighting in the Joy That Is Our Strength.* Wheaton, IL: Crossway, 2011.

———. "A Pastoral Theology of the Glory of God." In *The Glory of God,* edited by Christopher W. Morgan and Robert A. Peterson, 190–206. Wheaton, IL: Crossway, 2010.

Charleston Baptist Association. *The Minutes of the Charleston Baptist Association.* February 6, 1774. Charleston, SC: Charleston Baptist Association, 1774.

———. *The Minutes of the Charleston Baptist Association.* February 7, 1774. Charleston, SC: Charleston Baptist Association, 1774.

———. *The Minutes of the Charleston Baptist Association.* February 8, 1775. Charleston, SC: Charleston Baptist Association, 1775.

———. *The Minutes of the Charleston Baptist Association.* November 5, 1808. Charleston, SC: Charleston Baptist Association, 1808.

———. *The Minutes of the Charleston Baptist Association.* November 15, 1791. Charleston, SC: Charleston Baptist Association, 1791.

———. *A Summary of Church Discipline: Shewing the Qualifications and Duties, of the Officers and Members of a Gospel Church.* Edited by Oliver Hart et al. Charleston, SC: Riley, 1831.

Chenault, John Cable, and Jonathan Truman Dorris. *Old Cane Springs—a Story of the War between the States in Madison County, Kentucky.* Louisville: Standard, 1936.

Cherry, Constance M. *The Worship Architect: A Blueprint for Designing Culturally Relevant and Biblically Faithful Services.* Grand Rapids: Baker Academic, 2010.

"Choirs." *Alabama Baptist Advocate.* October 10, 1849.

The Christian's Duty, Exhibited, in a Series of Hymns: Collected from Various Authors, Designed for the Worship of God, and for the Edification of Christians. Germantown, PA: Peter Leibert, 1791.

"The Christian's Duty, Exhibited, in a Series of Hymns: Collected from Various Authors, Designed for the Worship of God, and for the Edification of Christians (1st ed.)." *Hymnary.org.* http://www.hymnary.org/hymnal/CD1791?page=3.

Chun, Chris. *The Legacy of Jonathan Edwards in the Theology of Andrew Fuller.* Boston: Brill, 2012.

Clark, David, ed. *Psalms and Hymns of Dr. Watts, Arranged by Dr. Rippon; with Dr. Rippon's Selection.* Philadelphia: David Clark, 1827.

Clark, James L. *To Set Them in Order: Some Influences of the Philadelphia Baptist Association upon Baptists in America to 1814.* Springfield, MO: Particular Baptist, 2001.

Clifford, Paul Rowntree. "Baptist Forms of Worship." *Foundations* 3 (1960) 221–33.

———. "The Structure and Ordering of Baptist Worship." *Foundations* 3 (1960) 348–61.

Cole, R. Alan. *Exodus.* Downers Grove: IVP Academic, 1973.

Conner, William T. *The Gospel of Redemption.* Nashville: Broadman, 1945.

Copan, Paul. "Jonathan Edwards's Philosophical Influences: Lockean or Malebranchean?" *Journal of the Evangelical Theological Society* 44 (2001) 107–24.

Cosper, Mike. *Rhythms of Grace: How the Church's Worship Tells the Story of the Gospel.* Wheaton, IL: Crossway, 2013.

Crosby, Thomas. *The History of the English Baptists.* Vol. 1. Lafayette, TN: Church History Research and Archives, 1738.

Cunningham, William. *The Reformation of the Church.* Edited by Iain Murray. London: Banner of Truth Trust, 1965.

Davies, Horton. *Christian Worship, Its History and Meaning.* New York: Abingdon, 1957.

———. *The Worship of the American Puritans.* Reprint. Morgan, PA: Soli Deo Gloria, 1999.

———. *The Worship of the English Puritans.* Reprint. Morgan, PA: Soli Deo Gloria, 1997.

Day, Judson Le Roy. "Spiritual Worship in Baptist Churches." *Foundations* 14 (1971) 271–83.

Deacon's Meetings Minutes: April 6, 1885–December 5, 1898. Louisville: Walnut Street Baptist Church, n.d.

"The Dedication." *Western Recorder,* November 20, 1902.

"Dedication of the Tremont Temple." *Alabama Baptist Advocate.* June 6, 1844.

Descartes, René. *Discourse on Method of Rightly Conducting One's Reason and of Seeking Truth in the Sciences.* Reprint. Auckland, New Zealand: The Floating, 2009.

DeVotie, James. *Personal Journals: 1855–1891.* Manuscript notes, sermons, and papers of J. H. DeVotie. Louisville: Boyce Centennial Library, Southern Baptist Historical Library and Archives.

Dictionary of Canadian Biography. "McMaster, William." Toronto: University of Toronto, 2003. http://www.biographi.ca/en/bio/mcmaster_william_11E.html.

Dix, Gregory. *The Shape of the Liturgy*. Westminster: Dacre, 1949.

Dixon, Warren. "Sandy Creek Separate Baptist Church." *Randolph County*. http://www. co.randolph.nc.us/hlpc/downloads/sandyCreek.pdf.

Doane, W. H., and E. H. Johnson, eds. *The Baptist Hymnal for Use in Church and Home*. Philadelphia: American Baptist Publication Society, 1883.

Doriani, Daniel M. *Getting the Message: A Plan for Interpreting and Applying the Bible*. Phillipsburg, NJ: P & R, 1996.

Due, Noel. *Created for Worship: From Genesis to Revelation to You*. Fearn, Scotland: Mentor, 2005.

Duff, Paul B. "Transformed from 'Glory to Glory': Paul's Appeal to the Experience of His Readers in 2 Corinthians 3:18." *Journal of Biblical Literature* 127 (2008) 759–80.

Duncan, Pope Alexander. "Influence of Andrew Fuller on Calvinism." PhD diss., Southern Baptist Theological Seminary, 1955.

Dunn, James D. G. *Unity and Diversity in the New Testament: An Inquiry in the Character of Earliest Christianity*. London: SCM, 2006.

Durham, John I. *Exodus*. Word Biblical Commentary 3. Waco, TX: Word, 1987.

Dutton, Anne. *Thoughts on the Lord's Supper, Relating to the Nature, Subjects, and the Right Partaking of This Solemn Ordinance*. London: Hart, 1748.

Duvall, Jim. "Old Cane Springs Baptist Church, Madison County, Kentucky." *Baptist History Homepage*. http://baptisthistoryhomepage .com/ky.madison.old.cane. sprng.html.

Eaton, T. T. "2nd Commandment." Box 8. Thomas Treadwell Eaton Papers, Archives and Special Collections, James P. Boyce Centennial Library, The Southern Baptist Theological Seminary. N.d: Louisville, n.d.

———. *Colossians 3:16*. Manuscript. Box 10. Thomas Treadwell Eaton Papers, Archives and Special Collections. Louisville: James P. Boyce Centennial Library, The Southern Baptist Theological Seminary.

———. "Defense of the Philadelphia Confession of Faith." In *Pillars of Orthodoxy; or, Defenders of the Faith*, edited by Ben M. Bogard, 110–11. Louisville: Baptist Book Concern, 1900.

———. *The Faith of Baptists*. Louisville: Baptist Book Concern, 1895.

———. *How to Behave as a Church Member*. Louisville: n.d., 1898.

———. "Right Use of the Bible in Public Worship." In The Third Annual Baptist Autumnal Conference for the Discussion of Current Questions, Held at Philadelphia, PA, November 11–13, 1884. Boston: Baptist Missionary Rooms, 1885.

———. "Some Hymns." Box 10. Thomas Treadwell Eaton Papers, Archives and Special Collections, James P. Boyce Centennial Library, The Southern Baptist Theological Seminary. N.d.: Louisville, n.d.

———. "What Is Baptism?" In *Pillars of Orthodoxy; or, Defenders of the Faith*, edited by Ben M. Bogard, 1–11. Louisville: Baptist Book Concern, 1900.

———. "Worship Excerpt." Box 2, folder 2. Thomas Treadwell Eaton Papers, Archives and Special Collections, James P. Boyce Centennial Library, The Southern Baptist Theological Seminary. N.d.: Louisville, n.d.

Eaton, T. T., et al. *History of the Walnut Street Baptist Church of Louisville, Kentucky*. Louisville: Western Recorder, 1937.

Edwards, Jonathan. "A Divine and Supernatural Light." In *Sermons and Discourses 1730–1733*, edited by Wilson H. Kimnach, 405–26. Works of Jonathan Edwards 17. New Haven, CT: Yale University Press, 1999.

———. *Religious Affections*. Edited by John E. Smith. Vol. 2 of *The Works of Jonathan Edwards*. New Haven, CT: Yale University Press, 1959.

Edwards, Morgan. *The Customs of Primitive Churches; or, A Set of Propositions Relative to the Name, Materials, Constitution, Power, Officers, Ordinances, Rites, Business, Worship, Discipline, Government, Etc. of a Church: To Which Are Added Their Proofs from Scripture; and Historical Narratives of the Manner in Which Most of Them Have Been Reduced to Practice*. Philadelphia: Andrew Steuart, 1768.

———. *Materials towards a History of American Baptists*. Philadelphia: Joseph Crukshank and Isaac Collins, 1770.

Eliot, John, et al. *The Bay Psalm Book: A Facsimile Reprint of the First Edition of 1640*. Chicago: University of Chicago Press, 1956.

Ellis, Christopher J. *Approaching God: A Practical Guide to Leading Worship*. Norwich: Canterbury, 2009.

———. "Duty and Delight: Baptist Worship and Identity." *Review & Expositor* 100 (2003) 329–49.

———. *Gathering: A Theology and Spirituality of Worship in Free Church Tradition*. Norwich: Canterbury, 2004.

———. "Gathering around the Word: Baptists, Scripture, and Worship." In *"Plainly Revealed" Word of God? Baptist Hermeneutics in Theory and Practice*, edited by Helen Dare and Simon Woodman, 101–21. Macon, GA: Mercer University Press, 2011.

———. "Who Is Worship For? Dispatches from the War Zone." *Perspectives in Religious Studies* 36 (2009) 179–85.

Emlet, Michael R. *Cross Talk: Where Life and Scripture Meet*. Greensboro, NC: New Growth, 2009.

Ensor, John M., and John Piper. *The Great Work of the Gospel: How We Experience God's Grace*. Wheaton, IL: Crossway, 2006.

Eskew, Harry. *Singing Baptists: Studies in Baptist Hymnody in America*. Nashville: LifeWay Christian Resources, 1995.

Fagerberg, David W. *Theologia Prima: What Is Liturgical Theology?* Chicago: Hillenbrand, 2004.

Fairborn, Patrick. *The Typology of Scripture; or, The Doctrine of Types*. Philadelphia: Daniels & Smith, 1852.

Felde, Marcus. "Truly Vernacular Worship for the Sake of the Gospel." *International Review of Mission* 87 (1998) 39–47.

Ferguson, Sinclair. *The Holy Spirit*. Downers Grove: InterVarsity, 1996.

———. *In Christ Alone: Living the Gospel-Centered Life*. Orlando: Reformation Trust, 2007.

Fiddes, Paul S., ed. *Under the Rule of Christ: Dimensions in Baptist Spirituality*. Macon, GA: Smyth & Helwys, 2008.

Fiddes, Paul S., and Stephen Finamore. *Baptists and Spirituality: A Rule of Life*. Macon, GA: Smyth & Helwys, 2008.

Finn, Nathan A. "Answering My Great Question about 'The Great Question Answered.'" *Historia Ecclesiastica*. http://www.andrewfullercenter .org/blog/2014/02/answering-my-great-question-about-the-great-question-answered/.

First Baptist Church. "The First Baptist Church in America, 325th Anniversary Year, May 5, 1963." Worship Bulletin. Providence: First Baptist Church, 1963.

———. "First Day, April 9, 1995." Worship Bulletin. West Palm Beach, FL: First Baptist Church, 1995.

———. "March 27, 1949." Worship Bulletin. West Palm Beach, FL: First Baptist Church, 1949.

Fitch, Titus. *The Baptists in Canada*. Toronto: The Standard, 1907.

Flynt, Wayne. *Alabama Baptists: Southern Baptists in the Heart of Dixie*. Tuscaloosa: University of Alabama Press, 1998.

Ford, Samuel H. *Baptist Waymarks*. Philadelphia: American Baptist Publication Society, 1903. http://geocitiessites.com/baptist_documents/waymarks.ford.contents.html.

Frame, John M. *Contemporary Worship Music: A Biblical Defense*. Phillipsburg, NJ: P & R, 1997.

———. "A Fresh Look at the Regulative Principle: A Broader View." *Frame and Poythress*. June 4, 2012. https://frame-poythress.org/a-fresh-look-at-the-regulative-principle-a-broader-view/.

Fuller, A. James. *Chaplain to the Confederacy: Basil Manly and Baptist Life in the Old South*. Baton Rouge: Louisiana State University Press, 2000.

Fuller, Andrew. *The Works of Andrew Fuller*. Edited by Andrew Gunton Fuller. Carlisle, PA: Banner of Truth Trust, 2007.

Fuller, Andrew, et al. *The Works of Andrew Fuller*. Carlisle, PA: Banner of Truth Trust, 2007.

Fuller, Andrew, and Andrew Gunton Fuller. *The Complete Works of the Rev. Andrew Fuller: With a Memoir of His Life*. Boston: Gould, Kendall, and Lincoln, 1836.

Fuller, Andrew, and Joseph Belcher. *The Last Remains of the Rev. Andrew Fuller: Sermons, Essays, Letters, and Other Miscellaneous Papers, Not Included in His Published Works*. Philadelphia: American Baptist Publication Society, 1856.

Fuller, Andrew, and Michael A. G Haykin. *The Armies of the Lamb: The Spirituality of Andrew Fuller*. Dundas, Ontario: Joshua, 2001.

Fuller Richard, et al. *The Baptist Praise Book: For Congregational Singing*. New York: Barnes, 1871.

Furman, Wood. *A History of the Charleston Association of Baptist Churches in the State of South Carolina*. Charleston, SC: Hoff, 1811.

Garrett, James Leo, Jr. *Baptist Church Discipline*. Nashville: Broadman, 1962.

George, Timothy, and Denise George, eds. *Baptist Confessions, Covenants, and Catechisms*. Nashville: Broadman & Holman, 1996.

Gilbert, Greg. *What Is the Gospel?* Wheaton, IL: Crossway, 2010.

Gillette, A. D., ed. *The Minutes of the Philadelphia Baptist Association from A.D. 1707 to A. D. 1807 Being the First One Hundred Years of Its Existence*. Philadelphia: American Baptist Publication Society, 1851.

Goldsworthy, Graeme. *According to Plan: The Unfolding Revelation of God in the Bible*. Downers Grove: IVP Academic, 2002.

———. *Gospel-Centered Hermeneutics: Foundations and Principles of Evangelical Biblical Interpretation*. Downers Grove: IVP Academic, 2010.

———. *Preaching the Whole Bible as Christian Scripture: The Application of Biblical Theology to Expository Preaching*. Grand Rapids: Eerdmans, 2000.

Goertz, Donald. "Alexander Grant: Pastor, Evangelist, Visionary." In *Costly Vision: The Baptist Pilgrimage in Canada*, edited by Jarold K. Zeman, 16–22. Burlington, ON: Welch, 1988.

Goodspeed, Calvin. *The Peculiar Principles of Baptists*. Toronto: Dudley and Burns, 1878.

Gore, Ralph Jackson, Jr. *Covenantal Worship: Reconsidering the Puritan Regulative Principle*. Phillipsburg, NJ: P & R, 2002.

———. "The Pursuit of Plainness: Rethinking the Puritan Regulative Principle of Worship." PhD diss., Westminster Theological Seminary, 1988.

The Gospel Witness: A History of Jarvis Street Baptist Church. Jarvis Street Baptist Church, 2012. DVD.

Green, Joel B. *The Gospel of Luke*. New International Commentary on the New Testament. Grand Rapids: Eerdmans, 1997.

Gregory, David Louis. "Southern Baptist Hymnals (1956, 1975, 1991) as Sourcebooks for Worship in Southern Baptist Churches." MCM thesis, Southern Baptist Theological Seminary, 1994.

Grenz, Stanley. *Isaac Backus—Puritan and Baptist*. Macon, GA: Mercer University Press, 1983.

Grindheim, Sigurd. "The Law Kills but the Gospel Gives Life: The Letter-Spirit Dualism in 2 Corinthians 3.5–18." *Journal for the Study of the New Testament* 84 (2001) 97–115.

Hafemann, Scott J. *2 Corinthians*. NIV Application Commentary. Grand Rapids: Zondervan, 2000.

Hall, E. Eugene. "The Word as Worship." *Theological Educator* 38 (1988) 56–70.

Harmon, Steven R. *Towards Baptist Catholicity: Essays on Tradition and the Baptist Vision*. Waynesboro, GA: Paternoster, 2006.

Hart, Oliver. *A Copy of Original Diary of Rev. Oliver Hart of Charlestown, Pastor of the Baptist Church of Charleston, 1741*. Typewritten Copy: Loulie Latimer Owens, 1949. E-text Collection, Archives and Special Collections, James P. Boyce Centennial Library, The Southern Baptist Theological Seminary, Louisville, Kentucky.

———. *A Gospel Church Portrayed, and Her Orderly Service Pointed Out—A Sermon, Delivered in the City of Philadelphia at the Opening of the Baptist Association, October 4, 1791*. Trenton, NJ: Collins, 1791.

———. *An Humble Attempt to Repair the Christian Temple—A Sermon, Shewing the Business of Officers and Private Members in the Church of Christ, and How Their Work Should Be Performed; with Some Motives to Excite Professors Ardently to Engage in It. Preached in the City of Philadelphia, October 21st, 1783 at the Opening of the Association and Published at Their Request*. Philadelphia: Aitken, 1785.

Haykin, Michael A. G. *The Armies of the Lamb: The Spirituality of Andrew Fuller*. Dundas, Ontario: Joshua, 2001.

———. *"At the Pure Fountain of Thy Word:" Andrew Fuller as an Apologist*. Carlisle, PA: Paternoster, 2004.

———. "'Dr. Thomas of Toronto:' The Life and Ministry of Benjamin Daniel Thomas (1843–1917)." June 2008. http://www.andrewfullercenter.org/files/bd-thomas-for-gw-june-2008.pdf.

Haykin, Michael A. G., et al. *Soldiers of Christ: Selections from the Writings of Basil Manly, Sr., and Basil Manly, Jr*. Cape Coral, FL: Founders, 2009.

Henderson, Samuel. *Christianity Exemplified: A Memorial Service of Rev. Basil Manly, Sr., D.D.* Atlanta: Franklin Stream, 1870.

Hill, Andrew E. *Enter His Courts with Praise! Old Testament Worship for the New Testament Church.* Grand Rapids: Baker, 1997.

Hinson, Glenn E. "Baptists and Spirituality: A Community at Worship." *Review and Expositor* 84 (1987) 649–58.

"History of Samford University: Biography." http://www.samford.edu/universityhistory/biography.aspx.

"History of Siloam Baptist Church." *Alabama Baptist Advocate.* September 12, 1849.

Holcombe, Hosea. *A History of the Rise and Progress of the Baptists in Alabama.* Philadelphia: King and Baird, 1840.

Holmes, Stephen. "Religious Affections by Jonathan Edwards (1702–1758)." In *The Devoted Life: An Invitation to the Puritan Classics,* edited by Kelly M. Kapic and Randall C. Gleason, 285–97. Downers Grove: InterVarsity, 2004.

Hoon, Paul Waitman. *The Integrity of Worship: Ecumenical and Pastoral Studies in Liturgical Theology.* Nashville: Abingdon, 1971.

Hotz, Kendra G., and Matthew T. Mathews. *Shaping the Christian Life: Worship and the Religious Affections.* Louisville: Westminster John Knox, 2006.

Howell, R. B. C. *The Early Baptists of Virginia.* Philadelphia: Bible and Publication Society, 1857.

Hughes, D. Ian. "'No Principle at Second-Hand': Influences upon the Thought of Andrew Fuller in 'The Gospel of All Acceptation.'" ThM thesis, Westminster Theological Seminary, 2012.

Hughes, Graham. *Worship as Meaning: A Liturgical Theology for Late Modernity.* Cambridge: Cambridge University Press, 2003.

Hughes, Philip E. *The Second Epistle to the Corinthians.* New International Commentary on the New Testament. Grand Rapids: Eerdmans, 1992.

Hughes, R. Kent. *2 Corinthians: Power in Weakness.* Preaching the Word. Wheaton, IL: Crossway, 2006.

Huntingdon. "A Tribute to Dr. Edwin T. Winkler, August 25, 1872." Handwritten, August 25, 1872. Siloam Baptist Church Parlor Collection of Historical Artifacts, Marion, Alabama.

Hurtado, Larry. *At the Origins of Christian Worship.* Grand Rapids: Eerdmans, 2000.

Hustad, Donald P. "Baptist Worship Forms: Uniting the Charleston and Sandy Creek Traditions." *Review and Expositor* 85 (1988) 31–42.

"The Institute for Worship Studies." *The Institute for Worship Studies.* http://iws.edu/about/mission/.

Irwin, Kevin W. *Liturgical Theology: A Primer.* Collegeville, MN: Liturgical, 1990.

"James DeVotie." *Alabama Baptist Advocate.* April 17, 1849.

Jarvis Street Baptist Church Deacon's Book: May 1882–June 1899. Toronto: Jarvis Street Baptist Church, n.d.

Jarvis Street Minute Book: 1892–1910. Toronto: Jarvis Street Baptist Church, n.d.

Jones, Horatio Gates. *Historical Sketch of the Lower Dublin (or Pennepek) Baptist Church.* Morrisania, NY: n.d., 1869.

Jones, Samuel. *A Century Sermon: Delivered in Philadelphia, at the Opening of the Philadelphia Baptist Association, October 6th, 1807.* Philadelphia: Bartram and Reynolds, 1807.

Jones, Samuel, and Burgiss Allison, eds. *Selection of Psalms and Hymns Done under the Appointment of the Philadelphian Association*. Philadelphia: Aitken, 1790.

Johnson, William B. "Reminiscences of William B. Johnson." Edited by J. Glenwood Clayton. *Journal of the South Carolina Baptist Historical Society* 4 (1978) 1–11.

Julian, John, ed. "Doxologies." In *A Dictionary of Hymnology: Setting Forth the Origin and History of Christian Hymns of All Ages and Nations*, 308. New York: Scribner, 1892.

Kauflin, Bob. *Worship Matters: Leading Others to Encounter the Greatness of God*. Wheaton, IL: Crossway, 2008.

Kavanagh, Aidan. *On Liturgical Theology*. New York: Pueblo, 1984.

Keach, Benjamin. *The Breach Repaired in God's Worship*. London: Hancock, 1691.

———. *A Golden Mine Opened; or, The Glory of God's Rich Grace Displayed in the Mediator to Believers*. London: Marshall, 1694.

Keach, Elias. *A Banquetting-House Full of Spiritual Delights; or, Hymns and Spiritual Songs on Several Occasions*. London: Harris, 1696.

———. *The Glory and Ornament of a True Gospel-Constituted Church*. London, 1697. http://baptiststudiesonline.com/wp-content/uploads/2006/11/The-Glory-and-Ornament-of-a-True-Gospel-Church.pdf.

———. *A Plain and Familiar Discourse on Justification Being the Substance of Four Sermons, Preach'd at the Morning-Lecture, at Pinners-Hall, in Broad Street, the Third, Tenth, Seventeenth, and Twenty Fourth Days of September, 1693*. Ann Arbor, MI: University of Michigan, Digital Library Production Service. http://name.umdl.umich.edu/A47098.0001.001.

Keen, William Williams, ed. *First Baptist Church Philadelphia: Bi-centennial Celebration*. Philadelphia: American Baptist Publication Society, 1899.

Keown, Harlice E. "The Preaching of Andrew Fuller." ThM thesis, Southern Baptist Theological Seminary, 1957.

Keywood, Jay. "Jonathan Edwards' Religious Affections and True Religion in the Local Church." *Founders Journal* 85 (2011) 14–22.

Kidd, Reggie M. *With One Voice: Discovering Christ's Song in Our Worship*. Grand Rapids: Baker, 2005.

Kidd, Thomas S. "'Do the Holy Scriptures Countenance Such Wild Disorder?' Baptist Growth in the Eighteenth-Century American South." In *Baptists and Missions: Papers from the Fourth International Conference on Baptist Studies*, edited by Ian M. Randall and Anthony R. Cross, 109–29. Milton Keynes, UK: Paternoster, 2007.

The Great Awakening: The Roots of Evangelical Christianity in Colonial America. New Haven, CT: Yale University Press, 2007.

Kiffin, William. *A Sober Discourse of Right to Church-Communion*. London: Prosser, 1681.

Kimbrough, B. T. *The History of the Walnut Street Baptist Church, Louisville, Kentucky*. Louisville: Press of Western Recorder, 1949.

Kittel, Gerhard, ed. *Theological Dictionary of the New Testament*. Translated by Geoffrey W. Bromiley. Grand Rapids: Eerdmans, 1967.

Knight, Richard. *History of the General or Six Principle Baptists, in Europe and America*. New York: Arno, 1980.

Knollys, Hanserd. *An Exposition of the Whole Book of the Revelation*. London: Marshall, 1689.

———. *The Parable of the Kingdom of Heaven Expounded*. London: Harris, 1674.

————. *The World That Now Is; and the World That Is to Come: Or the First and Second Coming of Jesus Christ*. London: Snowdon, 1681.

Lathrop, Gordon W. *Holy Things: A Liturgical Theology*. Minneapolis: Fortress, 1998.

————. "New Pentecost of Joseph's Britches? Reflections on the History and Meaning of the Worship Ordo in the Megachurches." *Worship* 72 (2001) 521–38.

Leafblad, Bruce. "Evangelical Worship: A Biblical Model for Worship in the Twenty-First Century." In *Experience God in Worship*, edited by Michael D. Warden, 93–114. Loveland, CO: Group, 2000.

LeBaron, J. Hugh. *Sketches from the Life of Charles Crow, 1770–1845*. J. Hugh LeBaron, 1995. http://www.angelfire.com/al2/crowe/sketches.html.

Lee, Simon S. *Jesus' Transfiguration and the Believers' Transformation: A Study of the Transfiguration and Its Development in Early Christian Writings*. Tubingen, Germany: Mohr Siebeck, 2009.

Leland, John. *The Writings of the Late Elder John Leland, Including Some Events in His Life, Written by Himself; with Additional Sketches, &c by L. F. Greene*. Edited by L. F. Greene. Gallatin, TN: Church History Research and Archives, 1986.

Lemons, J. Stanley. *First Baptist, Providence*. Baptists in Early North America 2. Macon, GA: Mercer University Press, 2013.

————. *The First Baptist Church in America*. Macon, GA: Charitable Baptist Society, 1988.

Leonard, Bill J. *Baptists in America*. New York: Columbia University Press, 2005.

————. *Community in Diversity: A History of Walnut Street Baptist Church, 1815–1990*. Louisville: Simons-Neely, 1990.

Leonard, Richard C. *The Biblical Foundations of Christian Worship*. Edited by Robert E. Webber. Complete Library of Christian Worship 2. Peabody, MA: Hendrickson, 1993.

Levy, I. Judson. *Come, Let Us Worship: A Guide for Public Worship*. St. Stephen, New Brunswick: Print 'n Press, 1979.

Lindman, Janet Moore. *Bodies of Belief: Baptist Community in Early America*. Early American Studies. Philadelphia: University of Pennsylvania Press, 2008.

Litwa, David M. "2 Corinthians 3:18 and Its Implications for Theosis." *Journal of Theological Interpretation* 2 (2008) 117–33.

Lock, William Rowland. *Ontario Church Choirs and Choral Societies, 1818–1918*. Ann Arbor: University Microfilms, 1973.

Loftis, John F. "Factors in Southern Baptist Identity as Reflected by Ministerial Role Models, 1750–1925." PhD diss., Southern Baptist Theological Seminary, 1987.

Lovelace, Julia Murfee. *A History of Siloam Baptist Church, Marion, Alabama*. Birmingham: Birmingham, 1943.

Lovette, Roger. "'Eleven O'clock on Sunday Morning': Proclamation in the Context of Worship." *Review and Expositor* 84 (1987) 87–97.

————. *Jonathan Edwards: The Holy Spirit in Revival*. Darlington: Evangelical, 2005.

————. "A Sweet Flame": Piety in the Letters of Jonathan Edwards*. Grand Rapids: Reformation Heritage, 2007.

Lucas, Sean Michael. *God's Grand Design*. Wheaton, IL: Crossway, 2011.

Lumpkin, William L. *Baptist Confessions of Faith*. Philadelphia: Judson, 1959.

————. *Baptist Foundations in the South*. Nashville: Broadman, 1961.

MacArthur, John. *2 Corinthians*. MacArthur New Covenant Commentary. Chicago: Moody, 2003.

Mahaney, C. J. *Living the Cross-Centered Life: Keeping the Gospel the Main Thing*. Sisters, OR: Multnomah, 2006.

Mallory, Charles D. *Memoirs of Elder Edmund Botsford*. Charleston, SC: Riley, 1832.

Man, Ron. *Proclamation and Praise: Hebrews 2:12 and the Christology of Worship*. Eugene, OR: Wipf & Stock, 2007.

Manly, Basil, ed. *Baptist Chorals: A Tune and Hymn Book Designed to Promote General Congregational Singing; Containing One Hundred and Sixty-Four Tunes, Adapted to about Four Hundred Choice Hymns*. Richmond, VA: Starke, 1859.

———, ed. *Manly's Choice: A New Selection of Approved Hymns for Baptist Churches; with Music*. Louisville: Baptist Book Concern, 1892.

———. *Mercy and Judgment, a Discourse Containing Some Fragments of the History of the Baptist Church in Charleston, South Carolina, Delivered at the Request of the Corporation of Said Church, September 23rd and 30th, A.D. 1832*. Charleston, SC: Knowles and Vose, 1837.

Manly, Basil, and Basil Manly, Jr., eds. *The Baptist Psalmody: A Selection of Hymns for the Worship of God*. New York: Sheldon, 1850.

Manly, Basil, et al. *The Baptist Psalmody: A Selection of Hymns for the Worship of God*. Charleston, SC: Southern Baptist Publication Society, 1850.

Marsden, George. *Jonathan Edwards: A Life*. New Haven, CT: Yale University Press, 2003.

Marshall, Walter. *The Gospel-Mystery of Sanctification*. Reprint. Grand Rapids: Zondervan, 1954.

Martin, Ralph P. *Worship in the Early Church*. London: Marshall, Morgan & Scott, 1964.

McBeth, H. Leon. *A Sourcebook for Baptist Heritage*. Nashville: Broadman, 1990.

McBeth, Leon. "Baptist Beginnings." *Baptist History and Heritage* 15 (1980) 36–41.

McCartney, Dan, and Charles Clayton. *Let the Reader Understand: A Guide to Interpreting and Applying the Bible*. Phillipsburg, NJ: P & R, 2002.

McCollum, David. "A Study of Evangelicals and Revival Exercises from 1730–1805: Tracing the Development of Exercise Traditions through the First Great Awakening Period to the Southern Great Revival." PhD diss., Southeastern Baptist Theological Seminary, 2009.

McDormand, Thomas Bruce. *The Art of Building Worship Services*. Nashville: Broadman, 1942.

McElrath, Hugh T. *Sing with Understanding: An Introduction to Christian Hymnology*. Nashville: Genevox, 1995.

McKibbens, Thomas R. "Our Baptist Heritage in Worship." *Review and Expositor* 80 (1983) 53–69.

McLoughlin, William G. *Soul Liberty*. Hanover, NH: Brown University Press, 1991.

Mears, Amy Lee. "Worship in Selected Churches of the Charleston Baptist Association, 1682–1795." PhD diss., Southern Baptist Theological Seminary, 1995.

Measels, Donald Clark. "A Catalog of Source Readings in Southern Baptist Church Music, 1828–1890." DMA project, Southern Baptist Theological Seminary, 1986.

Meikleham, Marget H. C. "Caldicott, Thomas Ford." In *Dictionary of Canadian Biography*. Toronto: University of Toronto, 2008. http://www.biographi.ca/en/bio/caldicott_thomas_ford_9E.html.

Miller, H. New *Selection of Psalms, Hymns, and Spiritual Songs, from the Best Authors, Designed for Use in Conference Meetings, Private Circles, and Congregations*. Cincinnati: Miller, 1835.

Minutes from Olde Pennepack Record Books, 1687–1894. Philadelphia: Pennepack Baptist Church, 1894.

Mitchell, Carlton Turner. "Baptist Worship in Relation to Baptist Concepts of the Church, 1608–1865." PhD diss., New York University, 1962.

Mitman, F. Russell. *Worship in the Shape of Scripture.* Cleveland, OH: Pilgrim, 2001.

Morden, Peter J., and Ian M. Randall. *Offering Christ to the World: Andrew Fuller (1754–1815) and the Revival of Eighteenth-Century Particular Baptist Life.* Waynesboro, GA: Paternoster, 2003.

Morgan, Christopher W., and Robert A. Peterson, eds. *The Glory of God.* Wheaton, IL: Crossway, 2010.

Morrill, Bruce T. *Anamnesis as Dangerous Memory: Political and Liturgical Theology in Dialogue.* Collegeville, MN: Liturgical, 2000.

Murphy, Debra Dean. "Worship as Catechesis: Knowledge, Desire, and Christian Formation." *Theology Today* 58 (2001) 321–32.

Murrell, Irvin Henry, Jr. "Ardor and Order: Southern Antebellum Baptist Hymnody . . . and Beyond." In *Baptist History Celebration 2007: A Symposium on Our History, Theology, and Hymnody,* 36–47. Springfield, MO: Particular Baptist, 2008.

———. "An Examination of Southern Ante-Bellum Baptist Hymnals as Indicators of the Congregational Hymn and Tune Repertories of the Period with an Analysis of Representative Tunes." DMA project, New Orleans Baptist Theological Seminary, 1984.

Music, David W. "Baptists Hymnals as Shapers of Worship." *Baptist History and Heritage* 31 (1996) 7–17.

———. "Congregational Song Practices in Southern Baptist Churches." *Southern Baptist Church Music Journal* 9 (1992) 10–20.

———. "The Glorious Gospel: Our Worship Heritage." *Southwestern Journal of Theology* 34 (1992) 28–32.

———. *Hymnology: A Collection of Source Readings.* Lanham, MD: Scarecrow, 1996.

Music, David, and Paul A. Richardson. *"I Will Sing the Wondrous Story": A History of Baptist Hymnody in North America.* Macon, GA: Mercer University Press, 2008.

A Narrative of the Proceedings of the General Assembly of Divers Pastors, Messengers and Ministering-Brethren, Met Together in London. London, 1689.

Nettles, Tom J. *The Baptists: Key People Involved in Forming a Baptist Identity.* Vol. 2. Scotland: Christian Focus, 2005.

———. "Basil Manly, Fire from Light." Paper presented at the Founders Day Convocation, Southern Baptist Theological Seminary, Louisville, January 31, 1995.

———. "Biographical Sketch of John L. Dagg." *Founders.org.* http://founders.org/library/dagg_sketch/.

———. "Edwards and His Impact on Baptists." *Founders Journal* 53 (2003) 1–18.

Newman, A. H. *A History of the Baptist Churches in the United States.* New York: Christian Literature, 1894.

Noll, Mark A. *Wonderful Words of Life: Hymns in American Protestant History and Theology.* Grand Rapids: Eerdmans, 2004.

Nuttal, Geoffrey F. "Northamptonshire and the Modern Question: A Turning-Point in Eighteenth-Century Dissent." *Journal of Theological Studies* 16 (1965) 101–23.

O'Kelly, Steve. "The Influence of the Separate Baptists on Revivalistic Evangelism and Worship." PhD diss., Southwestern Baptist Theological Seminary, 1978.

Olford, Stephen F. "Restoring the Scriptures to Baptist Worship." *Review and Expositor* 85 (1988) 19–30.

Packer, J. I. *Grounded in the Gospel: Building Believers the Old-Fashioned Way*. Grand Rapids: Baker, 2010.

Parrett, Gary. "9.5 Theses on Christian Worship: A Disputation on the Role of Music." *Christianity Today* 49 (2005) 38–42.

Pennepack Baptist Church 275th Anniversary Program: Forward through the Ages. Philadelphia: Lower Dublin Baptist Church, 1963.

Peterson, David. *Encountering God: Biblical Patterns for Ministry and Worship*. Nottingham: InterVarsity, 2013.

Peterson, David G. *Encountering God Together: Leading Worship Services That Honor God, Minister to His People, and Build His Church*. Phillipsburg, NJ: P & R, 2014.

———. *Engaging with God: A Biblical Theology of Worship*. Downers Grove: IVP Academic, 2002.

Peterson, Eugene. *The Message: The Bible in Contemporary Language*. Colorado Springs: NavPress, 2002.

Pfatteicher, Philip H. *Liturgical Spirituality*. Valley Forge, PA: Trinity Press International, 1997.

Phifer, Kenneth G. *A Protestant Case for Liturgical Renewal*. Philadelphia: Westminster, 1965.

Phipps, William E. *Amazing Grace in John Newton: Slave Ship Captain, Hymn Writer, and Abolitionist*. Macon, GA: Mercer University Press, 2001.

Piper, John. *Desiring God: Meditations of a Christian Hedonist*. Colorado Springs: Multnomah, 2011.

———. *Future Grace*. Sisters, OR: Multnomah, 2005.

———. *God Is the Gospel: Meditations on God's Love as the Gift of Himself*. Wheaton, IL: Crossway, 2011.

———. *Seeing and Savoring Jesus Christ*. Wheaton, IL: Crossway, 2004.

———. *The Supremacy of God in Preaching*. Grand Rapids: Baker, 2004.

Piper, John, and Justin Taylor, eds. *A God Entranced Vision of All Things: The Legacy of Jonathan Edwards*. Wheaton, IL: Crossway, 2004.

Platt, Nathan Harold. "The Hymnological Contributions of Basil Manly Jr. to the Congregational Song of Southern Baptists." DMA project, The Southern Baptist Theological Seminary, 2004.

Poloma, Margaret M. "Giving Glory to God in Appalachia: Worship Practices of Six Baptist Subdenominations." *Journal of the American Academy of Religion* 58 (1990) 492–94.

Poti, Nancy Rock. "Gathered and Scattered: Worship That Embodies a Right Relationship with God." *Review and Expositor* 106 (2009) 235–47.

Pratt, Andrew. "A Community of Ministers: Pastors and Staff." In *Community in Diversity: A History of Walnut Street Baptist Church, 1815–1990*, by Bill J. Leonard, 61–82. Louisville: Simons-Neely, 1990.

Price, Charles P., and Louis Weil. *Liturgy for Living*. Harrisburg, PA: Morehouse, 2000.

Priestley, David T., ed. *Memory and Hope: Strands of Canadian Baptist History*. Waterloo, ON: Canadian Corporation for Studies in Religion, 1996.

"The Psalmist." *Alabama Baptist Advocate*, January 8, 1847.

Purefoy, George W. *A History of the Sandy Creek Association*. New York: Sheldon, 1859.

Ratliff, F. William. "The Place of the Lord's Supper: Afterthought or Central Focus?" *Review and Expositor* 80 (1983) 85–96.

Rawlyk, G. A., ed. *Canadian Baptists and Christian Higher Education*. Montreal: McGill-Queen's University Press, 1988.

Rayburn, Robert G. *O Come, Let Us Worship: Corporate Worship in the Evangelical Church*. Eugene, OR: Wipf & Stock, 2010.

Reid, Avery Hamilton. *Baptists in Alabama: Their Organization and Witness*. Montgomery, AL: Alabama Baptist State Convention, 1967.

Reisinger, Ernest C., and D. Matthew Allen. *Worship: The Regulative Principle and the Biblical Practice of Accommodation*. Cape Coral, FL: Founders, 2001.

Reynolds, William Jenson. "Baptist Hymnody in America." In *Handbook to The Baptist Hymnal*, edited by Jere V. Adams, 30–54. Nashville: Convention, 1992.

———. *A Survey of Christian Hymnody*. Carol Stream, IL: Hope, 1991.

Richardson, Paul A. "Hymnology: A Crucial Intersection." *Review and Expositor* 91 (1994) 421–35.

———. "Sing Them Over Again to Me: Scripture and Hymns." *Review and Expositor* 106 (2009) 189–206.

Rienstra, Debra K., and Ron Rienstra. *Worship Words: Discipling Language for Faithful Ministry*. Grand Rapids: Baker Academic, 2009.

Rivera, Ted. *Jonathan Edwards on Worship: Public and Private Devotion to God*. Eugene, OR: Pickwick, 2010.

Roberts, R. D. "John Rippon's 'Selection of Hymns' and Its Contributions to Baptist Hymnody." MCM thesis, Southwestern Baptist Theological Seminary, 1972.

Robertson, John Ross. *Sketches in City Churches*. Toronto: Robertson, 1886.

Robinson, Haddon W. *Biblical Preaching: The Development and Delivery of Expository Messages*. Grand Rapids: Baker Academic, 2001.

Roper, Cecil M. "A Response: Worship." *Southwestern Journal of Theology* 28 (1986) 25–27.

Rose, Richard Wayne. "'The Psalmist': A Significant Hymnal for Baptists in America during the Nineteenth Century." DMA project, Southwestern Baptist Theological Seminary, 1991.

Ross, Allen P. *Recalling the Hope of Glory: Biblical Worship from the Garden to the New Creation*. Grand Rapids: Kregel, 2006.

Rosser, F. T. "Fyfe, Robert Alexander." In *Dictionary of Canadian Biography*. Toronto: University of Toronto, 2003. http://www.biographi.ca/en/bio/fyfe_robert_alexander_10E.html.

Ryland, John. *The Life and Death of Andrew Fuller*. London: Button, 1816.

Sacred Performances at the Dedication of the Baptist Meeting-House in Charlestown, May 12, 1801. Boston: Manning and Loring, 1801. https://archive.org/stream/sacredperoofirs#page/n3/mode/2up.

Schaff, Philip, ed. *The Evangelical Protestant Creeds*. Vol. 3, *The Creeds of Christendom with a History and Critical Notes*. Grand Rapids: Baker, 1990.

Scharf, John Thomas, and Thompson Westcott. *History of Philadelphia: 1609–1884*. Philadelphia: Everts, 1884.

Schenkel, Albert Frederick. "New Wine and Baptist Wineskins: American and Southern Baptist Denominational Responses ot the Charismatic Renewal, 1960–80." In *Pentecostal Currents in American Protestantism*, edited by Edith L. Blumhofer et al., 152–67. Urbana: University of Illinois Press, 1999.

Schmemann, Alexander. *The Eucharist: Sacrament of the Kingdom.* Translated by Paul Kachur. Crestwood, NY: St. Vladimir's Seminary Press, 1988.

———. *Introduction to Liturgical Theology.* Translated by Asheleigh E. Moorhouse. Portland, ME: American Orthodox, 1966.

———. "Liturgical Theology: Remarks on Method." In *Liturgy and Tradition: Theological Reflections of Alexander Schmemann,* edited by Thomas Fisch, 137–44. Crestwood, NY: St. Vladimir's Seminary Press, 1982.

Schmit, Clayton J. *Sent and Gathered: A Worship Manual for the Missional Church.* Grand Rapids: Baker Academic, 2009.

Schreiner, Thomas R. *Paul: Apostle of God's Glory in Christ.* Downers Grove: IVP Academic, 2001.

Seerveld, Calvin. *Voicing God's Psalms.* Grand Rapid: Eerdmans, 2005.

Segler, Franklin M., and C. Randall Bradley. *Christian Worship: Its Theology and Its Practice.* Nashville, B & H Academic, 2006.

Semple, Robert Baylor. *A History of the Rise and Progress of the Baptists in Virginia.* Edited by G. W. Beale. Reprint. Lafayette, TN: Church History Research and Archives, 1894.

Senn, Frank. *Christian Liturgy: Catholic and Evangelical.* Minneapolis: Fortress, 1997.

Shepard, C. Edward. "Observing the Christian Year as a Means of Facilitating Christian Growth." *Review and Expositor* 106 (2009) 221–33.

Shepherd, Massey Hamilton, et al. *The Liturgical Renewal of the Church.* New York: Oxford University Press, 1960.

Sheppard, Lancelot C. *The People Worship: A History of the Liturgical Movement.* New York: Hawthorn, 1967.

Shurden, William. *Not an Easy Journey: Some Transitions in Baptist Life.* Macon: Mercer University Press, 2005.

Siloam Baptist Church. "The Constitution of Siloam Baptist Church." Typewritten copy. Siloam Baptist Church Parlor Collection of Historical Artifacts, Marion, Alabama. Marion, AL: 1850.

———. *Plan of Church Work, Adopted by Siloam Baptist Church, March 30, 1879.* Marion, AL: Siloam Baptist Church, 1879.

Simpson, Phillip L. *A Life of Gospel Peace: A Biography of Jeremiah Burroughs.* Grand Rapids: Reformation Heritage, 2011.

Singer, David. "God and Man in Baptist Hymnals, 1784–1844." *American Studies* 9 (1968) 14–26. https://journals.ku.edu/index.php/amerstud/article/viewFile/2157/2116.

Smith, Eric Coleman. "Order and Ardor: The Revival Spirituality of Regular Baptist Oliver Hart [1723–1795] of the Charleston Tradition." PhD prospectus, Southern Baptist Theological Seminary, 2015.

Smith, Karen E. "Community and Conflict: Theological Issues." In *Community in Diversity: A History of Walnut Street Baptist Church, 1815–1990,* edited by Bill J. Leopard, 156–74. Louisville: Simons-Neely, 1990.

Smith, James K. A. *Desiring the Kingdom: Worship, Worldview, and Cultural Formation.* Grand Rapids: Baker Academic, 2009.

———. *Imagining the Kingdom: How Worship Works.* Grand Rapids: Baker Academic, 2013.

Smith, Joseph F., ed. *The Latter Day Saints Memorial Star.* Vol. 39. London: Smith, 1877.

Smith, Peter. "Sojourn Community Church Balances 10 Years of Faith, Arts, Service." *Courier-Journal*, September 19, 2010. https://secure.pqarchiver.com/courier_journal/doc/751846613.html?FMT=FT.

Smyth, John. "The Differences of the Churches of the Separation." In *The Works of John Smyth*, edited by W. T. Whitley, 1:269–92. Cambridge: University Press, 1915.

South, Thomas J. "The Response of Andrew Fuller to the Sandemanian View of Saving Faith." ThD diss., Mid-America Baptist Theological Seminary, 1993.

Southern Baptist Convention. *The Proceedings of the Southern Baptist Convention, Convened at Nashville, Tennessee, on May 9th, 10th, 12th, and 13th*. Richmond, 1851.

Spann, C. Edward. "Singing among Baptists up to 1689." *Baptist History and Heritage* 3 (1968) 51–59.

Spencer, David. *The Early Baptists of Philadelphia*. Philadelphia: Syckelmoore, 1877.

Spilsbury, John. *A Treatise Concerning the Lawfull Subject of Baptisme*. London, 1643.

Sponseller, Edwin H. *Northampton and Jonathan Edwards*. Shippensburg, PA: Shippensburg State College, 1966.

Sprague, William B. *Annals of the American Baptist Pulpit*. Vol. 7. New York: Carter, 1860.

Stein, Robert H. *Luke*. New American Commentary 24. Nashville: Broadman & Holman, 1992.

Stillman, Samuel. *A Good Minister of Jesus Christ: A Sermon, Preached in Boston, September 15, 1797 at the Ordination of the Rev. Mr. Stephen Smith Nelson*. Boston, MA: Manning & Loring, 1797. http://ezproxy.sbts.edu:2048/login?url=http://opac.newsbank.com/select/evans/32882.

Stow, Baron, and S. F. Smith, eds. *The Psalmist: A New Collection of Hymns for the Use of the Baptist Churches*. Boston: Gould, Kendall and Lincoln, 1845.

Talbot, Mark. "Godly Emotions (Religious Affections)." In *A God Entranced Vision of All Things*, edited by John Piper and Justin Taylor. Wheaton, IL: Crossway, 2004.

Taylor, Michael J. *Liturgical Renewal in the Christian Churches*. Baltimore: Helicon, 1967.

"Thanksgiving Day in Missouri." *Alabama Baptist Advocate*, June 6, 1844.

Thomas, B. D. *"The Harp of Ten Strings" in A Souvenir of the Tenth Anniversary of the Settlement of B. D. Thomas with the Jarvis Street Baptist Church*. Toronto: Davis and Henderson, 1892.

———. "Memorial Sermon on William Mann of Philadelphia." 19. Philadelphia: n.d., 1881.

———. *"My Pastorate in Toronto": A Souvenir of the Tenth Anniversary of the Settlement of B. D. Thomas with the Jarvis Street Baptist Church*. Toronto: Davis and Henderson, 1892.

———. *Sermons Preached in the Jarvis Street Baptist Church, Toronto*. Toronto: Briggs, 1911.

Thomas, Derek W. H. *How the Gospel Brings Us All the Way Home*. Orlando: Reformation Trust, 2011.

Thompson, Philip E. "Baptists and Liturgy: The Very Idea!" *Review and Expositor* 100 (2003) 317–26.

———. "Re-Envisioning Baptist Identity: Historical, Theological, and Liturgical Analysis." *Perspectives in Religious Studies* 27 (2000) 287–302.

Thompson, William D. *Philadelphia's First Baptists: A Brief History of The First Baptist Church of Philadelphia, Founded 1698.* Philadelphia: First Baptist Church of the City of Philadelphia, n.d.

Tiffany, Henry W. "The History of Arminianism and Calvinism Among Baptists in America." ThD diss., Southern Baptist Theological Seminary, 1920.

Tombes, John. *Jehovah Jireh; or, God's Providence in Delivering the Godly.* London: Cotes, 1643.

Tomlinson, Glenn. *From Scotland to Canada: The Life of Pioneer Missionary Alexander Stewart.* Guelph, Ontario: Joshua, 2008.

Tomlinson, Glenn V., and Andrew M. Fountains, eds. *From Strength to Strength: A Pictorial History of Jarvis Street Baptist Church 1818–1993.* Toronto: Gospel Witness, 1993.

Torrance, James B. *Worship, Community and the Triune God of Grace.* Downers Grove: IVP Academic, 1997.

Townes, S. A. *The History of Marion: Sketches of Life, Etc. in Perry County, Alabama.* Reprint. Marion, AL: Cather, 1985.

Townsend, Leah. *South Carolina Baptists, 1670–1805.* Florence, SC: Florence Printing, 1935.

Tracy, Patricia J. *Jonathan Edwards, Pastor: Religion and Society in Eighteenth Century Northampton.* New York: Hill and Wang, 1980.

Trinier, Harold U. *A Century of Service: Story of the Canadian Baptist, 1854–1954.* Toronto: Board of Publication of the Baptist Convention of Ontario and Quebec, 1954.

Trites, Allison A. "Calvin Goodspeed: An Assessment of His Theological Contribution." In *Costly Vision: The Baptist Pilgrimage in Canada,* edited by Jarold K. Zeman, 23–39. Burlington, ON: Welch, 1988.

Tull, James E. *High-Church Baptists in the South: The Origin, Nature and Influence of Landmarkism.* Macon, GA: Mercer University Press, 2000.

Tupper, H. A. *The First Century of the First Baptist Church of Richmond, VA: 1780–1880.* Richmond: Carlton McCarthy, 1880.

———. *Two Centuries of the First Baptist Church of South Carolina.* Baltimore: Woodward, 1889.

Tyson, John R. *Sing Them Over Again to Me: Hymns and Hymnbooks in America.* Tuscaloosa: University Alabama Press, 2006.

Vaughan, Alden T. *The Puritan Tradition in America, 1620–1730.* Columbia: University of South Carolina Press, 1972.

Vogel, Dwight W., ed. *Primary Sources of Liturgical Theology: A Reader.* Collegeville, MN: Liturgical, 2000.

Wainwright, Geoffrey, and Karen B. Westerfield Tucker. *The Oxford History of Christian Worship.* New York: Oxford University Press, 2005.

Waldron, Samuel E. *Baptist Roots in America.* Boonton, NJ: Simpson, 1991.

Walker, Gavin Morton. *Philadelphia Baptist Development in Two Centuries and a Quarter.* Philadelphia: The Judson, 1932.

Walker, Robert Gary. "The Walnut Street Music Reader: A Documentary History of the Music Program of the Walnut Street Baptist Church, Louisville, Kentucky, 1844–1954." MCM thesis, Southern Baptist Theological Seminary, 1971.

Walnut Street Baptist Church. *Business Meeting Minutes.* June 15, 1849–November 28, 1858. Louisville: Walnut Street Baptist Church, 1858.

————. *Business Meeting Minutes*. December 10, 1858–October 11, 1872. Louisville: Walnut Street Baptist Church, 1872.

————. *Business Meeting Minutes*. December 6, 1872–March 13, 1885. Louisville: Walnut Street Baptist Church, 1885.

————. *Business Meeting Minutes*. July 8, 1885–July 6, 1892. Louisville: Walnut Street Baptist Church, 1892.

————. *Business Meeting Minutes*. August 10, 1892–November 12, 1902. Louisville: Walnut Street Baptist Church, 1902.

————. "Celebrate a New Beginning, September 9, 2001." Louisville: Walnut Street Baptist Church. Church Archives.

————. "Centennial Celebration, October 9, 1949." Louisville: Walnut Street Baptist Church. Church Archives.

————. "Church Chimes, January 9, 1977." Louisville: Walnut Street Baptist Church, 1977.

————. *Manual of Operations and Policies*. Louisville: Walnut Street Baptist Church, n.d.

————. *Testimony in Full in the Case of Ford Against Everts for Slander, and in the Case of Hord against Ford for Immoral Conduct: Together with a Synopsis and Review of the Same, and Protest against the Precedent and Action of the Frankfort Council.* Louisville: Walnut Street Baptist Church, 1859.

Walsh, H. H. *The Christian Church in Canada*. Toronto: Ryerson, 1956.

Ward, Matthew. *Pure Worship: The Early English Baptist Distinctive*. Eugene, OR: Pickwick, 2014.

Warren, Timothy S. "Can Topical Preaching Also Be Expository?" In *The Art and Craft of Biblical Preaching: A Comprehensive Resource for Today's Communicators*, edited by Haddon W. Robinson and Craig Brian Larson, 418–20. Grand Rapids: Zondervan, 2005.

Weaver, C. Douglas. *In Search of the New Testament Church: The Baptist Story*. Macon, GA: Mercer University Press, 2008.

Weaver, Steve. "'The Plain Testimony of Scripture': How the Early English Baptists Employed the Regulative Principle to Argue for Believers Baptism." *Gospel Witness* (January 2012) 13–15.

Webber, Robert E. *Common Roots: The Original Call to an Ancient-Future Faith*. Grand Rapids: Zondervan, 2009.

————. *Worship Old and New*. Grand Rapids: Zondervan, 1994.

Webber, Robert E., and John Wilvliet. *Ancient-Future Worship: Proclaiming and Enacting God's Narrative*. Grand Rapids: Baker, 2008.

White, Blanche Sydnor. *First Baptist Church Richmond 1780–1955: One Hundred and Seventy-Five Years of Service to God and Man*. Richmond: Whittet & Shepperson, 1955.

White, James F. *A Brief History of Christian Worship*. Nashville: Abingdon, 1993.

————. *Documents of Christian Worship: Descriptive and Interpretive Sources*. Louisville: Westminster John Knox, 1992.

————. *Protestant Worship: Traditions in Transition*. Louisville: Westminster John Knox, 1989.

Whitley, William Thomas, ed. *The Works of John Smyth*. Vol. 1. Cambridge: Cambridge University Press, 1915.

Whitsitt, William H. *A Question in Baptist History: Whether the Anabaptists in England Practiced Baptism by Immersion before 1641?* Louisville: Dearing, 1896.

Williams, Barnett L. "An Investigation of Baptist Worship in America from 1620–1850." ThM thesis, Southern Baptist Theological Seminary, 1954.

Williams, Maurice F. "Structure and Form in Church Worship." *Baptist Quarterly* 18 (1960) 293–99.

Williams, Michael E. "The Influence of Calvinism on Colonial Baptists: An Ongoing Argument Emerging in the Past Decades of Baptist Life Revolves around the Theological Origins of Early Baptists Generally, Specifically in America, and the Role That Calvinist Theology Played in Baptist Development." *Baptist History and Heritage* 39 (2004) 26–39.

Williams, W. H. "History of Bethesda, Narbeth." In *Bethesda Baptist Church, Narbeth, 1808–1958,* 13–20. Narbeth, Wales: Walters, 1958.

Wills, Gregory A. *Southern Baptist Theological Seminary, 1859–2009.* New York: Oxford University Press, 2009.

Wilson, Jared C. *Gospel Wakefulness.* Wheaton, IL: Crossway, 2011.

Wilson, Mabel Ponder, et al. *Some Early Alabama Churches (Founded before 1870).* Birmingham: Daughters of the American Revolution, 1973.

Wilson, Paul R. "Baptists and Business: Central Canadian Baptists and the Secularization of the Businessman at Toronto's Jarvis Street Baptist Church, 1848–1921." PhD diss., University of Western Ontario, 1996.

Wilson, Robert S., ed. *An Abiding Conviction: Maritime Baptists and Their World.* Hantsport: Lancelot, 1988.

Windsor, Jerry M. "Preaching Up a Storm from 1839–1889." *Alabama Baptist Historian* 29 (1993) 13–20.

Witvliet, John D. "The Cumulative Power of Transformation in Public Worship." In *Worship That Changes Lives: Multidisciplinary and Congregational Perspectives on Spiritual Transformation,* edited by Alexis D. Abernathy, 41–58. Grand Rapids: Baker Academic, 2008.

———— *Worship Seeking Understanding: Windows into Christian Practice.* Grand Rapids: Baker Academic, 2003.

Wolever, Terry. *The Life and Ministry of John Gano.* Springfield, MO: Particular Baptist, 1998.

Wood, Nathan E. *The History of the First Baptist Church of Boston.* Edited by Constance C. Hanson. Salem, NH: Ayer, 1990.

Wren, Brian. *Praying Twice: The Music and Words of Congregational Song.* Louisville: Westminster John Knox, 2000.

Wright, Tim, and Jan Wright, eds. *Contemporary Worship: A Sourcebook for Spirited-Traditional, Praise and Seeker Services.* Nashville: Abingdon, 1997.

York, Terry W. "Trends in Church Music in Southern Baptist Churches: Implications for Study and Practices." *Theological Educator* 49 (1994) 157–65.

Made in the USA
Monee, IL
15 January 2022

88967234R00157